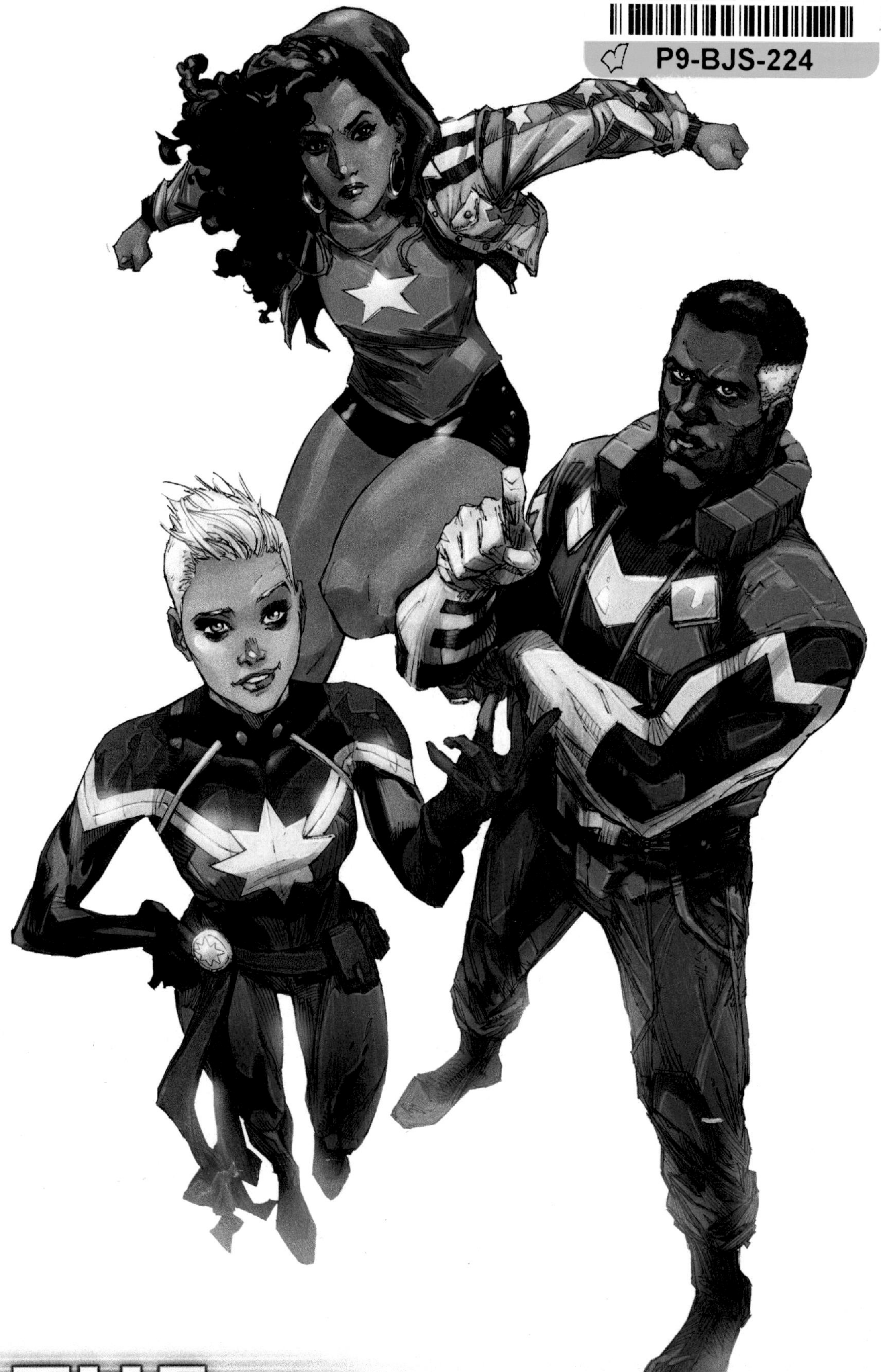

THE ULTIMATES

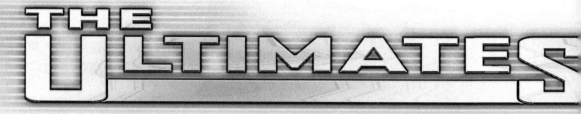

THE ULTIMATES

START WITH THE IMPOSSIBLE

AL EWING
writer

KENNETH ROCAFORT (#1-5) &
CHRISTIAN WARD (#6)
artists

DAN BROWN (#1-5) WITH
KENNETH ROCAFORT (#4)
color artists

VC's JOE SABINO
letterer

KENNETH ROCAFORT WITH **EDGAR DELGADO** (#1) &
RICHARD ISANOVE (AVENGERS #0)
cover art

CHRIS ROBINSON AND
CHARLES BEACHAM
assistant editors

WIL MOSS WITH **JON MOISAN,**
MARK PANICCIA AND **EMILY SHAW**
editors

TOM BREVOORT
executive editor

COLLECTION EDITOR **SARAH BRUNSTAD**
ASSOCIATE MANAGING EDITOR **KATERI WOODY**
EDITOR, SPECIAL PROJECTS **MARK D. BEAZLEY**
SENIOR EDITOR, SPECIAL PROJECTS **JENNIFER GRÜNWALD**
VP PRODUCTION & SPECIAL PROJECTS **JEFF YOUNGQUIST**
SVP PRINT, SALES & MARKETING **DAVID GABRIEL**
BOOK DESIGNER **ADAM DEL RE**

EDITOR IN CHIEF **AXEL ALONSO**
CHIEF CREATIVE OFFICER **JOE QUESADA**
PUBLISHER **DAN BUCKLEY**
EXECUTIVE PRODUCER **ALAN FINE**

ULTIMATES: OMNIVERSAL VOL. 1 — START WITH THE IMPOSSIBLE. Contains material originally published in magazine form as ULTIMATES #1-6 and AVENGERS #0. Second printing 2017. ISBN# 978-0-7851-9670-9. Published by MARVEL WORLDWIDE, INC., a subsidiary of MARVEL ENTERTAINMENT, LLC. OFFICE OF PUBLICATION: 135 West 50th Street, New York, NY 10020. **Printed in the U.S.A.** ALAN FINE, President, Marvel Entertainment; DAN BUCKLEY, President, TV, Publishing & Brand Management; JOE QUESADA, Chief Creative Officer; TOM BREVOORT, SVP of Publishing; DAVID BOGART, SVP of Business Affairs & Operations, Publishing & Partnership; C.B. CEBULSKI, VP of Brand Management & Development, Asia; DAVID GABRIEL, SVP of Sales & Marketing, Publishing; JEFF YOUNGQUIST, VP of Production & Special Projects; DAN CARR, Executive Director of Publishing Technology; ALEX MORALES, Director of Publishing Operations; SUSAN CRESPI, Production Manager; STAN LEE, Chairman Emeritus. For information regarding advertising in Marvel Comics or on Marvel.com, please contact Vit DeBellis, Integrated Sales Manager, at vdebellis@marvel.com. For Marvel subscription inquiries, please call 888-511-5480. **Manufactured between 11/23/2016 and 12/26/2016 by QUAD/GRAPHICS WASECA, WASECA, MN, USA.**

10 9 8 7 6 5 4 3 2

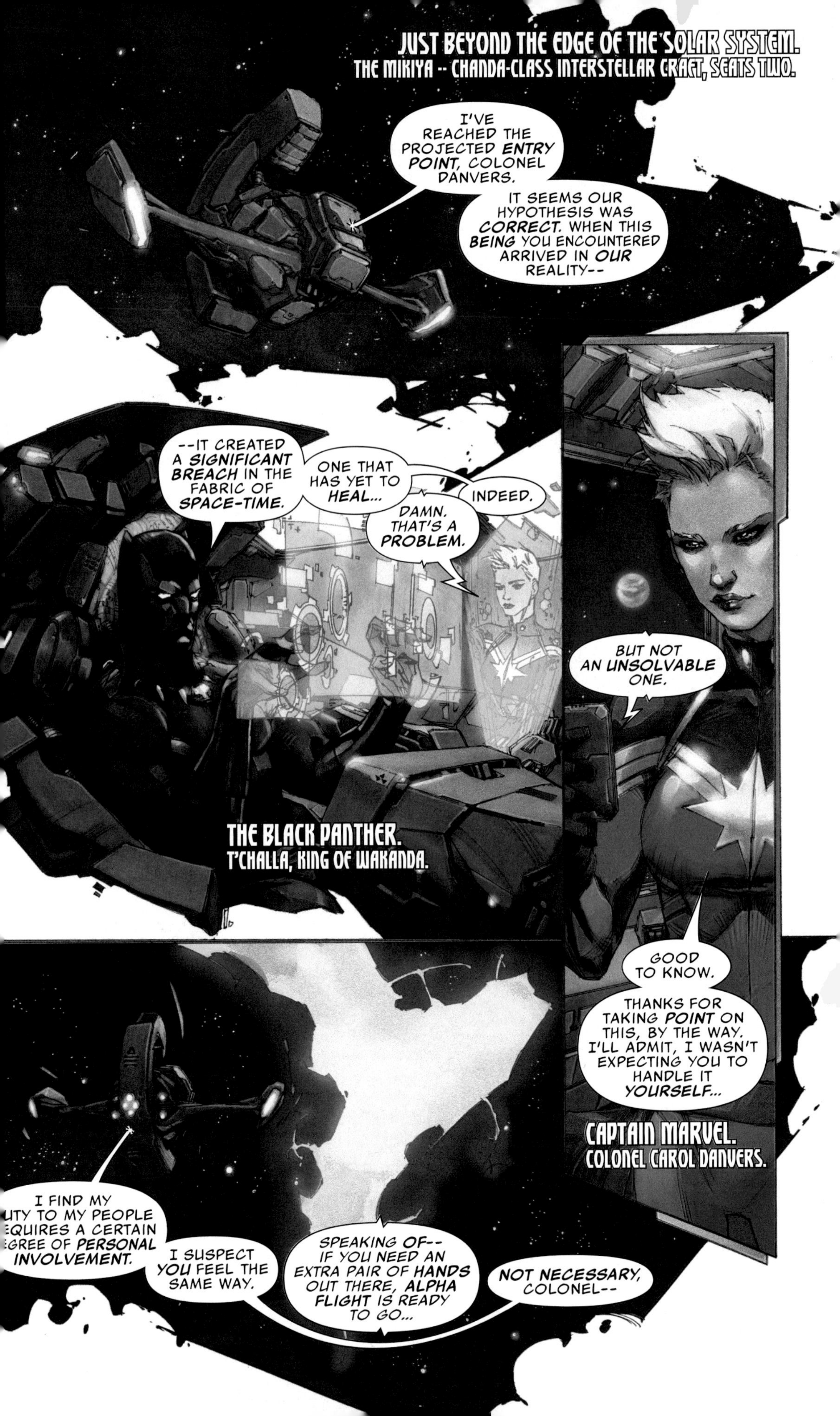
JUST BEYOND THE EDGE OF THE SOLAR SYSTEM.
THE MIKIYA -- CHANDA-CLASS INTERSTELLAR CRAFT, SEATS TWO.
I'VE REACHED THE PROJECTED ENTRY POINT, COLONEL DANVERS.
IT SEEMS OUR HYPOTHESIS WAS CORRECT. WHEN THIS BEING YOU ENCOUNTERED ARRIVED IN OUR REALITY--
--IT CREATED A SIGNIFICANT BREACH IN THE FABRIC OF SPACE-TIME.
ONE THAT HAS YET TO HEAL...
INDEED.
DAMN. THAT'S A PROBLEM.
BUT NOT AN UNSOLVABLE ONE.
THE BLACK PANTHER.
T'CHALLA, KING OF WAKANDA.
GOOD TO KNOW.
THANKS FOR TAKING POINT ON THIS, BY THE WAY. I'LL ADMIT, I WASN'T EXPECTING YOU TO HANDLE IT YOURSELF...
CAPTAIN MARVEL.
COLONEL CAROL DANVERS.
I FIND MY UTY TO MY PEOPLE EQUIRES A CERTAIN EGREE OF PERSONAL INVOLVEMENT.
I SUSPECT YOU FEEL THE SAME WAY.
SPEAKING OF-- IF YOU NEED AN EXTRA PAIR OF HANDS OUT THERE, ALPHA FLIGHT IS READY TO GO...
NOT NECESSARY, COLONEL--

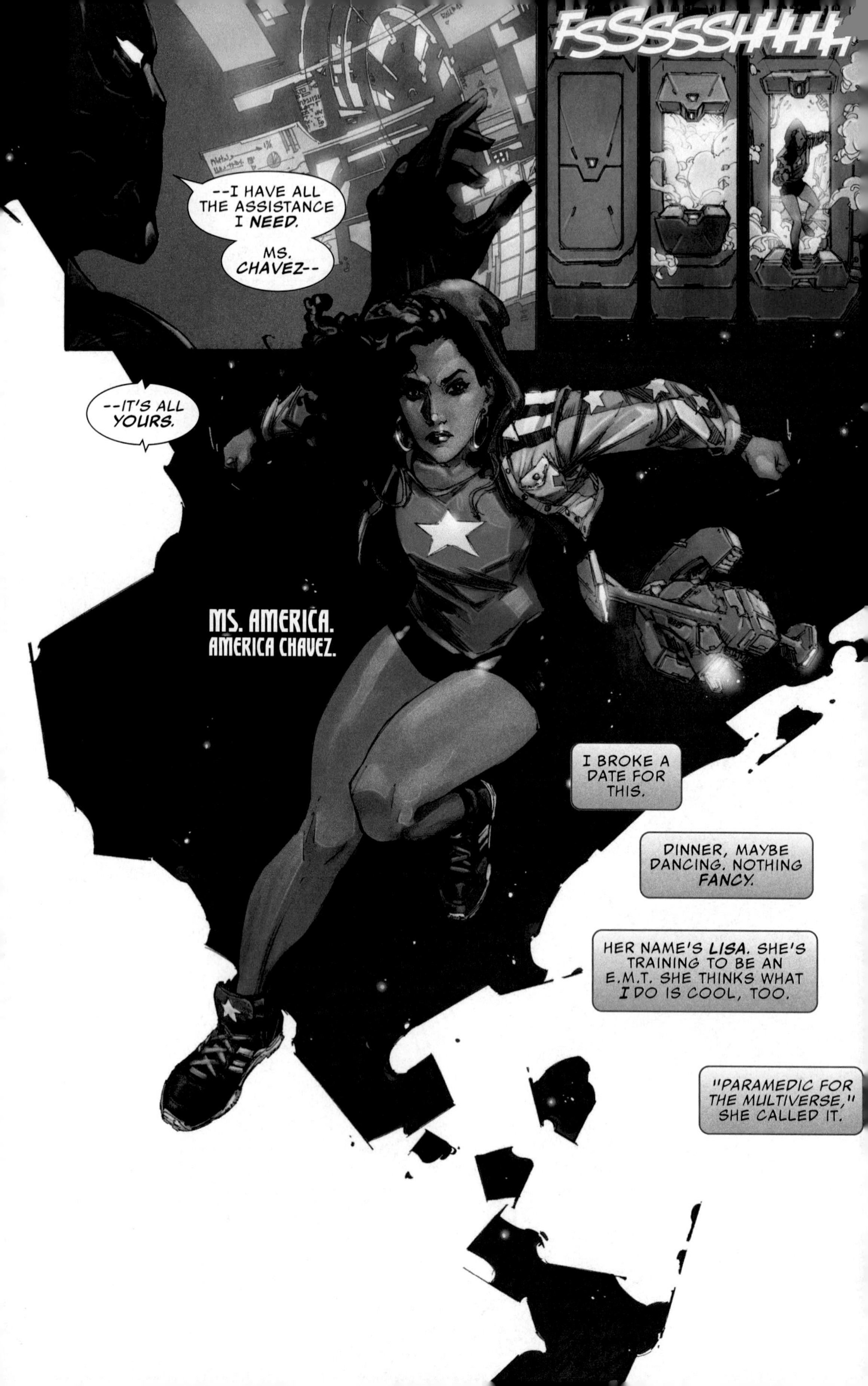
FSSSSSHHHH
--I HAVE ALL THE ASSISTANCE I NEED.
MS. CHAVEZ--
--IT'S ALL YOURS.
MS. AMERICA. AMERICA CHAVEZ.
I BROKE A DATE FOR THIS.
DINNER, MAYBE DANCING. NOTHING FANCY.
HER NAME'S LISA. SHE'S TRAINING TO BE AN E.M.T. SHE THINKS WHAT I DO IS COOL, TOO.
"PARAMEDIC FOR THE MULTIVERSE," SHE CALLED IT.

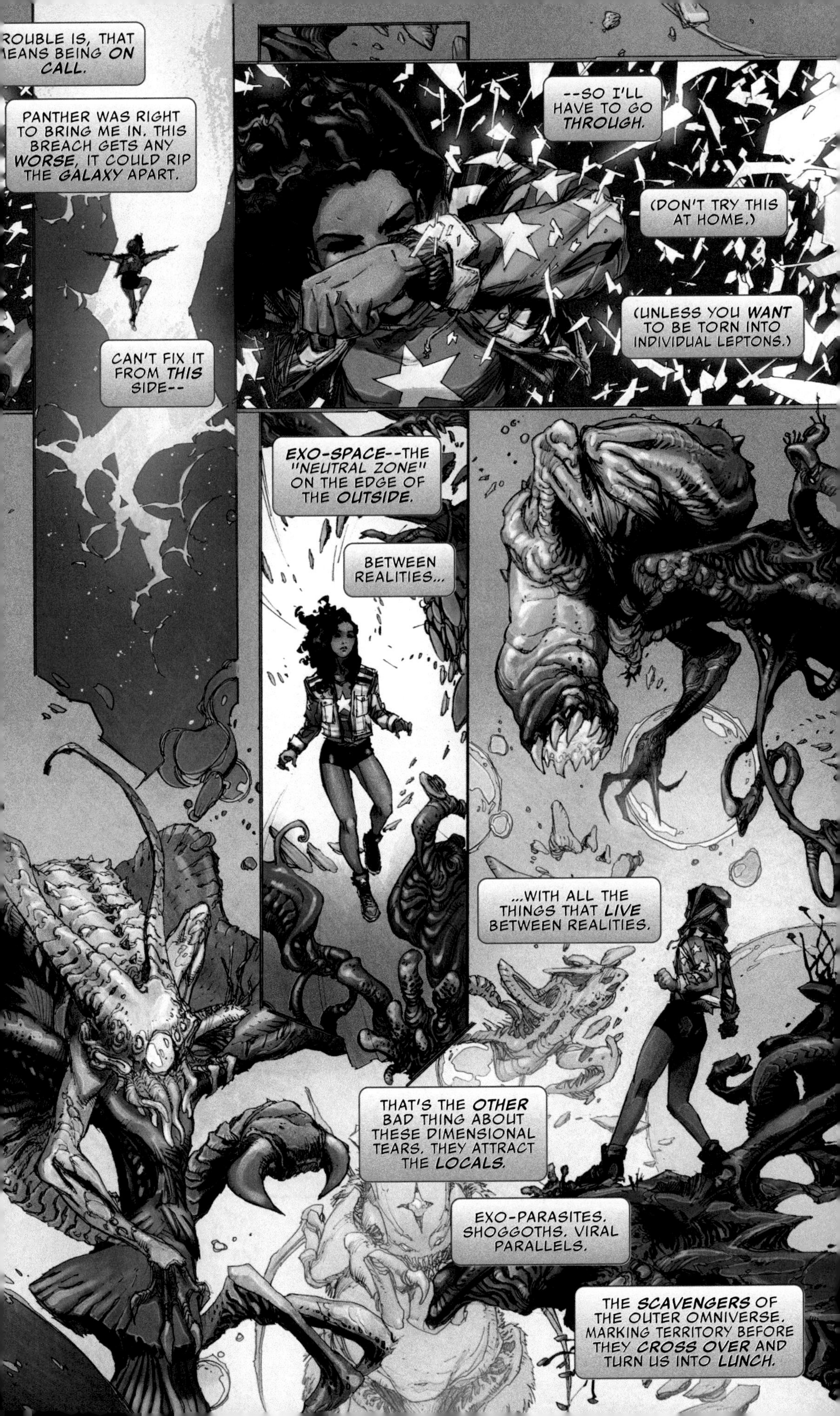
ROUBLE IS, THAT MEANS BEING ON CALL.
PANTHER WAS RIGHT TO BRING ME IN. THIS BREACH GETS ANY WORSE, IT COULD RIP THE GALAXY APART.
CAN'T FIX IT FROM THIS SIDE--
--SO I'LL HAVE TO GO THROUGH.
(DON'T TRY THIS AT HOME.)
(UNLESS YOU WANT TO BE TORN INTO INDIVIDUAL LEPTONS.)
EXO-SPACE--THE "NEUTRAL ZONE" ON THE EDGE OF THE OUTSIDE.
BETWEEN REALITIES...
...WITH ALL THE THINGS THAT LIVE BETWEEN REALITIES.
THAT'S THE OTHER BAD THING ABOUT THESE DIMENSIONAL TEARS. THEY ATTRACT THE LOCALS.
EXO-PARASITES. SHOGGOTHS. VIRAL PARALLELS.
THE SCAVENGERS OF THE OUTER OMNIVERSE. MARKING TERRITORY BEFORE THEY CROSS OVER AND TURN US INTO LUNCH.

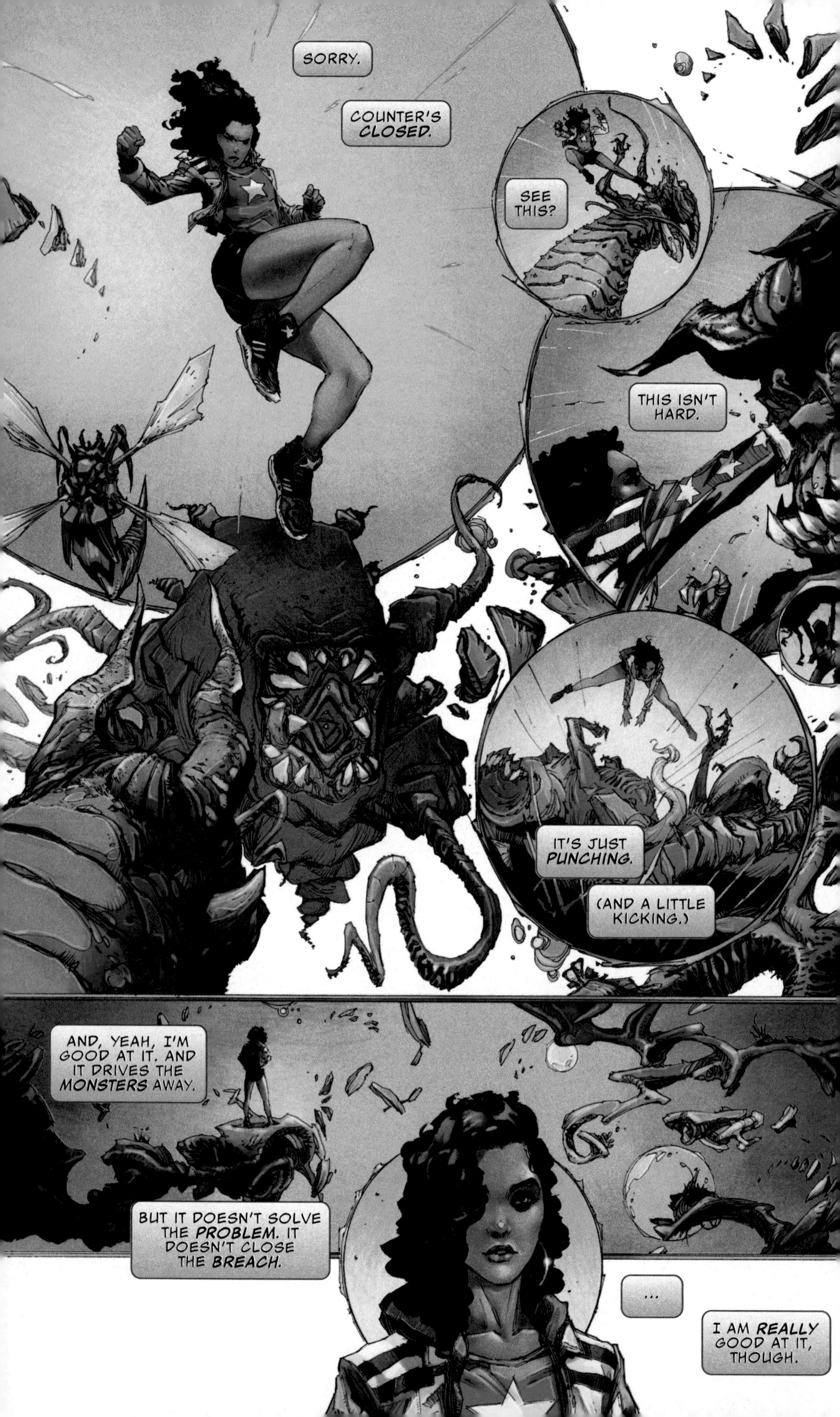
SORRY.
COUNTER'S CLOSED.
SEE THIS?
THIS ISN'T HARD.
IT'S JUST PUNCHING.
(AND A LITTLE KICKING.)
AND, YEAH, I'M GOOD AT IT. AND IT DRIVES THE MONSTERS AWAY.
BUT IT DOESN'T SOLVE THE PROBLEM. IT DOESN'T CLOSE THE BREACH.
...
I AM REALLY GOOD AT IT, THOUGH.

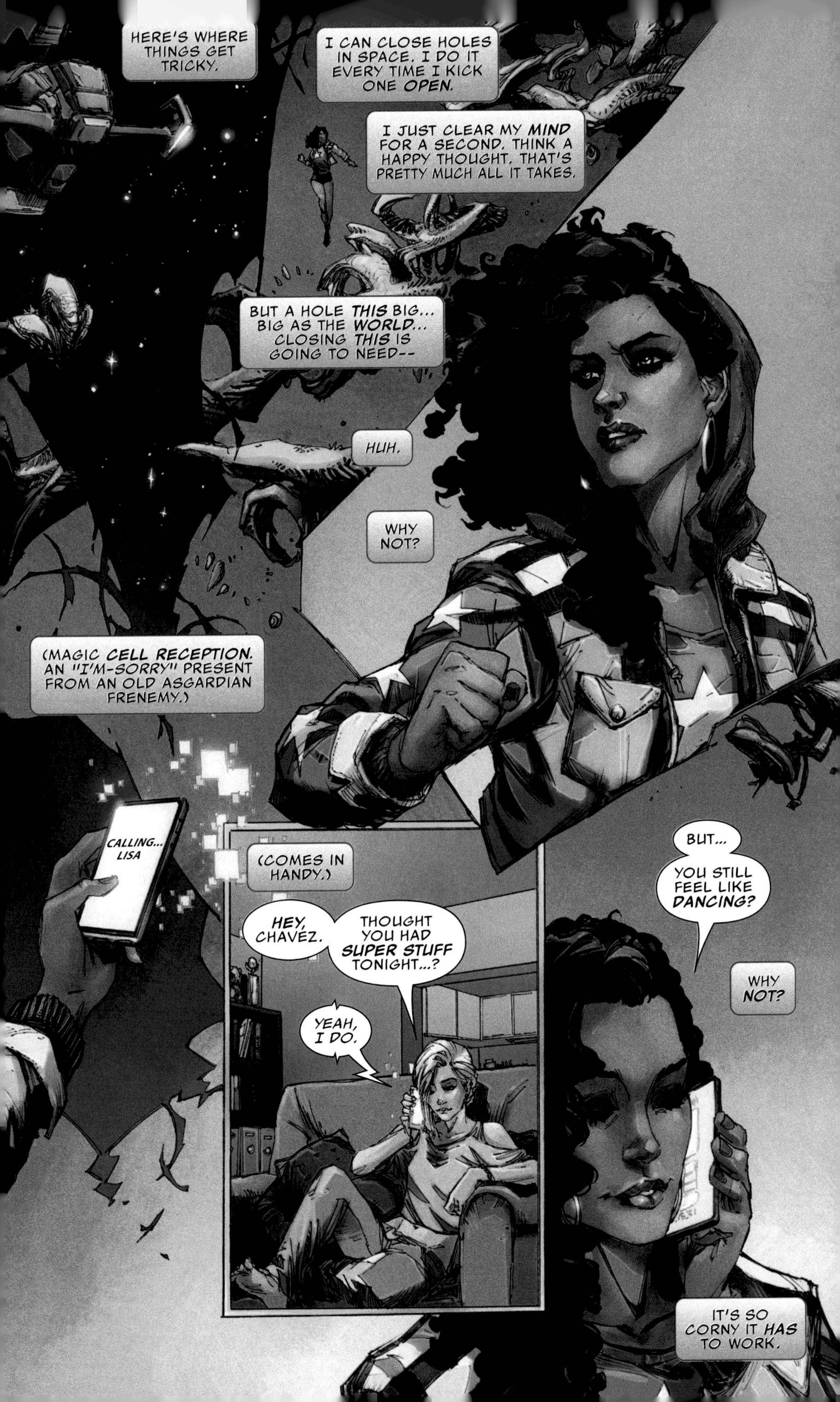
HERE'S WHERE THINGS GET TRICKY.
I CAN CLOSE HOLES IN SPACE. I DO IT EVERY TIME I KICK ONE OPEN.
I JUST CLEAR MY MIND FOR A SECOND. THINK A HAPPY THOUGHT. THAT'S PRETTY MUCH ALL IT TAKES.
BUT A HOLE THIS BIG... BIG AS THE WORLD... CLOSING THIS IS GOING TO NEED--
HUH.
WHY NOT?
(MAGIC CELL RECEPTION. AN "I'M-SORRY" PRESENT FROM AN OLD ASGARDIAN FRENEMY.)
CALLING... LISA
(COMES IN HANDY.)
HEY, CHAVEZ.
THOUGHT YOU HAD SUPER STUFF TONIGHT...?
YEAH, I DO.
BUT...
YOU STILL FEEL LIKE DANCING?
WHY NOT?
IT'S SO CORNY IT HAS TO WORK.

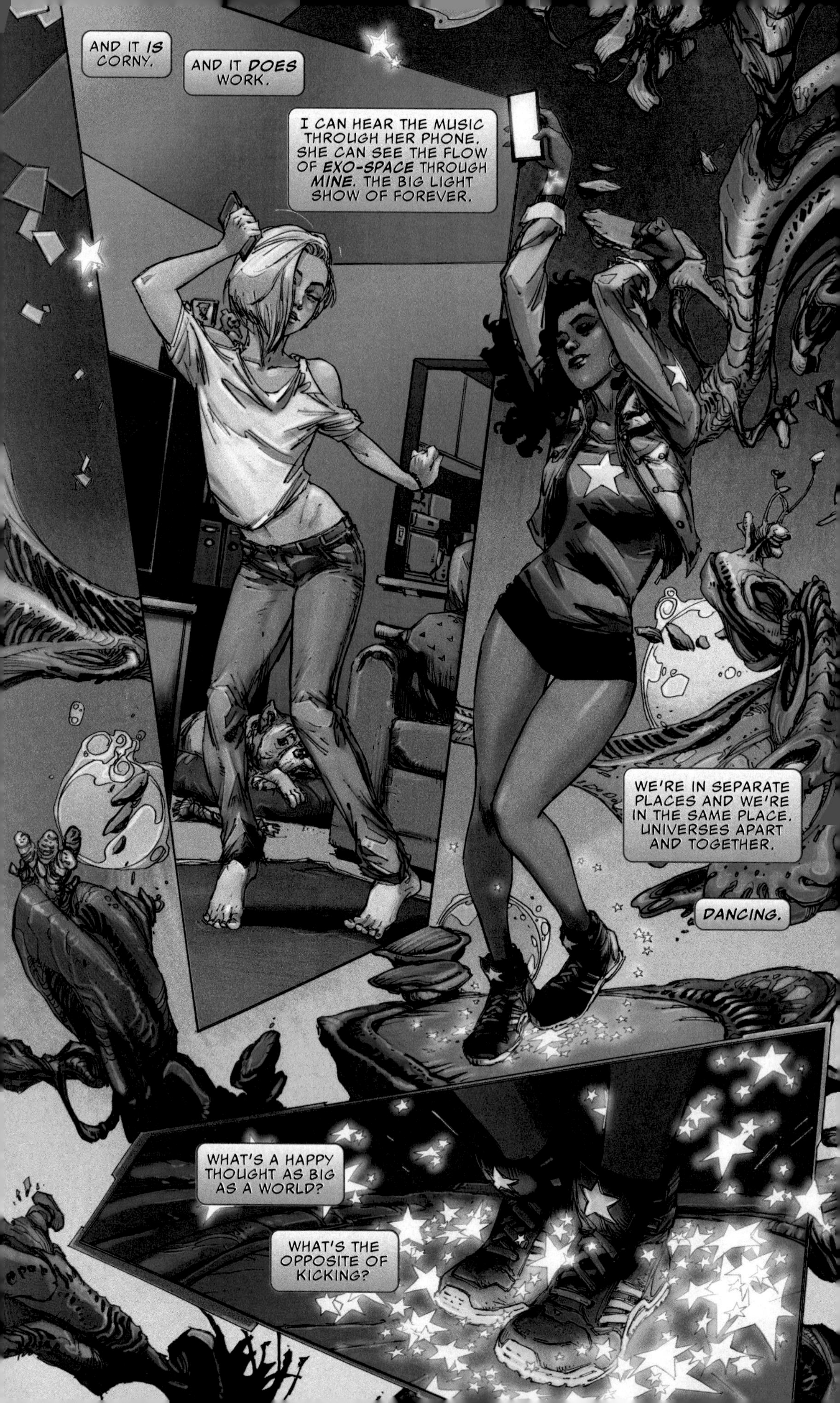
AND IT IS CORNY.
AND IT DOES WORK.
I CAN HEAR THE MUSIC THROUGH HER PHONE. SHE CAN SEE THE FLOW OF EXO-SPACE THROUGH MINE. THE BIG LIGHT SHOW OF FOREVER.
WE'RE IN SEPARATE PLACES AND WE'RE IN THE SAME PLACE. UNIVERSES APART AND TOGETHER.
DANCING.
WHAT'S A HAPPY THOUGHT AS BIG AS A WORLD?
WHAT'S THE OPPOSITE OF KICKING?

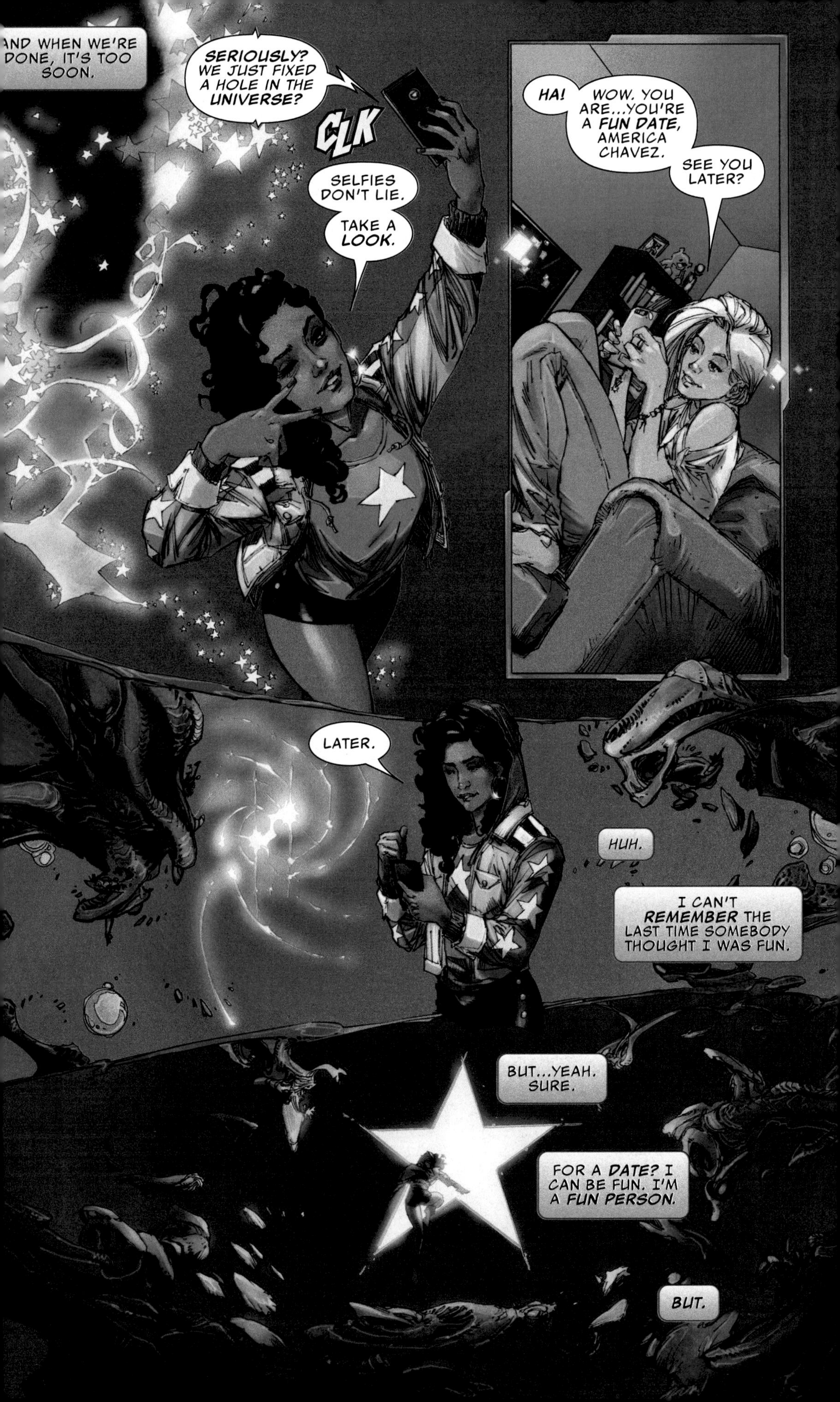
AND WHEN WE'RE DONE, IT'S TOO SOON.
SERIOUSLY? WE JUST FIXED A HOLE IN THE UNIVERSE?
CLK
SELFIES DON'T LIE.
TAKE A LOOK.
HA!
WOW. YOU ARE...YOU'RE A FUN DATE, AMERICA CHAVEZ.
SEE YOU LATER?
LATER.
HUH.
I CAN'T REMEMBER THE LAST TIME SOMEBODY THOUGHT I WAS FUN.
BUT...YEAH. SURE.
FOR A DATE? I CAN BE FUN. I'M A FUN PERSON.
BUT.

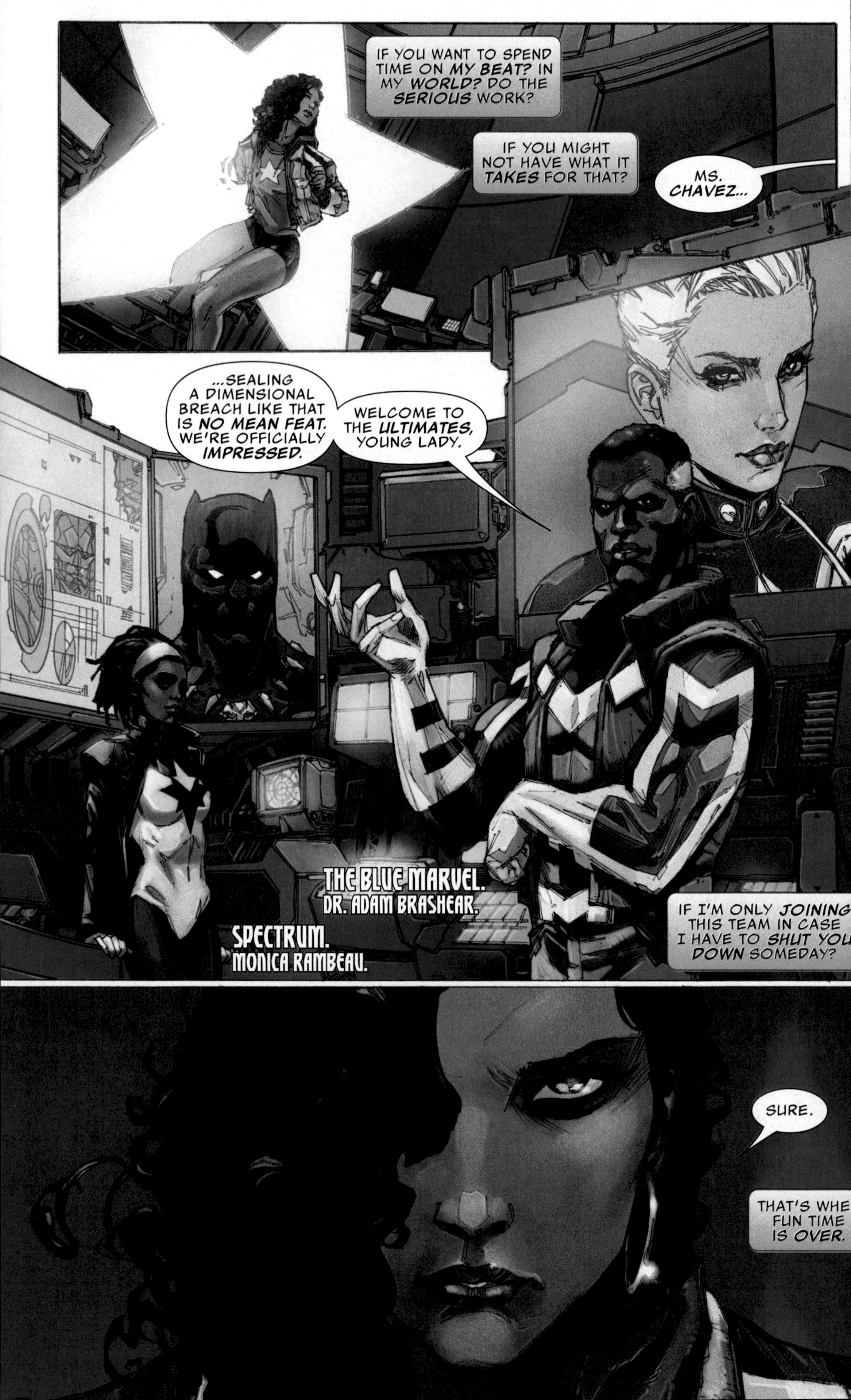
IF YOU WANT TO SPEND TIME ON MY BEAT? IN MY WORLD? DO THE SERIOUS WORK?
IF YOU MIGHT NOT HAVE WHAT IT TAKES FOR THAT?
MS. CHAVEZ...
...SEALING A DIMENSIONAL BREACH LIKE THAT IS NO MEAN FEAT. WE'RE OFFICIALLY IMPRESSED.
WELCOME TO THE ULTIMATES, YOUNG LADY.
THE BLUE MARVEL. DR. ADAM BRASHEAR.
SPECTRUM. MONICA RAMBEAU.
IF I'M ONLY JOINING THIS TEAM IN CASE I HAVE TO SHUT YOU DOWN SOMEDAY?
SURE.
THAT'S WHE FUN TIME IS OVER.

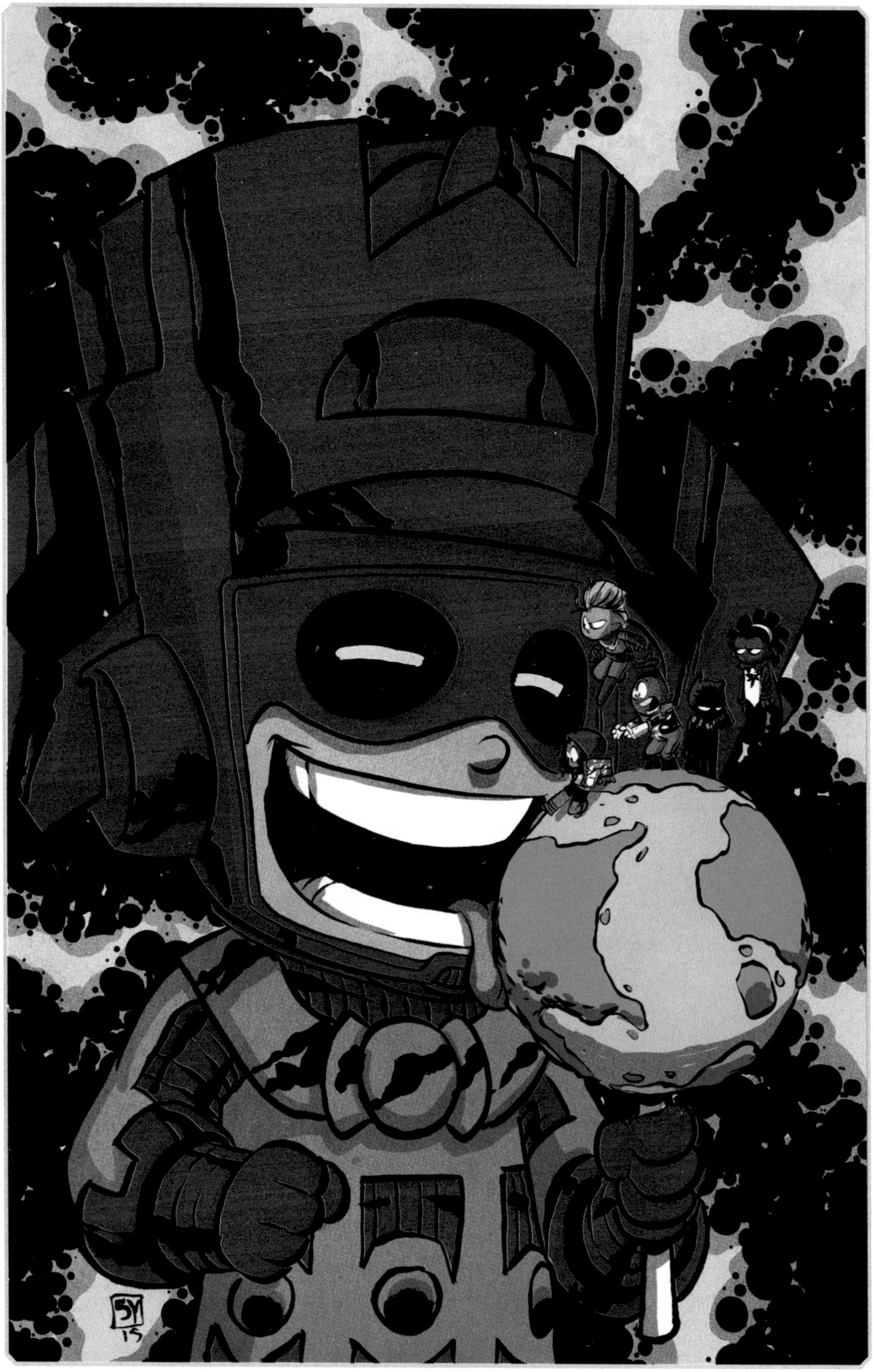

#1 VARIANT BY SKOTTIE YOUNG

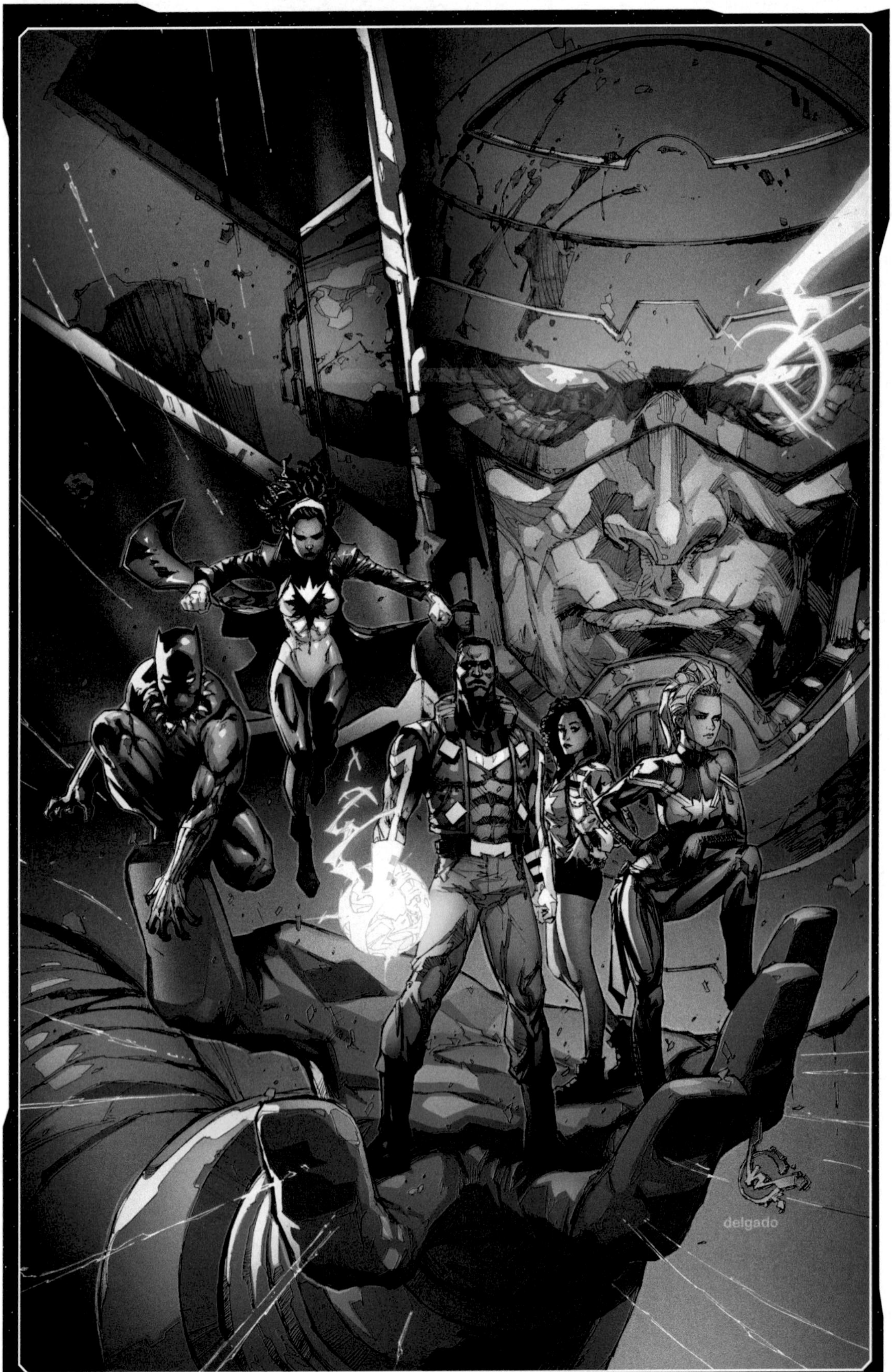
delgado

1

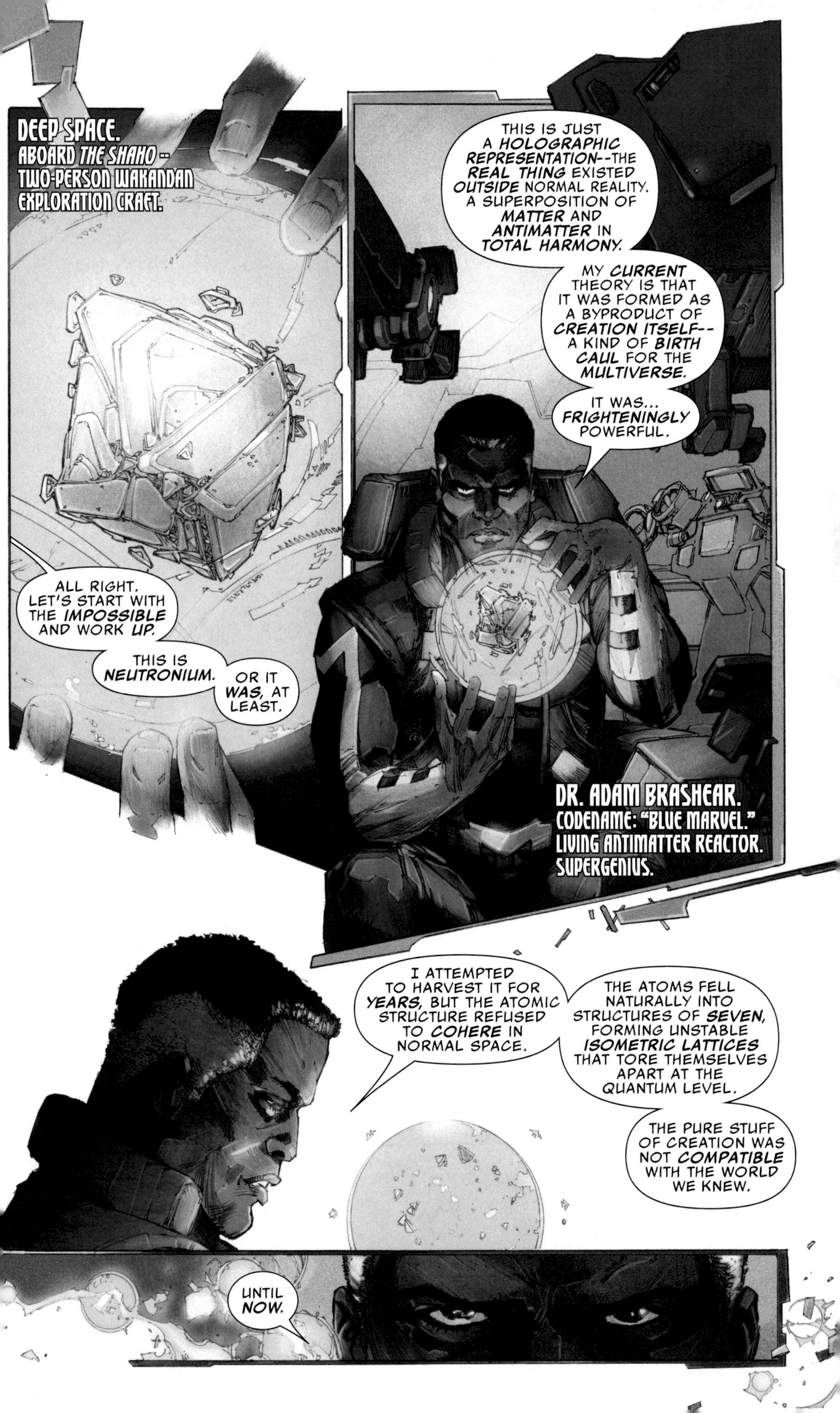
DEEP SPACE.
ABOARD THE SHAHO -- TWO-PERSON WAKANDAN EXPLORATION CRAFT.
ALL RIGHT. LET'S START WITH THE IMPOSSIBLE AND WORK UP.
THIS IS NEUTRONIUM.
OR IT WAS, AT LEAST.
THIS IS JUST A HOLOGRAPHIC REPRESENTATION--THE REAL THING EXISTED OUTSIDE NORMAL REALITY. A SUPERPOSITION OF MATTER AND ANTIMATTER IN TOTAL HARMONY.
MY CURRENT THEORY IS THAT IT WAS FORMED AS A BYPRODUCT OF CREATION ITSELF--A KIND OF BIRTH CAUL FOR THE MULTIVERSE.
IT WAS... FRIGHTENINGLY POWERFUL.
DR. ADAM BRASHEAR.
CODENAME: "BLUE MARVEL."
LIVING ANTIMATTER REACTOR.
SUPERGENIUS.
I ATTEMPTED TO HARVEST IT FOR YEARS, BUT THE ATOMIC STRUCTURE REFUSED TO COHERE IN NORMAL SPACE.
THE ATOMS FELL NATURALLY INTO STRUCTURES OF SEVEN, FORMING UNSTABLE ISOMETRIC LATTICES THAT TORE THEMSELVES APART AT THE QUANTUM LEVEL.
THE PURE STUFF OF CREATION WAS NOT COMPATIBLE WITH THE WORLD WE KNEW.
UNTIL NOW.

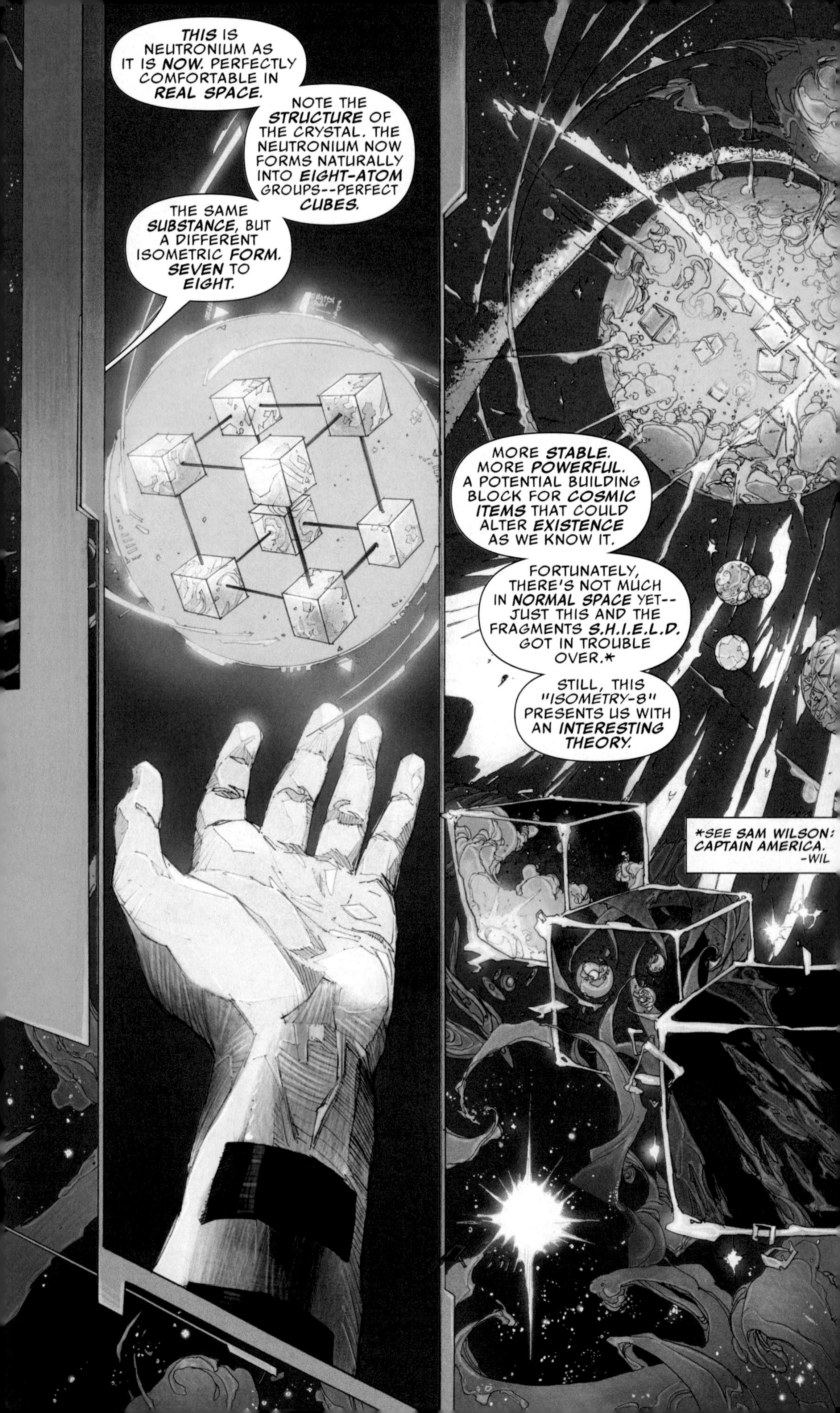
THIS IS NEUTRONIUM AS IT IS NOW. PERFECTLY COMFORTABLE IN REAL SPACE.
NOTE THE STRUCTURE OF THE CRYSTAL. THE NEUTRONIUM NOW FORMS NATURALLY INTO EIGHT-ATOM GROUPS--PERFECT CUBES.
THE SAME SUBSTANCE, BUT A DIFFERENT ISOMETRIC FORM. SEVEN TO EIGHT.
MORE STABLE. MORE POWERFUL. A POTENTIAL BUILDING BLOCK FOR COSMIC ITEMS THAT COULD ALTER EXISTENCE AS WE KNOW IT.
FORTUNATELY, THERE'S NOT MUCH IN NORMAL SPACE YET--JUST THIS AND THE FRAGMENTS S.H.I.E.L.D. GOT IN TROUBLE OVER.*
STILL, THIS "ISOMETRY-8" PRESENTS US WITH AN INTERESTING THEORY.
*SEE SAM WILSON: CAPTAIN AMERICA. -WIL

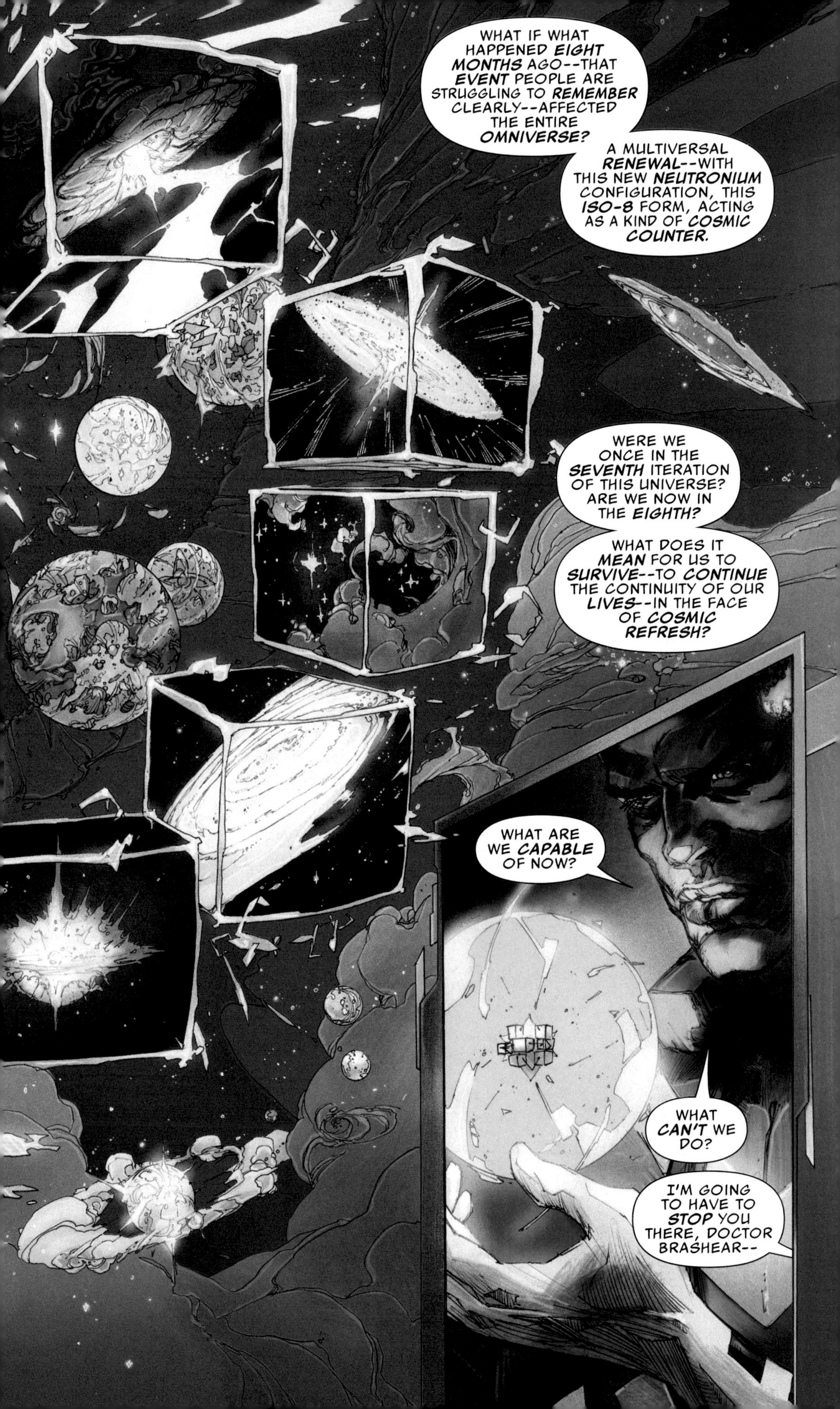
WHAT IF WHAT HAPPENED EIGHT MONTHS AGO--THAT EVENT PEOPLE ARE STRUGGLING TO REMEMBER CLEARLY--AFFECTED THE ENTIRE OMNIVERSE?
A MULTIVERSAL RENEWAL--WITH THIS NEW NEUTRONIUM CONFIGURATION, THIS ISO-8 FORM, ACTING AS A KIND OF COSMIC COUNTER.
WERE WE ONCE IN THE SEVENTH ITERATION OF THIS UNIVERSE? ARE WE NOW IN THE EIGHTH?
WHAT DOES IT MEAN FOR US TO SURVIVE--TO CONTINUE THE CONTINUITY OF OUR LIVES--IN THE FACE OF COSMIC REFRESH?
WHAT ARE WE CAPABLE OF NOW?
WHAT CAN'T WE DO?
I'M GOING TO HAVE TO STOP YOU THERE, DOCTOR BRASHEAR--

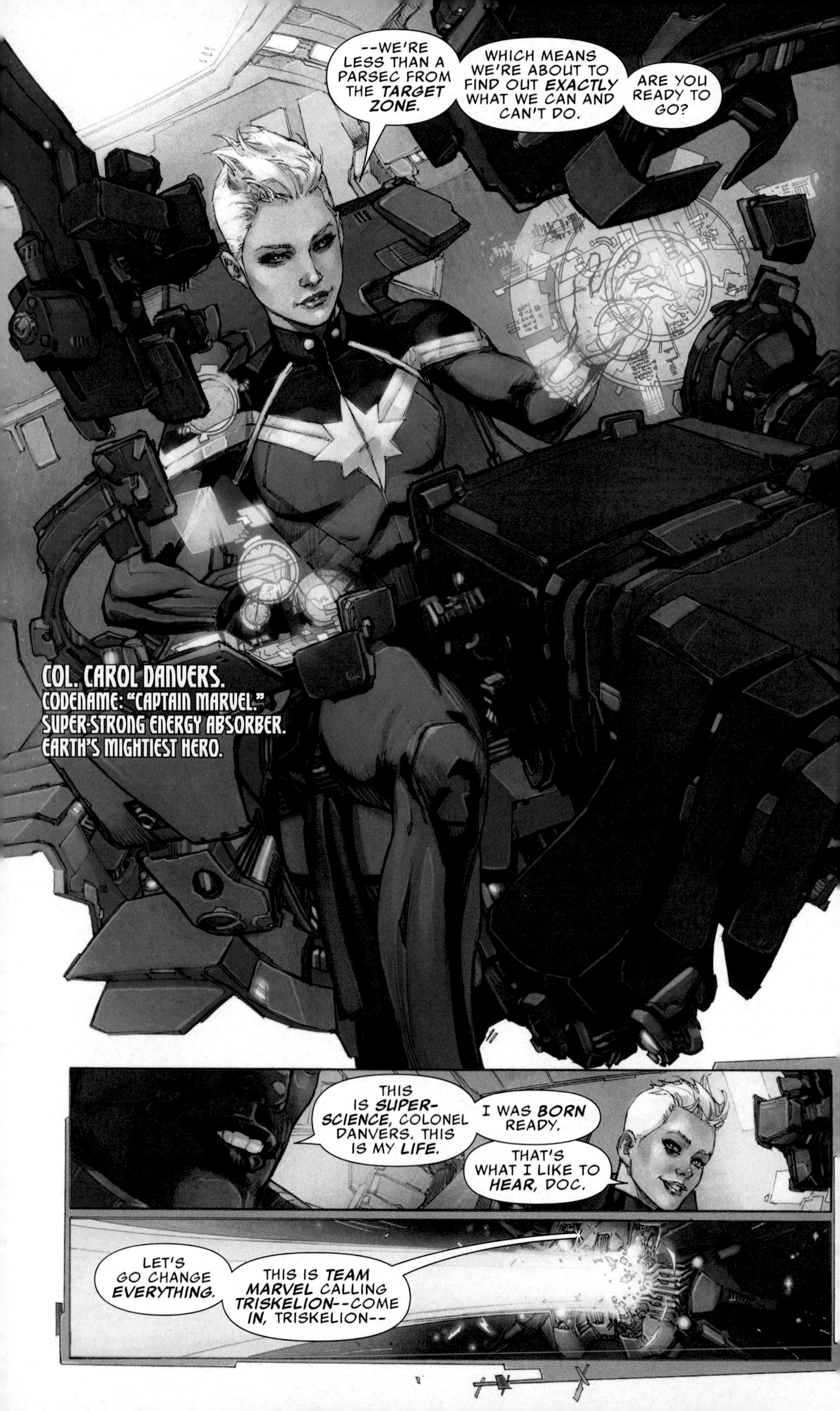
--WE'RE LESS THAN A PARSEC FROM THE TARGET ZONE.
WHICH MEANS WE'RE ABOUT TO FIND OUT EXACTLY WHAT WE CAN AND CAN'T DO.
ARE YOU READY TO GO?
COL. CAROL DANVERS.
CODENAME: "CAPTAIN MARVEL."
SUPER-STRONG ENERGY ABSORBER.
EARTH'S MIGHTIEST HERO.
THIS IS SUPER-SCIENCE, COLONEL DANVERS. THIS IS MY LIFE.
I WAS BORN READY.
THAT'S WHAT I LIKE TO HEAR, DOC.
LET'S GO CHANGE EVERYTHING.
THIS IS TEAM MARVEL CALLING TRISKELION--COME IN, TRISKELION--

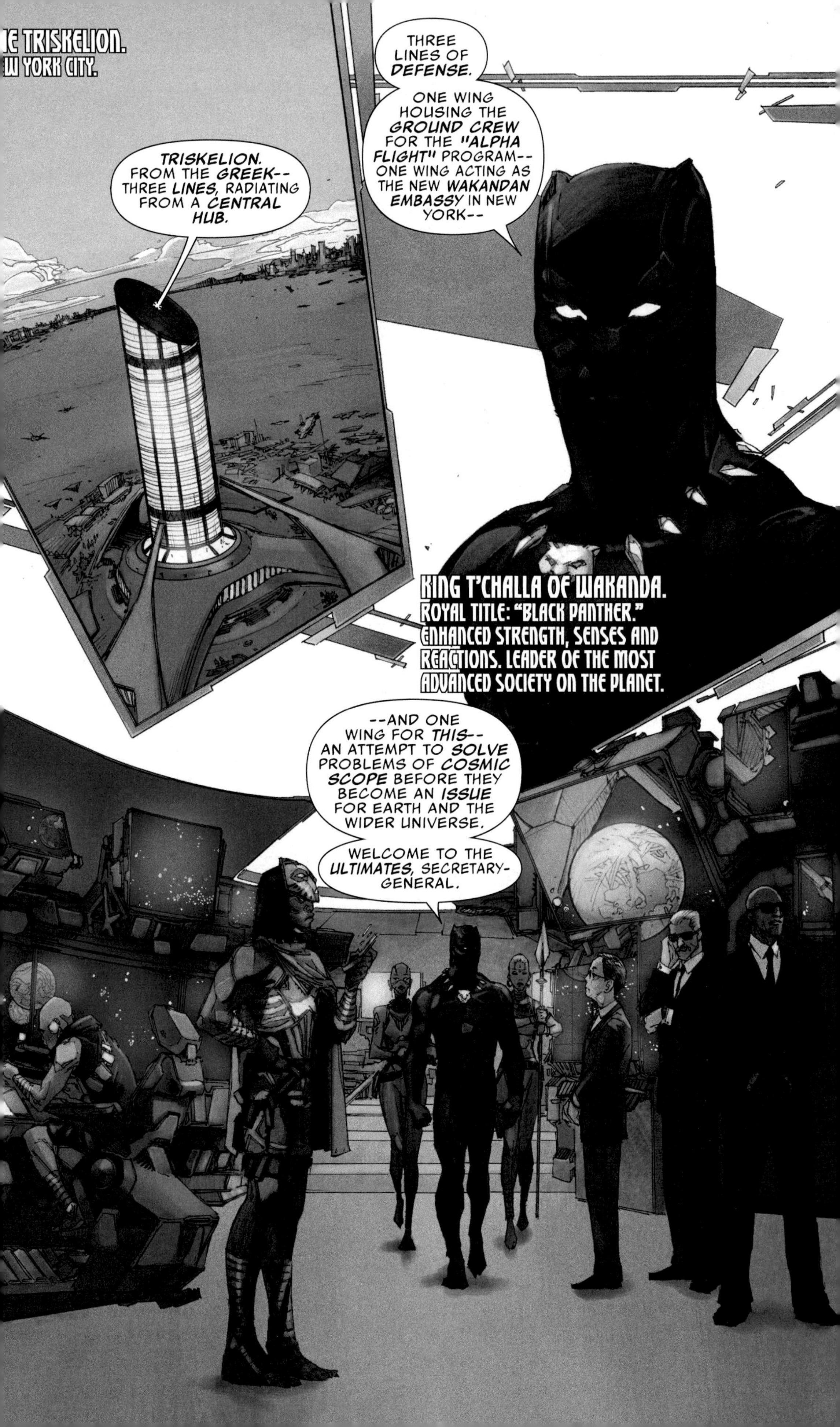

E TRISKELION.
W YORK CITY.
TRISKELION. FROM THE GREEK-- THREE LINES, RADIATING FROM A CENTRAL HUB.
THREE LINES OF DEFENSE.
ONE WING HOUSING THE GROUND CREW FOR THE "ALPHA FLIGHT" PROGRAM-- ONE WING ACTING AS THE NEW WAKANDAN EMBASSY IN NEW YORK--
KING T'CHALLA OF WAKANDA.
ROYAL TITLE: "BLACK PANTHER." ENHANCED STRENGTH, SENSES AND REACTIONS. LEADER OF THE MOST ADVANCED SOCIETY ON THE PLANET.
--AND ONE WING FOR THIS-- AN ATTEMPT TO SOLVE PROBLEMS OF COSMIC SCOPE BEFORE THEY BECOME AN ISSUE FOR EARTH AND THE WIDER UNIVERSE.
WELCOME TO THE ULTIMATES, SECRETARY-GENERAL.

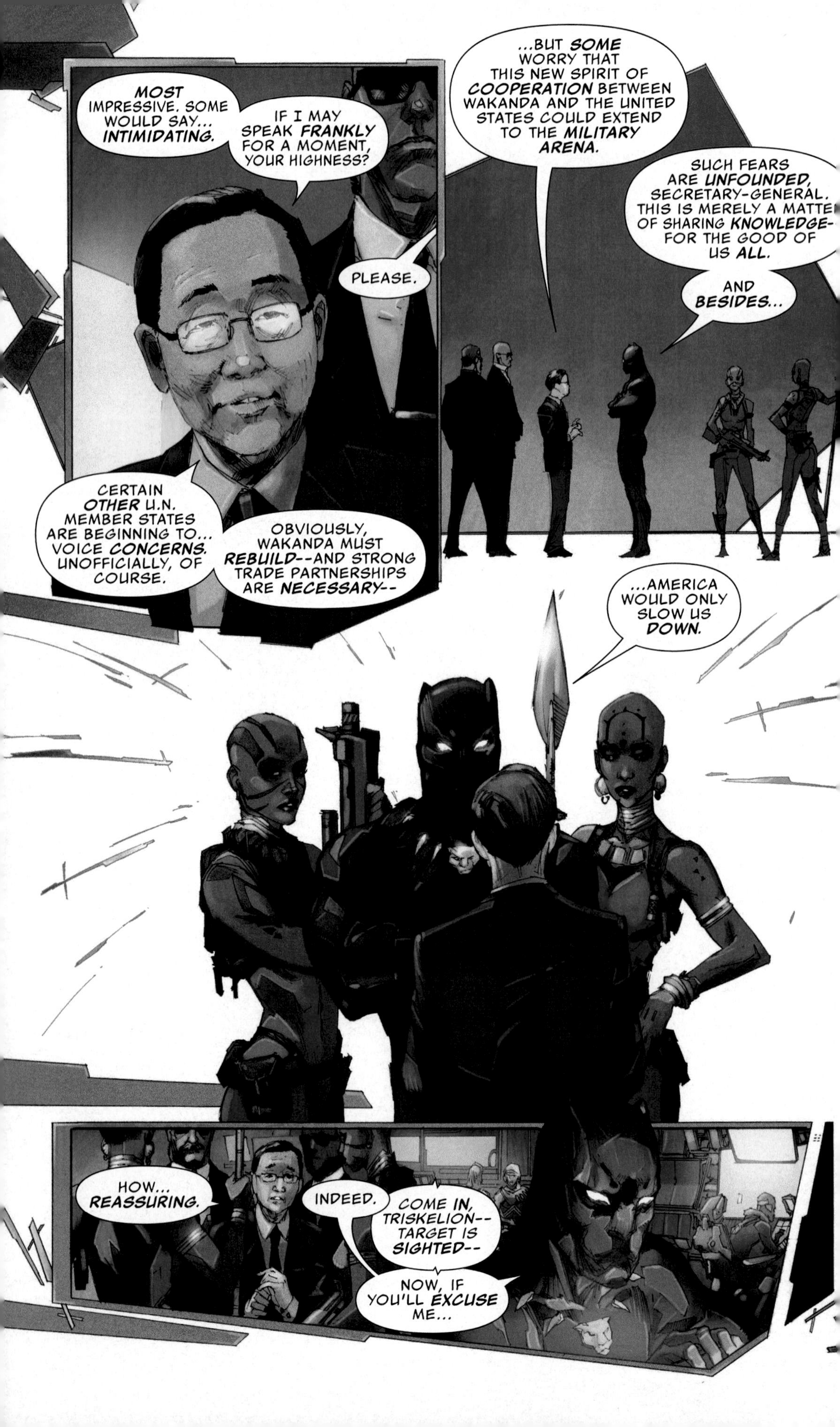
MOST IMPRESSIVE. SOME WOULD SAY... INTIMIDATING.
IF I MAY SPEAK FRANKLY FOR A MOMENT, YOUR HIGHNESS?
PLEASE.
CERTAIN OTHER U.N. MEMBER STATES ARE BEGINNING TO... VOICE CONCERNS. UNOFFICIALLY, OF COURSE.
OBVIOUSLY, WAKANDA MUST REBUILD--AND STRONG TRADE PARTNERSHIPS ARE NECESSARY--
...BUT SOME WORRY THAT THIS NEW SPIRIT OF COOPERATION BETWEEN WAKANDA AND THE UNITED STATES COULD EXTEND TO THE MILITARY ARENA.
SUCH FEARS ARE UNFOUNDED, SECRETARY-GENERAL. THIS IS MERELY A MATTE OF SHARING KNOWLEDGE- FOR THE GOOD OF US ALL.
AND BESIDES...
...AMERICA WOULD ONLY SLOW US DOWN.
HOW... REASSURING.
INDEED.
COME IN, TRISKELION-- TARGET IS SIGHTED--
NOW, IF YOU'LL EXCUSE ME...

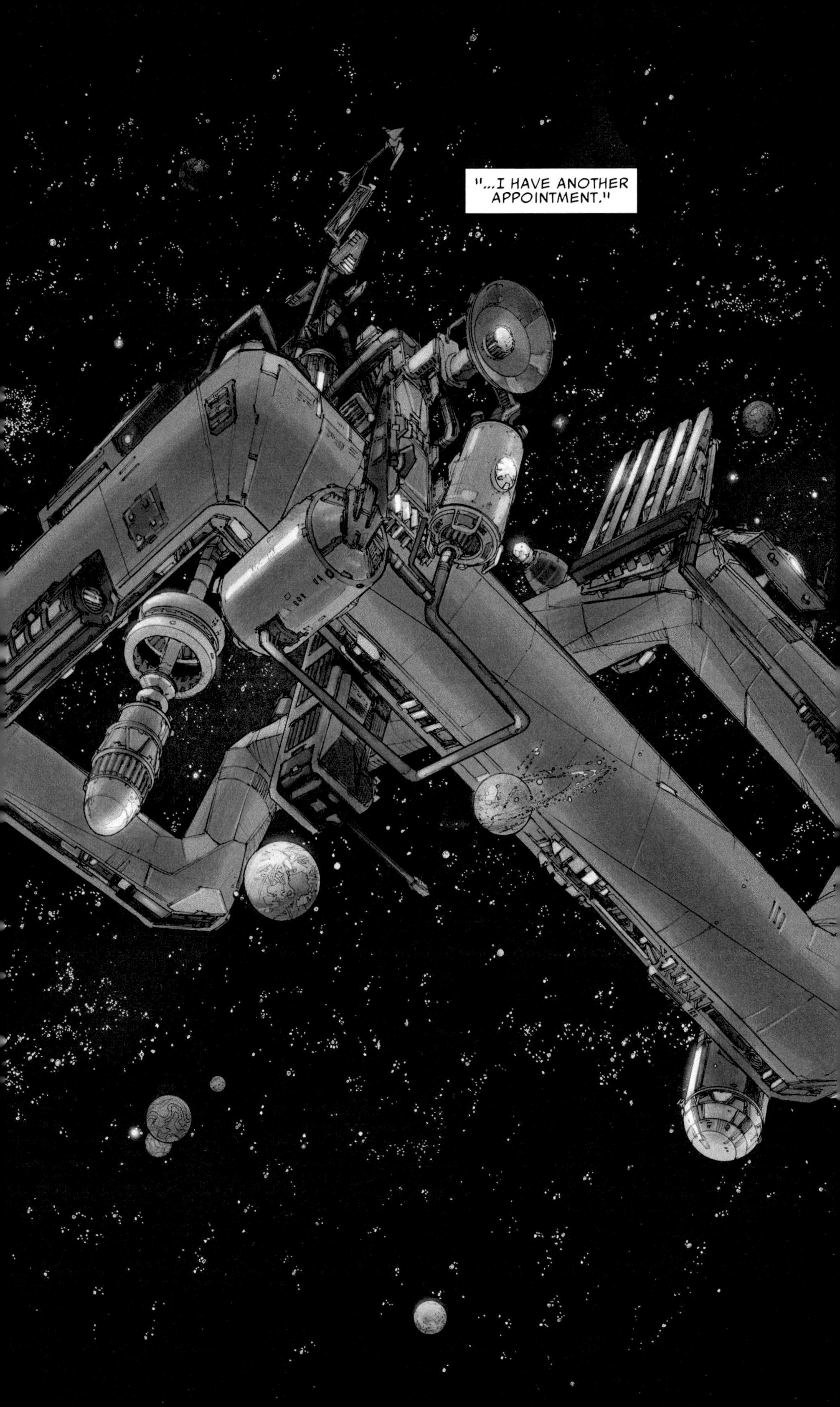
"...I HAVE ANOTHER APPOINTMENT."

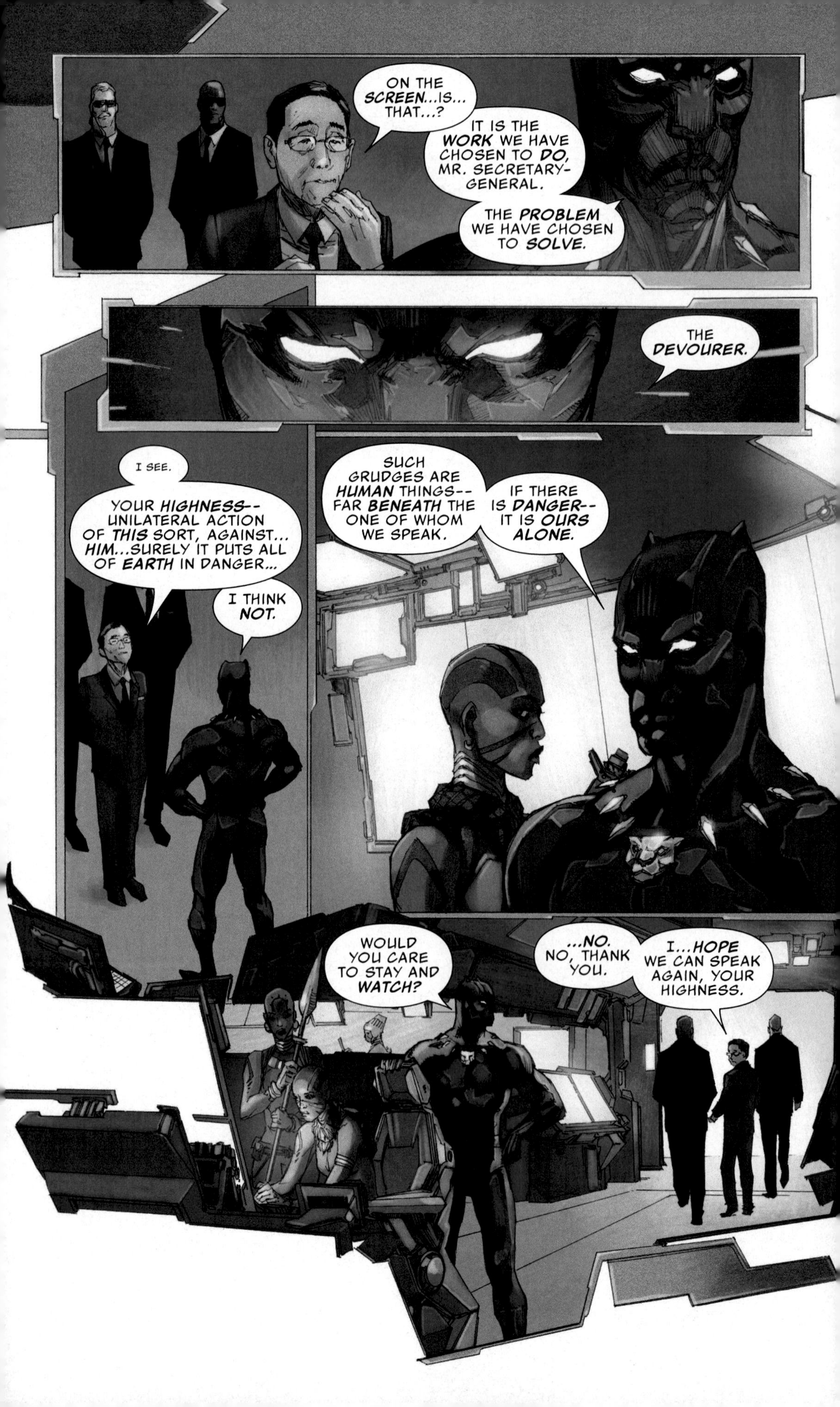

ON THE SCREEN...IS... THAT...?
IT IS THE WORK WE HAVE CHOSEN TO DO, MR. SECRETARY-GENERAL.
THE PROBLEM WE HAVE CHOSEN TO SOLVE.
THE DEVOURER.
I SEE.
YOUR HIGHNESS-- UNILATERAL ACTION OF THIS SORT, AGAINST... HIM...SURELY IT PUTS ALL OF EARTH IN DANGER...
I THINK NOT.
SUCH GRUDGES ARE HUMAN THINGS-- FAR BENEATH THE ONE OF WHOM WE SPEAK.
IF THERE IS DANGER-- IT IS OURS ALONE.
WOULD YOU CARE TO STAY AND WATCH?
...NO. NO, THANK YOU.
I...HOPE WE CAN SPEAK AGAIN, YOUR HIGHNESS.

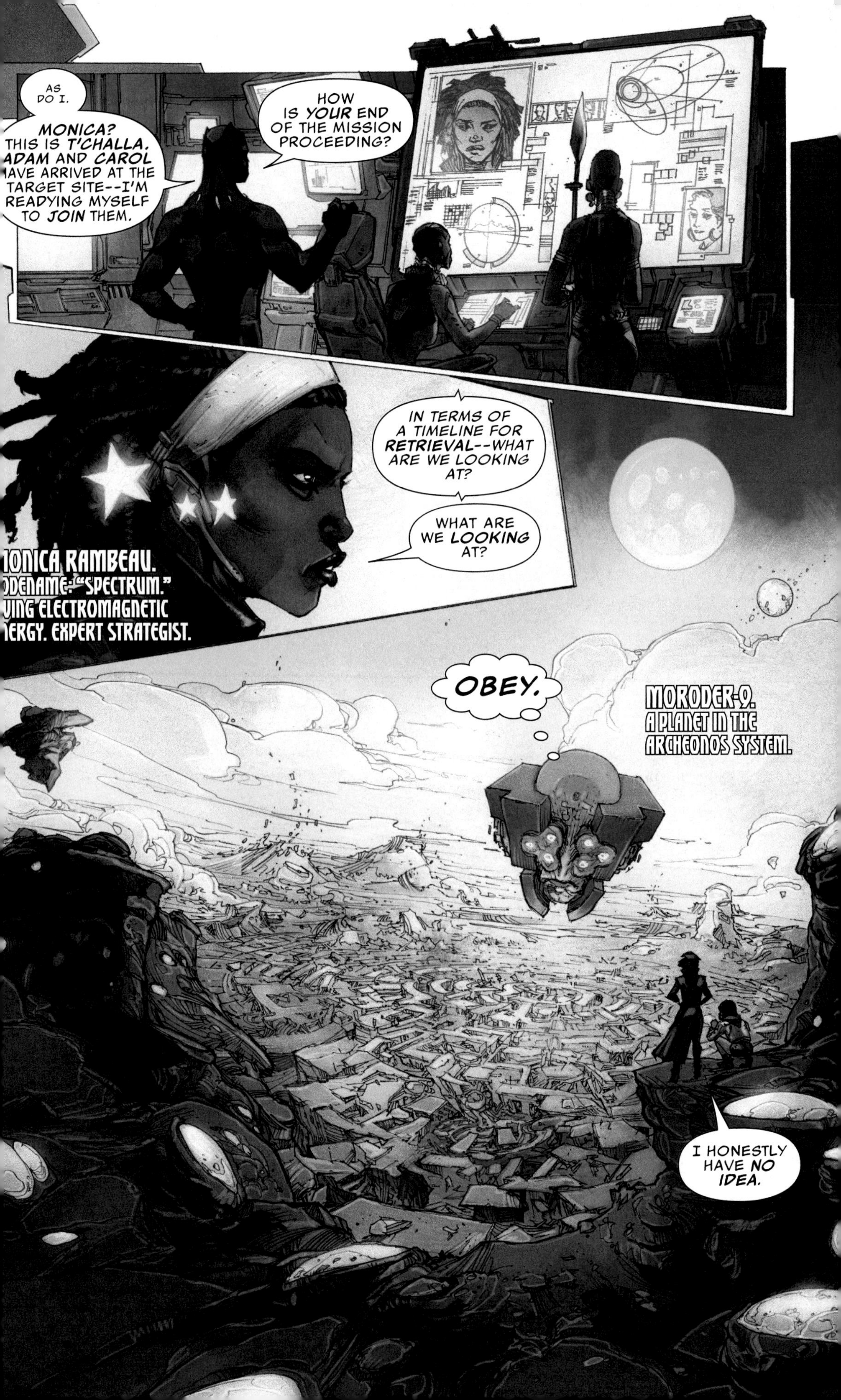
AS DO I.
MONICA? THIS IS T'CHALLA. ADAM AND CAROL HAVE ARRIVED AT THE TARGET SITE--I'M READYING MYSELF TO JOIN THEM.
HOW IS YOUR END OF THE MISSION PROCEEDING?
IN TERMS OF A TIMELINE FOR RETRIEVAL--WHAT ARE WE LOOKING AT?
WHAT ARE WE LOOKING AT?
ONICA RAMBEAU. ODENAME: "SPECTRUM." VING ELECTROMAGNETIC ERGY. EXPERT STRATEGIST.
OBEY.
MORODER-9. A PLANET IN THE ARCHEONOS SYSTEM.
I HONESTLY HAVE NO IDEA.

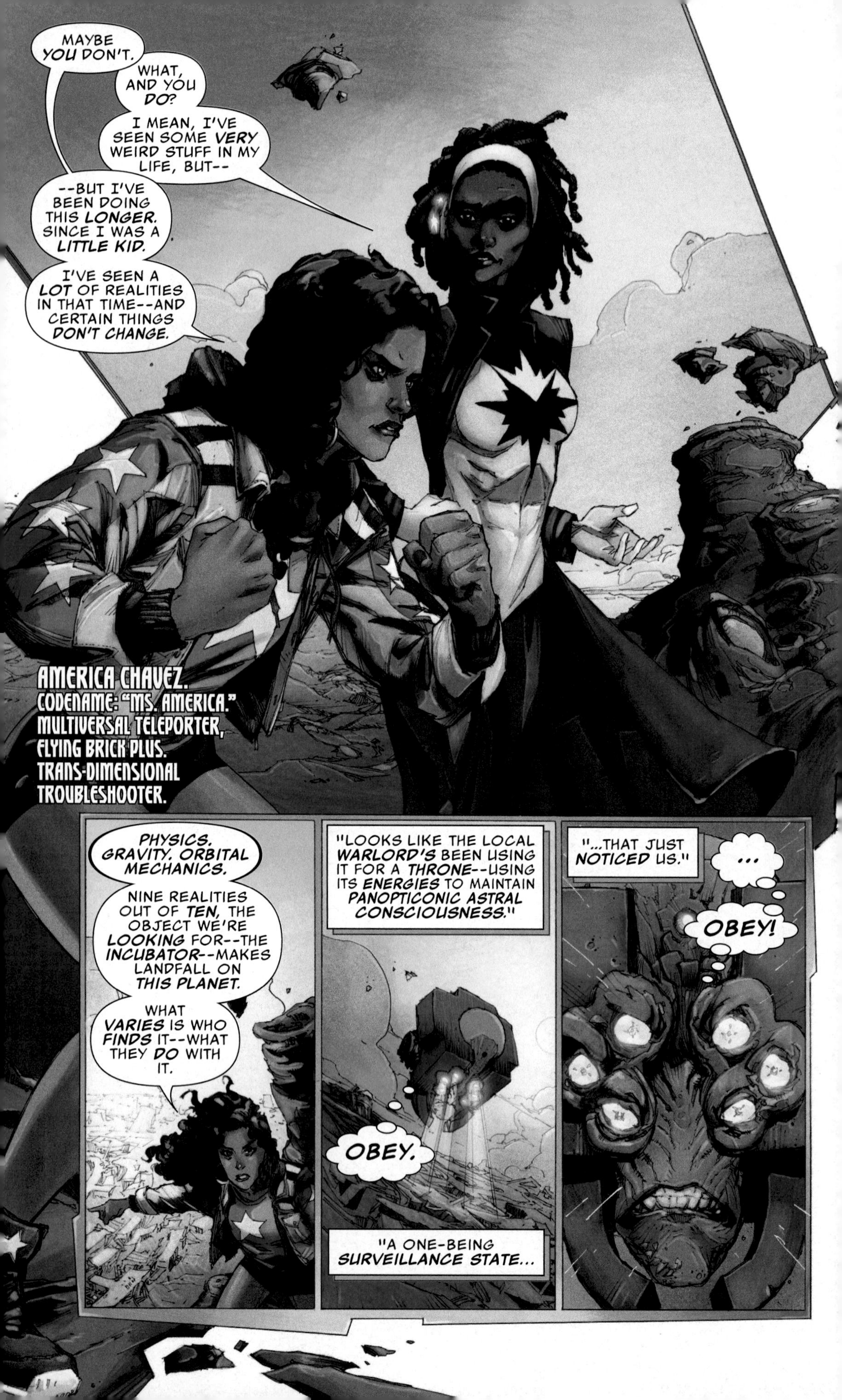

MAYBE YOU DON'T.
WHAT, AND YOU DO?
I MEAN, I'VE SEEN SOME VERY WEIRD STUFF IN MY LIFE, BUT--
--BUT I'VE BEEN DOING THIS LONGER. SINCE I WAS A LITTLE KID.
I'VE SEEN A LOT OF REALITIES IN THAT TIME--AND CERTAIN THINGS DON'T CHANGE.
AMERICA CHAVEZ. CODENAME: "MS. AMERICA." MULTIVERSAL TELEPORTER, FLYING BRICK PLUS. TRANS-DIMENSIONAL TROUBLESHOOTER.
PHYSICS. GRAVITY. ORBITAL MECHANICS.
NINE REALITIES OUT OF TEN, THE OBJECT WE'RE LOOKING FOR--THE INCUBATOR--MAKES LANDFALL ON THIS PLANET.
WHAT VARIES IS WHO FINDS IT--WHAT THEY DO WITH IT.
"LOOKS LIKE THE LOCAL WARLORD'S BEEN USING IT FOR A THRONE--USING ITS ENERGIES TO MAINTAIN PANOPTICONIC ASTRAL CONSCIOUSNESS."
OBEY.
"A ONE-BEING SURVEILLANCE STATE...
"...THAT JUST NOTICED US."
...
OBEY!

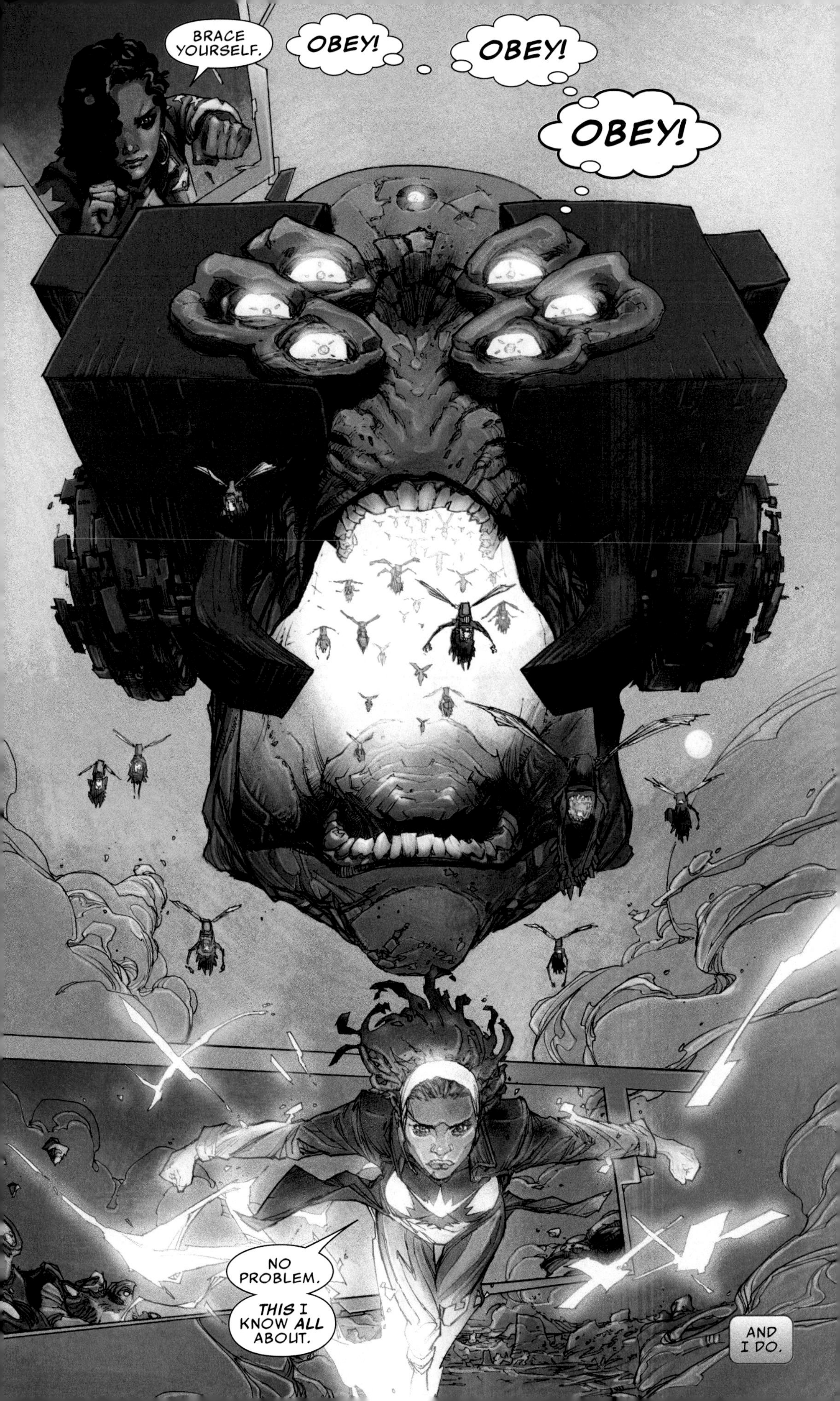
BRACE YOURSELF.
OBEY!
OBEY!
OBEY!
NO PROBLEM.
THIS I KNOW ALL ABOUT.
AND I DO.

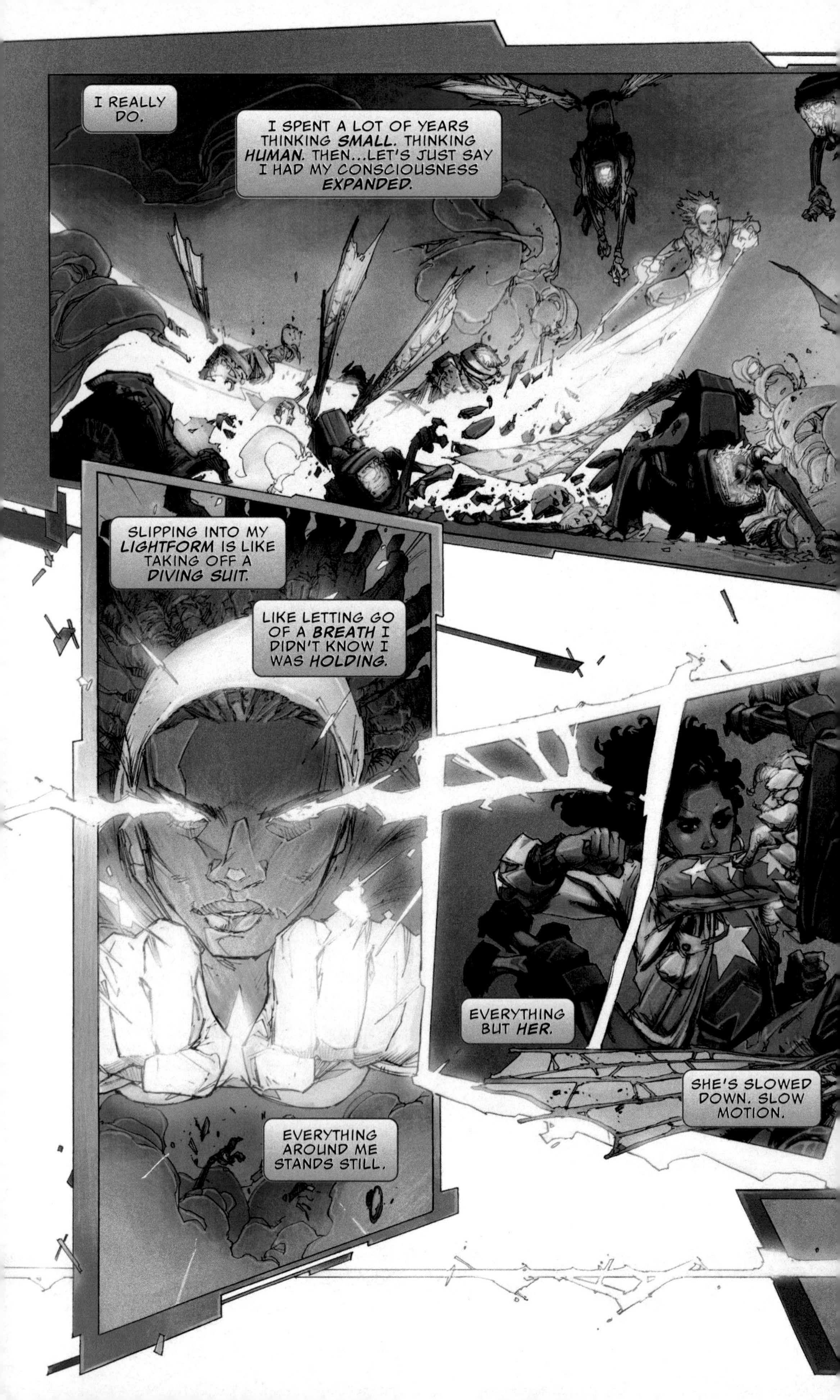
I REALLY DO.
I SPENT A LOT OF YEARS THINKING **SMALL**. THINKING ***HUMAN***. THEN...LET'S JUST SAY I HAD MY CONSCIOUSNESS ***EXPANDED***.
SLIPPING INTO MY ***LIGHTFORM*** IS LIKE TAKING OFF A ***DIVING SUIT***.
LIKE LETTING GO OF A ***BREATH*** I DIDN'T KNOW I WAS ***HOLDING***.
EVERYTHING AROUND ME STANDS STILL.
EVERYTHING BUT ***HER***.
SHE'S SLOWED DOWN. SLOW MOTION.

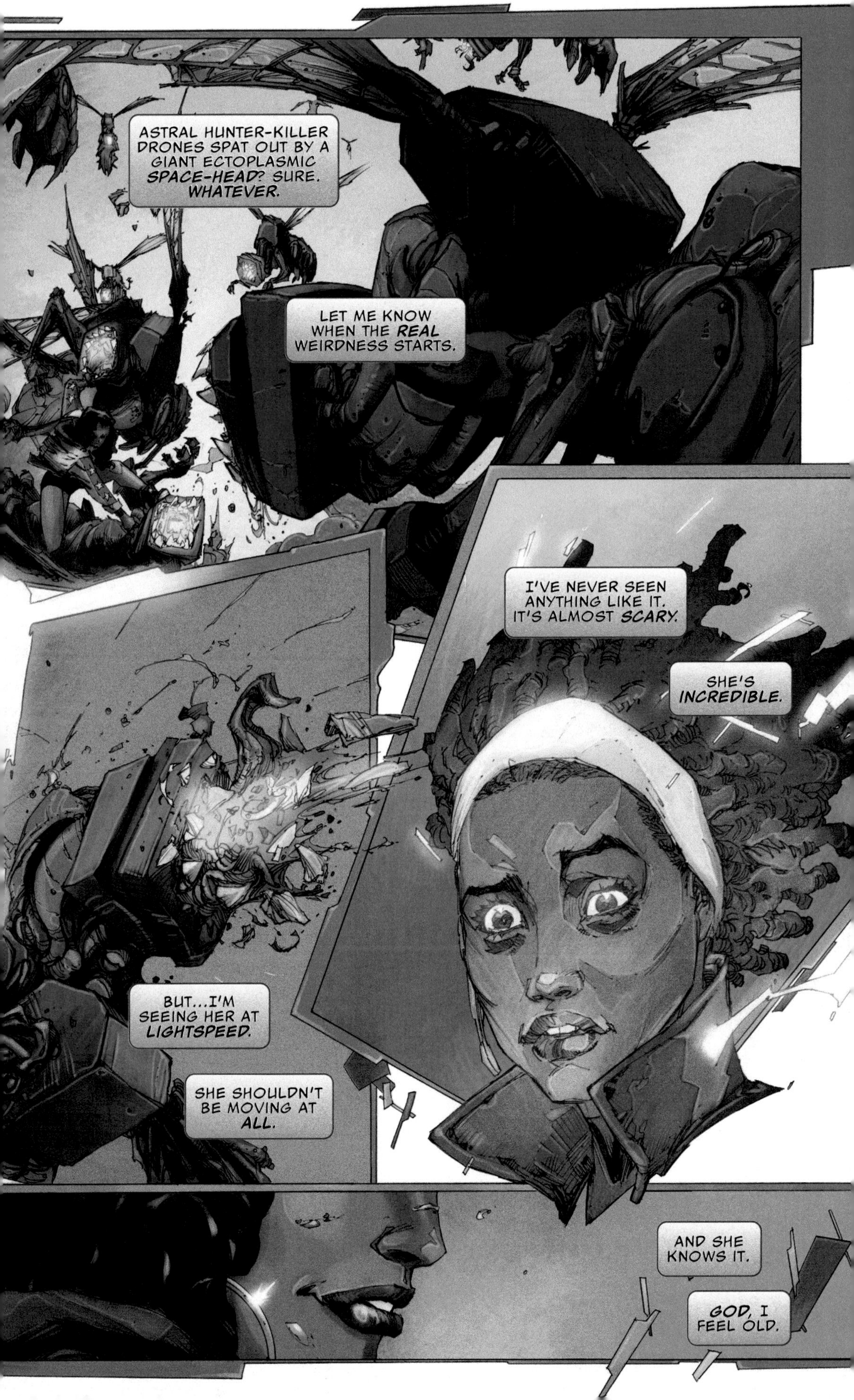
ASTRAL HUNTER-KILLER DRONES SPAT OUT BY A GIANT ECTOPLASMIC SPACE-HEAD? SURE. WHATEVER.
LET ME KNOW WHEN THE REAL WEIRDNESS STARTS.
I'VE NEVER SEEN ANYTHING LIKE IT. IT'S ALMOST SCARY.
SHE'S INCREDIBLE.
BUT...I'M SEEING HER AT LIGHTSPEED.
SHE SHOULDN'T BE MOVING AT ALL.
AND SHE KNOWS IT.
GOD, I FEEL OLD.

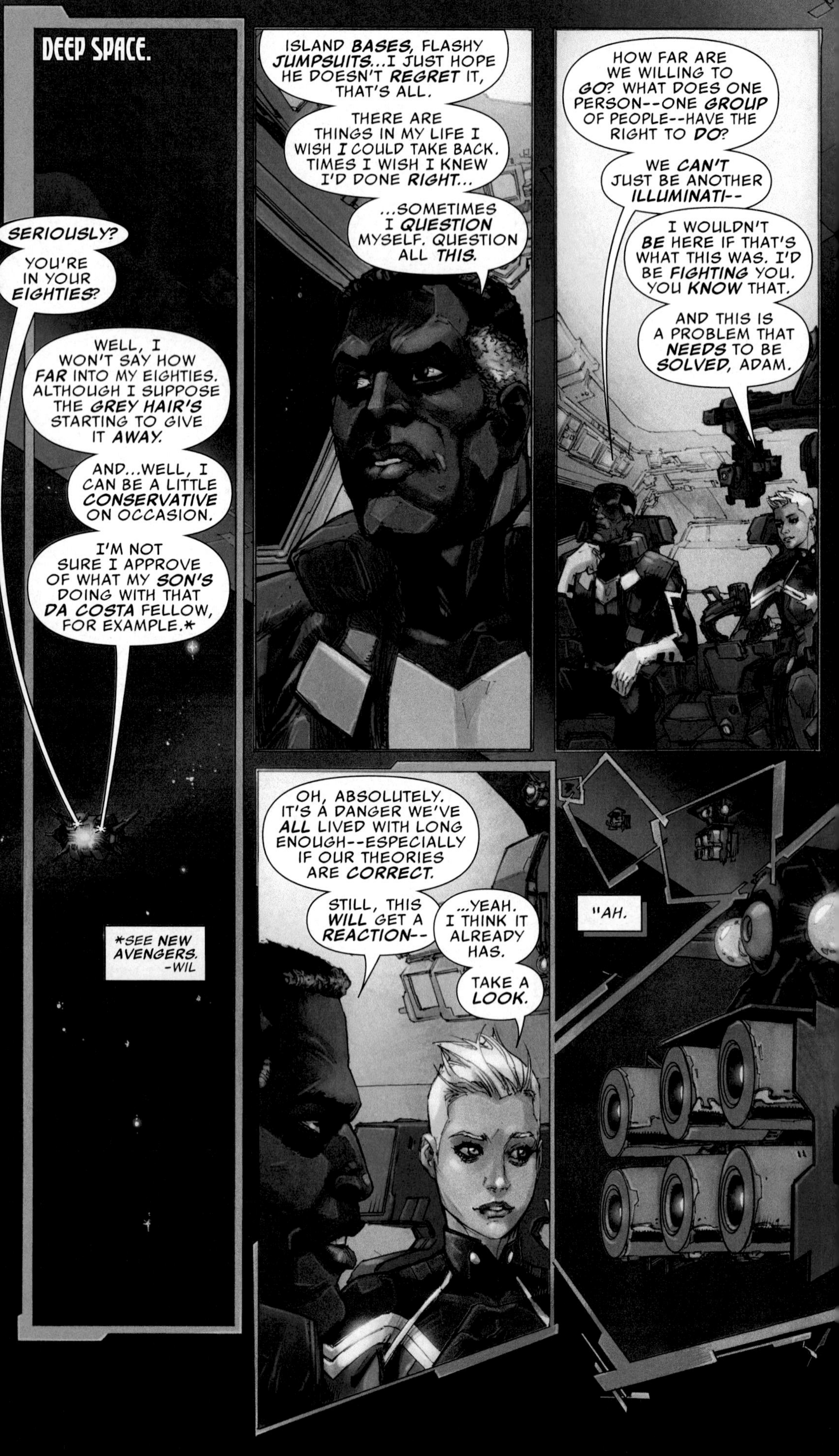
DEEP SPACE.
SERIOUSLY?
YOU'RE IN YOUR EIGHTIES?
WELL, I WON'T SAY HOW FAR INTO MY EIGHTIES. ALTHOUGH I SUPPOSE THE GREY HAIR'S STARTING TO GIVE IT AWAY.
AND...WELL, I CAN BE A LITTLE CONSERVATIVE ON OCCASION.
I'M NOT SURE I APPROVE OF WHAT MY SON'S DOING WITH THAT DA COSTA FELLOW, FOR EXAMPLE.*
*SEE NEW AVENGERS. -WIL
ISLAND BASES, FLASHY JUMPSUITS...I JUST HOPE HE DOESN'T REGRET IT, THAT'S ALL.
THERE ARE THINGS IN MY LIFE I WISH I COULD TAKE BACK. TIMES I WISH I KNEW I'D DONE RIGHT...
...SOMETIMES I QUESTION MYSELF. QUESTION ALL THIS.
HOW FAR ARE WE WILLING TO GO? WHAT DOES ONE PERSON--ONE GROUP OF PEOPLE--HAVE THE RIGHT TO DO?
WE CAN'T JUST BE ANOTHER ILLUMINATI--
I WOULDN'T BE HERE IF THAT'S WHAT THIS WAS. I'D BE FIGHTING YOU. YOU KNOW THAT.
AND THIS IS A PROBLEM THAT NEEDS TO BE SOLVED, ADAM.
OH, ABSOLUTELY. IT'S A DANGER WE'VE ALL LIVED WITH LONG ENOUGH--ESPECIALLY IF OUR THEORIES ARE CORRECT.
STILL, THIS WILL GET A REACTION--
...YEAH. I THINK IT ALREADY HAS.
TAKE A LOOK.
"AH.

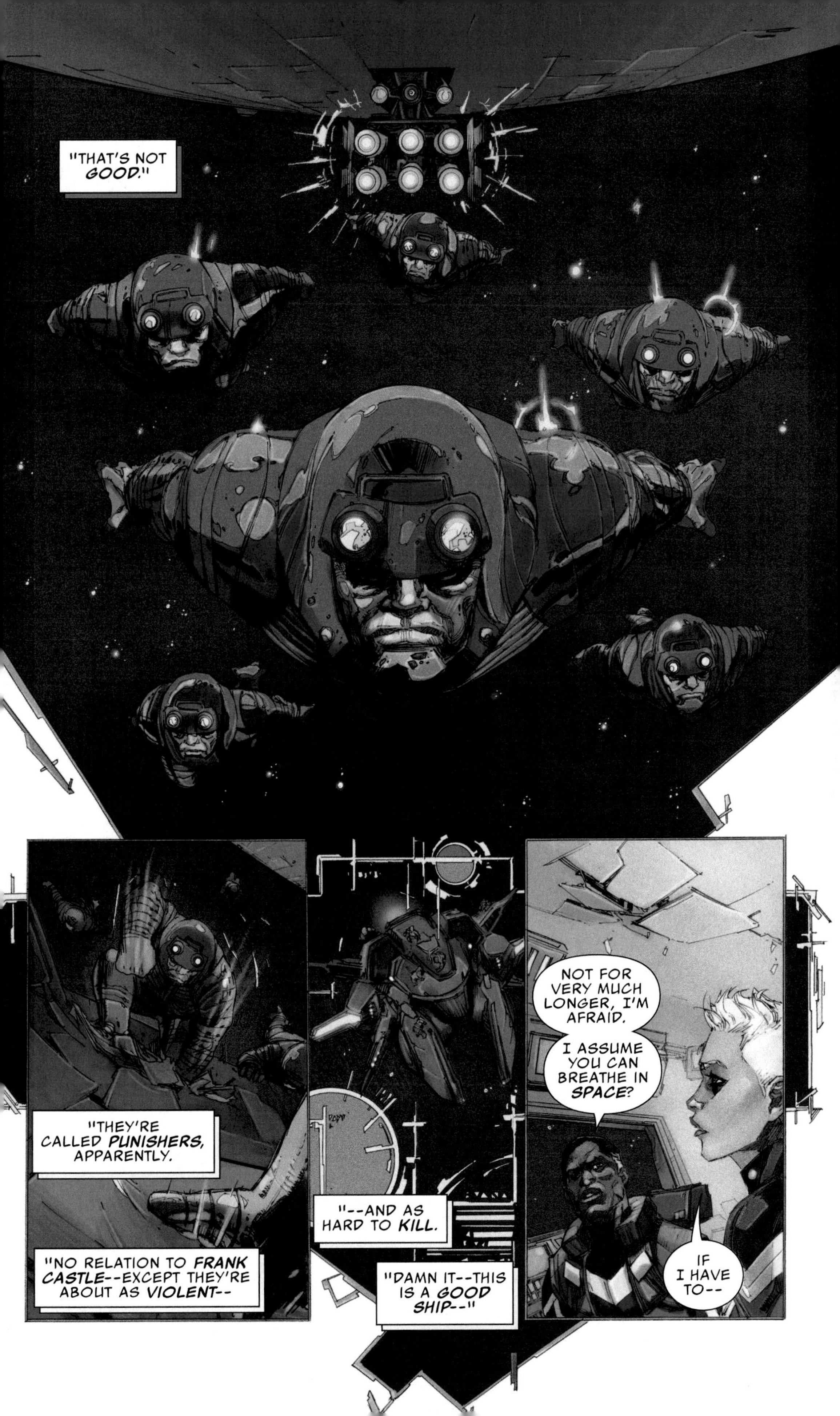
"THAT'S NOT GOOD."
"THEY'RE CALLED PUNISHERS, APPARENTLY.
"NO RELATION TO FRANK CASTLE--EXCEPT THEY'RE ABOUT AS VIOLENT--
"--AND AS HARD TO KILL.
"DAMN IT--THIS IS A GOOD SHIP--"
NOT FOR VERY MUCH LONGER, I'M AFRAID.
I ASSUME YOU CAN BREATHE IN SPACE?
IF I HAVE TO--

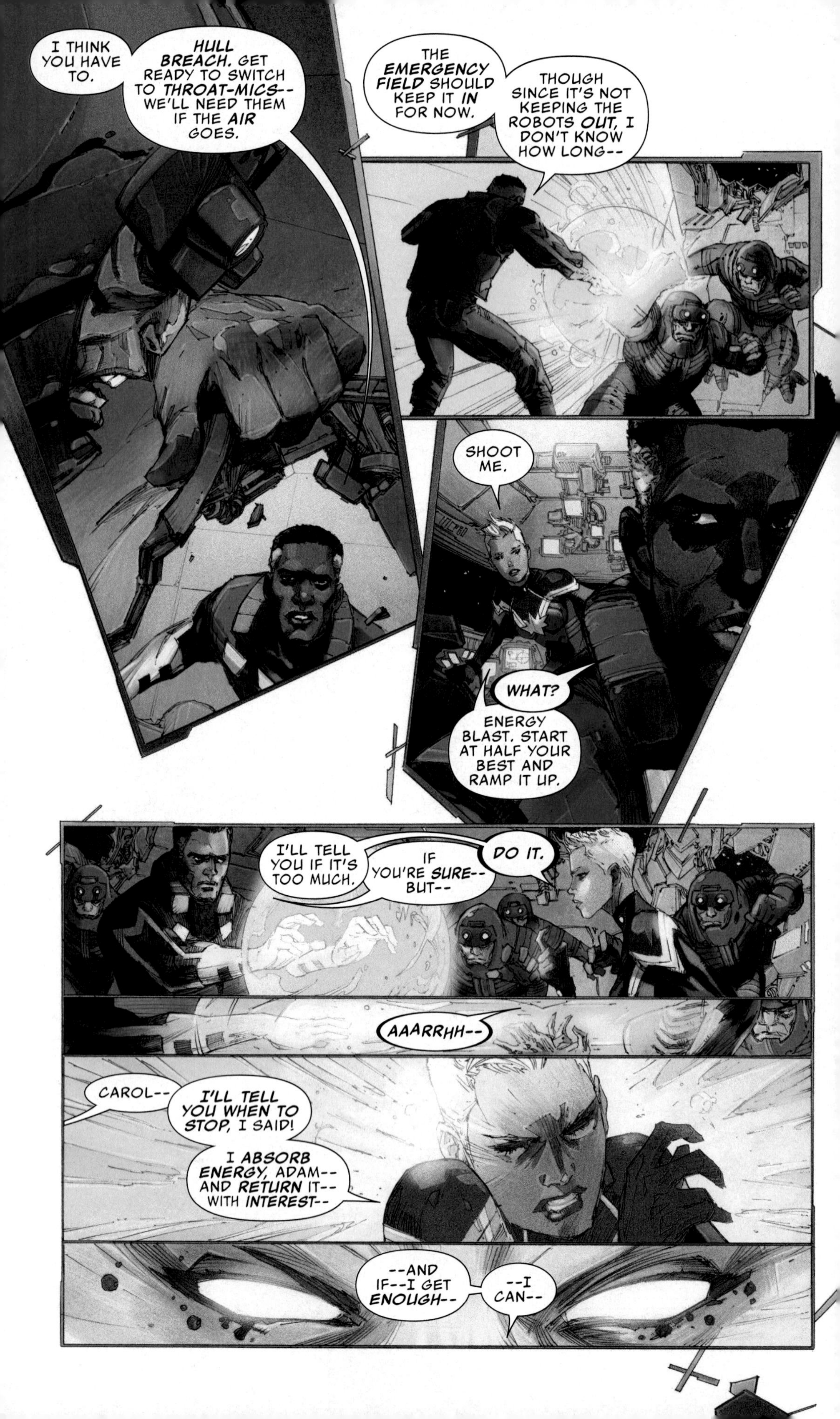
I THINK YOU HAVE TO.
HULL BREACH. GET READY TO SWITCH TO THROAT-MICS--WE'LL NEED THEM IF THE AIR GOES.
THE EMERGENCY FIELD SHOULD KEEP IT IN FOR NOW.
THOUGH SINCE IT'S NOT KEEPING THE ROBOTS OUT, I DON'T KNOW HOW LONG--
SHOOT ME.
WHAT?
ENERGY BLAST. START AT HALF YOUR BEST AND RAMP IT UP.
I'LL TELL YOU IF IT'S TOO MUCH.
IF YOU'RE SURE--BUT--
DO IT.
AAARRHH--
CAROL--
I'LL TELL YOU WHEN TO STOP, I SAID!
I ABSORB ENERGY, ADAM--AND RETURN IT--WITH INTEREST--
--AND IF--I GET ENOUGH--
--I CAN--

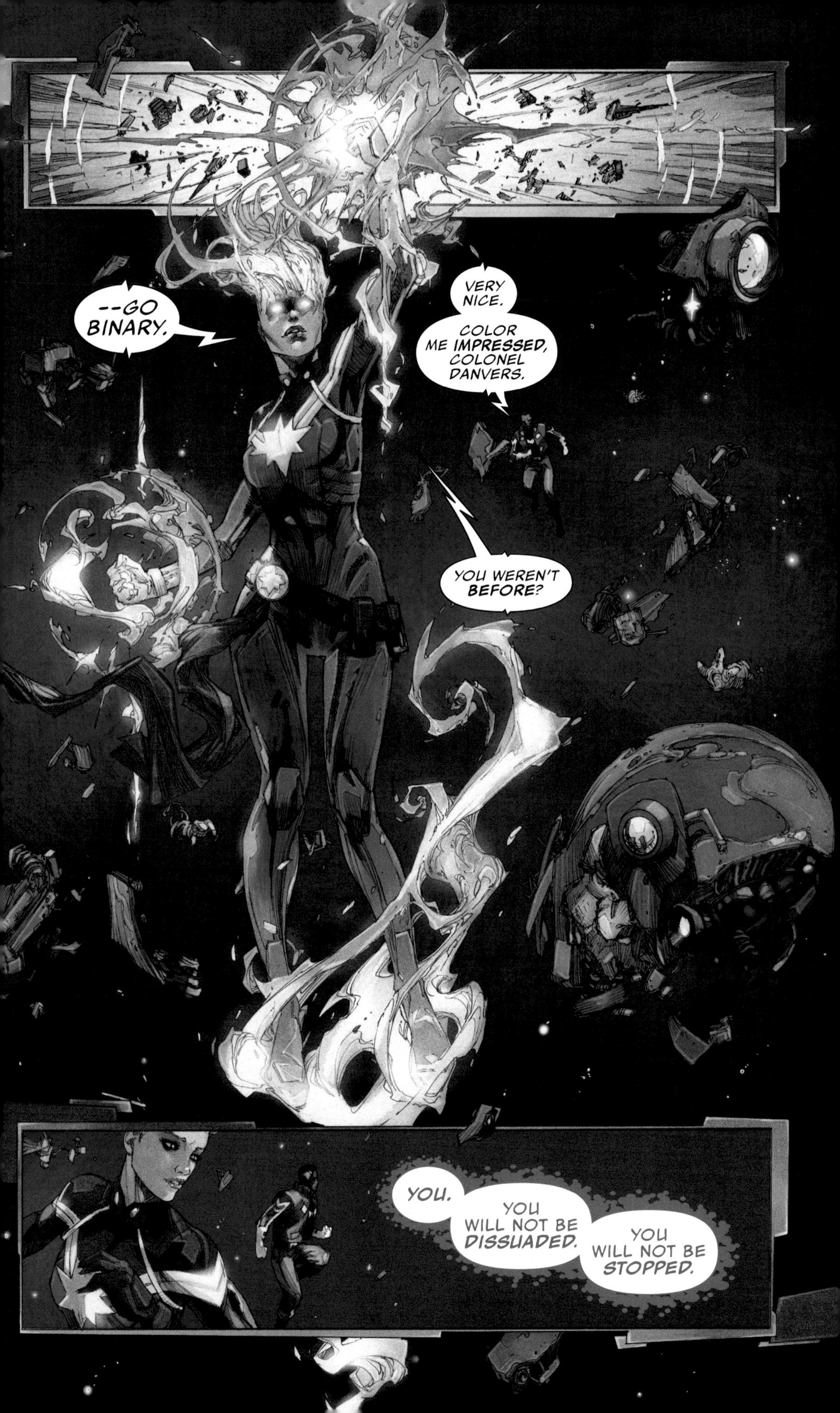
--GO BINARY.
VERY NICE.
COLOR ME IMPRESSED, COLONEL DANVERS.
YOU WEREN'T BEFORE?
YOU.
YOU WILL NOT BE DISSUADED.
YOU WILL NOT BE STOPPED.

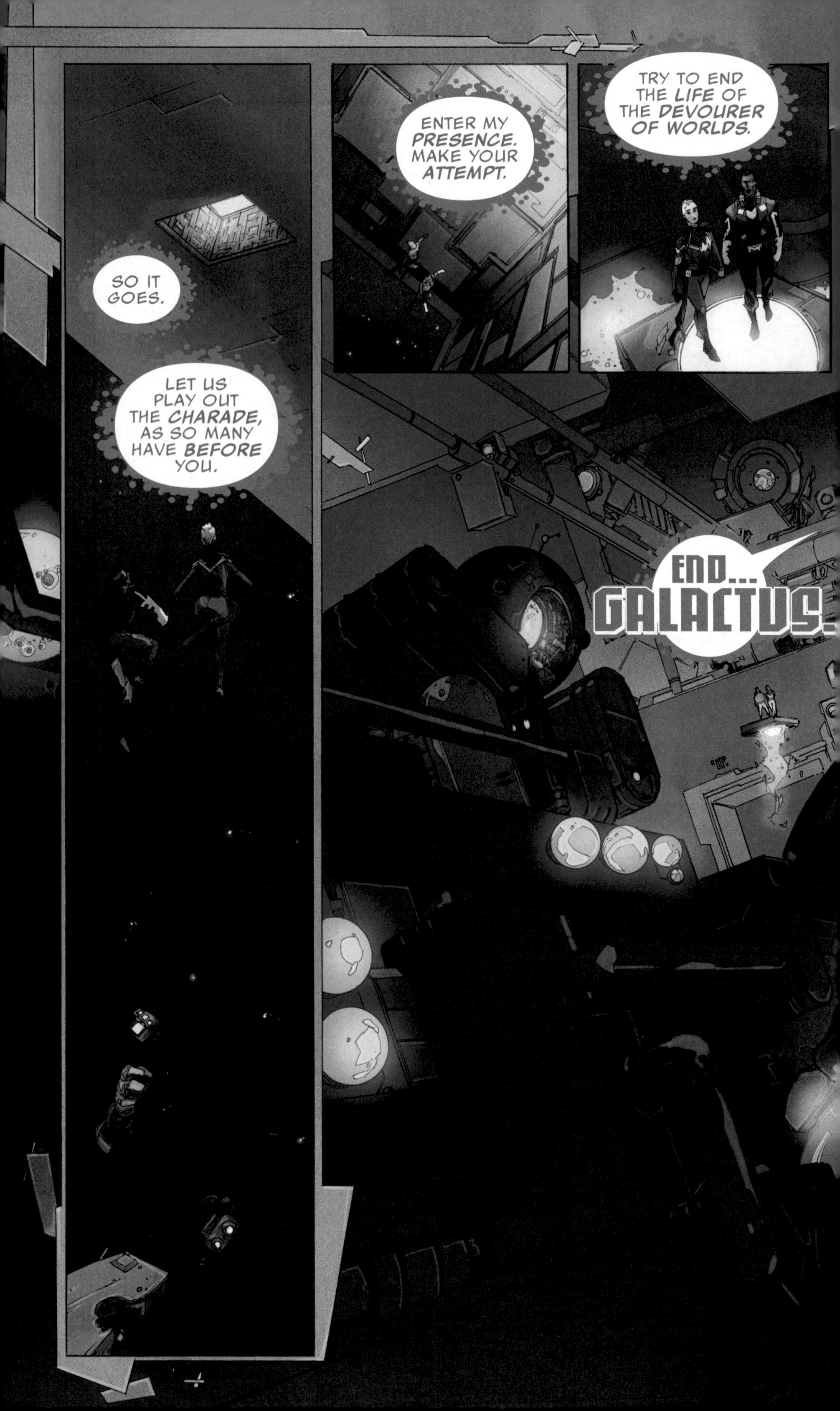

SO IT GOES.
LET US PLAY OUT THE CHARADE, AS SO MANY HAVE BEFORE YOU.
ENTER MY PRESENCE. MAKE YOUR ATTEMPT.
TRY TO END THE LIFE OF THE DEVOURER OF WORLDS.
END... GALACTUS.

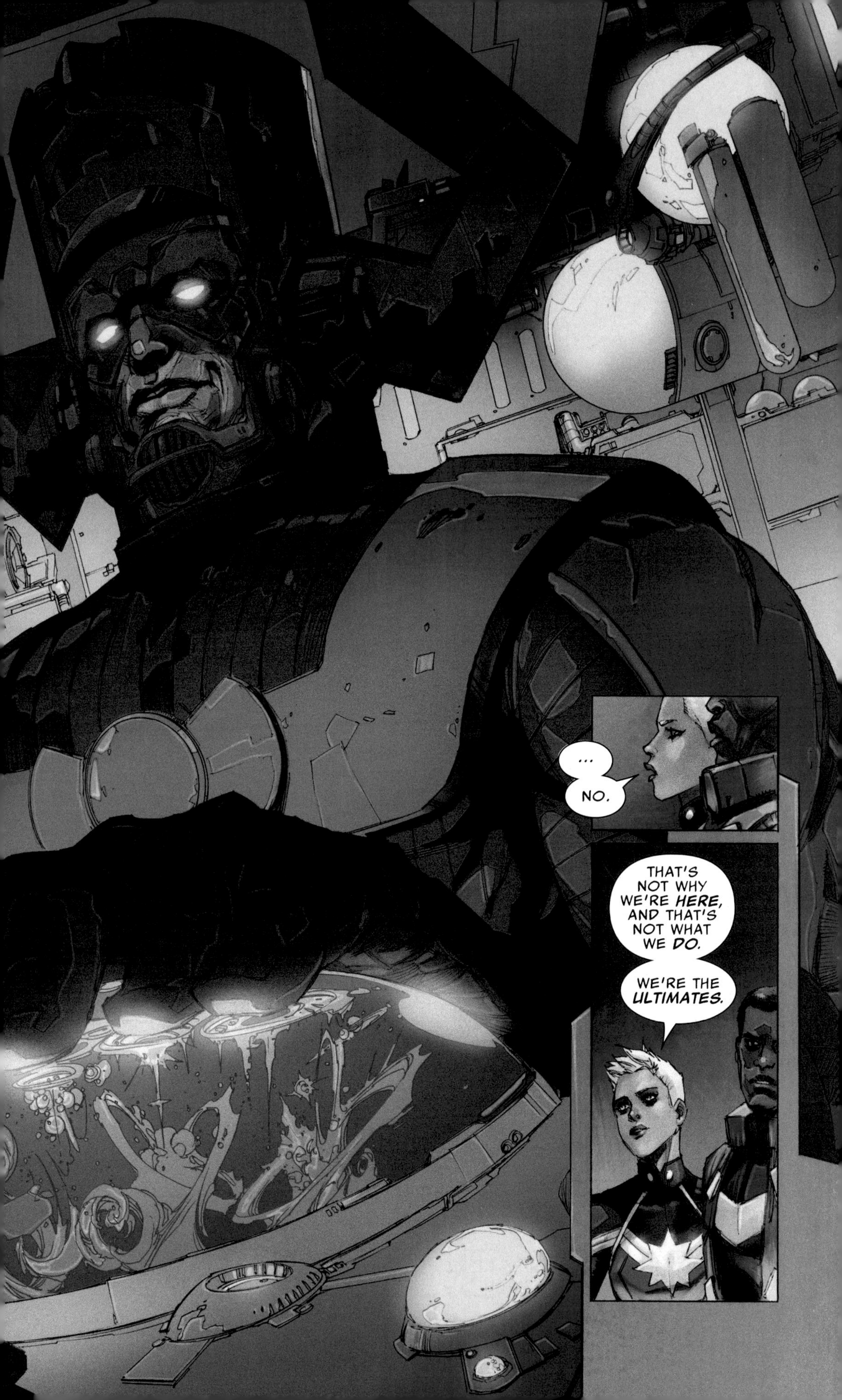
...
NO.
THAT'S NOT WHY WE'RE *HERE*, AND THAT'S NOT WHAT WE *DO*.
WE'RE THE *ULTIMATES*.

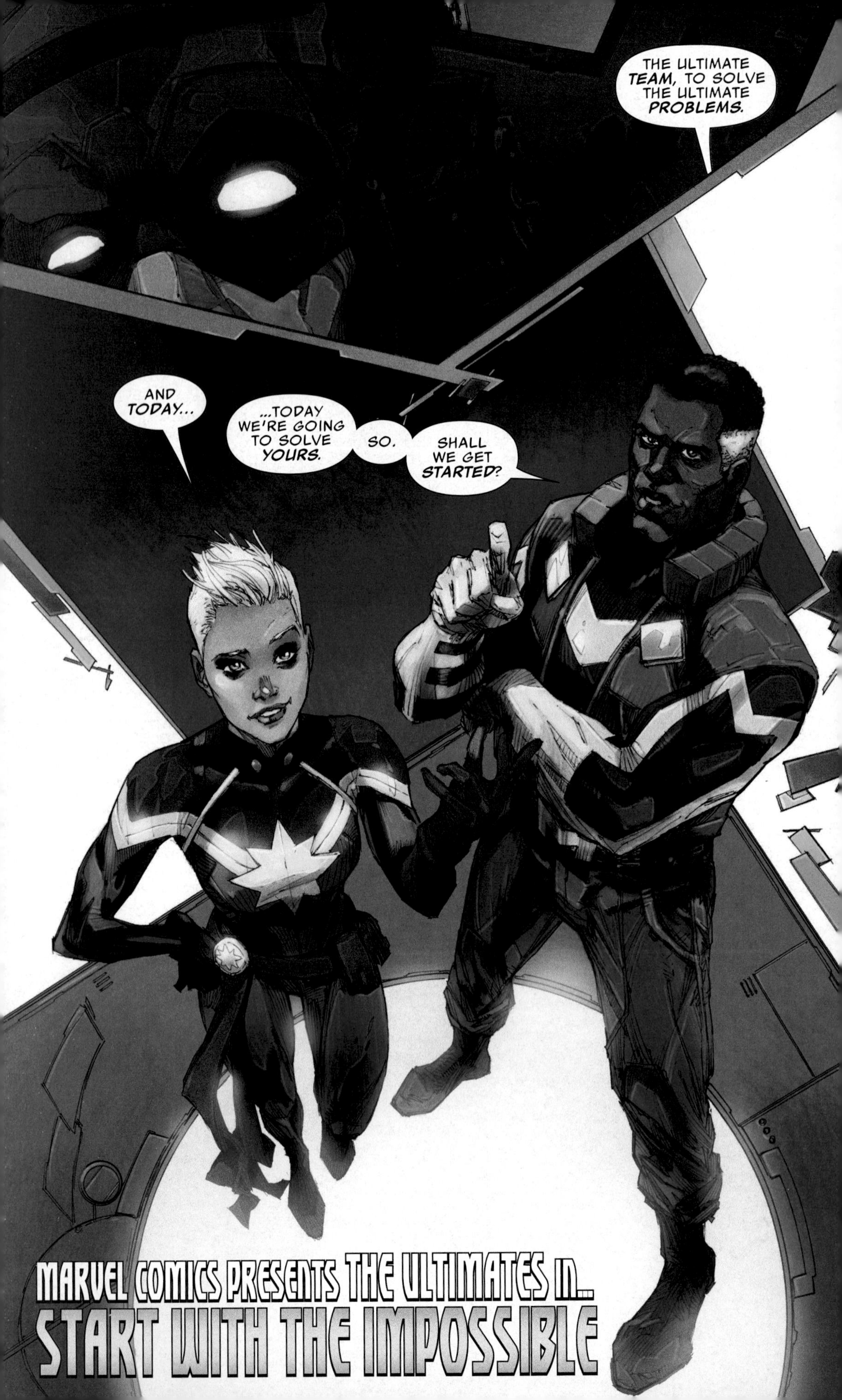
THE ULTIMATE TEAM, TO SOLVE THE ULTIMATE PROBLEMS.
AND TODAY...
...TODAY WE'RE GOING TO SOLVE YOURS.
SO.
SHALL WE GET STARTED?
MARVEL COMICS PRESENTS THE ULTIMATES IN...
START WITH THE IMPOSSIBLE

#1 VARIANT BY
ART ADAMS
& JASON KEITH

#1 VARIANT BY
TERRY DODSON &
RACHEL DODSON

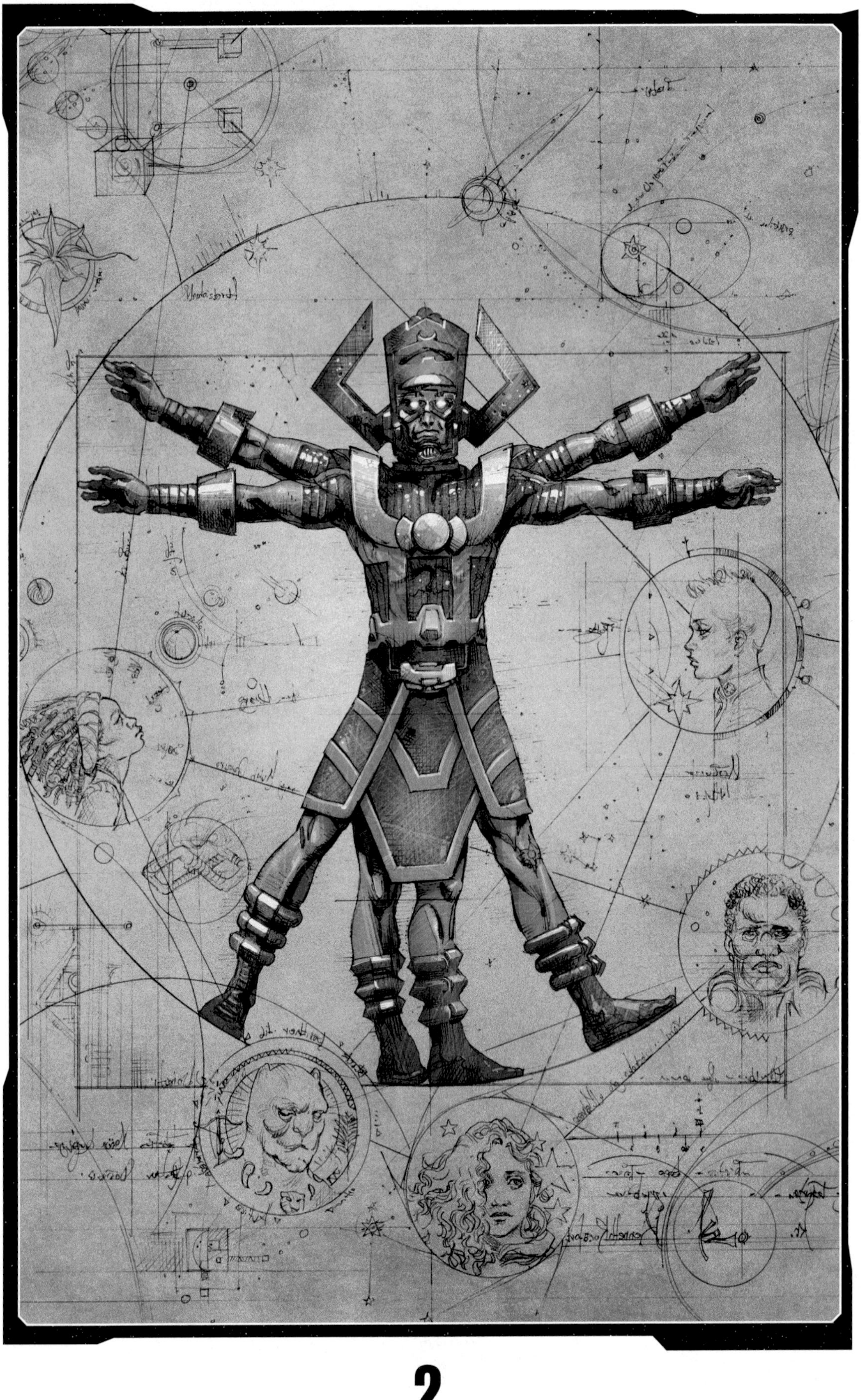

2

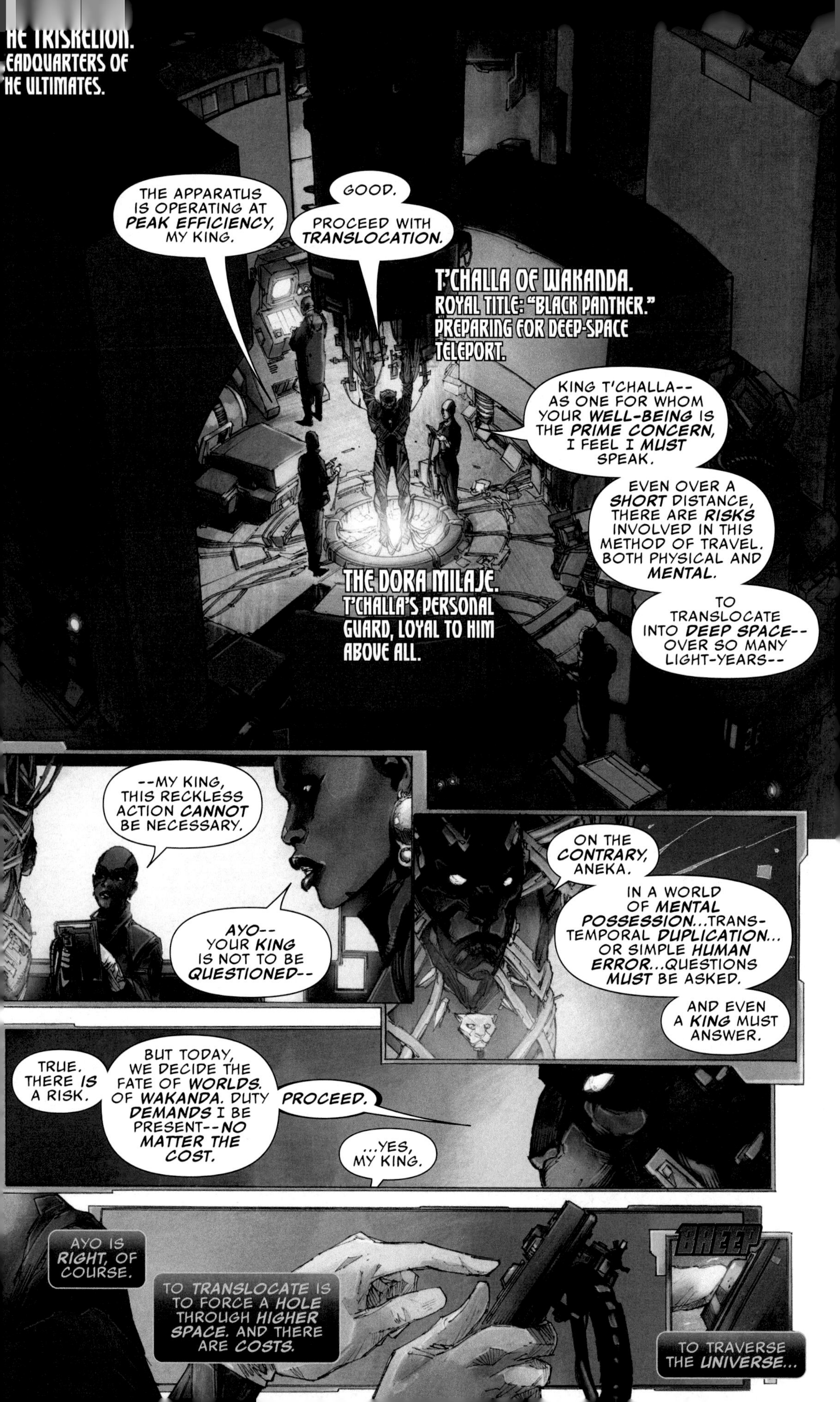
HE TRISKELION. EADQUARTERS OF HE ULTIMATES.
THE APPARATUS IS OPERATING AT PEAK EFFICIENCY, MY KING.
GOOD.
PROCEED WITH TRANSLOCATION.
T'CHALLA OF WAKANDA. ROYAL TITLE: "BLACK PANTHER." PREPARING FOR DEEP-SPACE TELEPORT.
KING T'CHALLA-- AS ONE FOR WHOM YOUR WELL-BEING IS THE PRIME CONCERN, I FEEL I MUST SPEAK.
EVEN OVER A SHORT DISTANCE, THERE ARE RISKS INVOLVED IN THIS METHOD OF TRAVEL. BOTH PHYSICAL AND MENTAL.
TO TRANSLOCATE INTO DEEP SPACE-- OVER SO MANY LIGHT-YEARS--
THE DORA MILAJE. T'CHALLA'S PERSONAL GUARD, LOYAL TO HIM ABOVE ALL.
--MY KING, THIS RECKLESS ACTION CANNOT BE NECESSARY.
AYO-- YOUR KING IS NOT TO BE QUESTIONED--
ON THE CONTRARY, ANEKA.
IN A WORLD OF MENTAL POSSESSION...TRANS-TEMPORAL DUPLICATION... OR SIMPLE HUMAN ERROR...QUESTIONS MUST BE ASKED.
AND EVEN A KING MUST ANSWER.
TRUE. THERE IS A RISK.
BUT TODAY, WE DECIDE THE FATE OF WORLDS. OF WAKANDA. DUTY DEMANDS I BE PRESENT--NO MATTER THE COST.
PROCEED.
...YES, MY KING.
AYO IS RIGHT, OF COURSE.
TO TRANSLOCATE IS TO FORCE A HOLE THROUGH HIGHER SPACE. AND THERE ARE COSTS.
BREEP
TO TRAVERSE THE UNIVERSE...

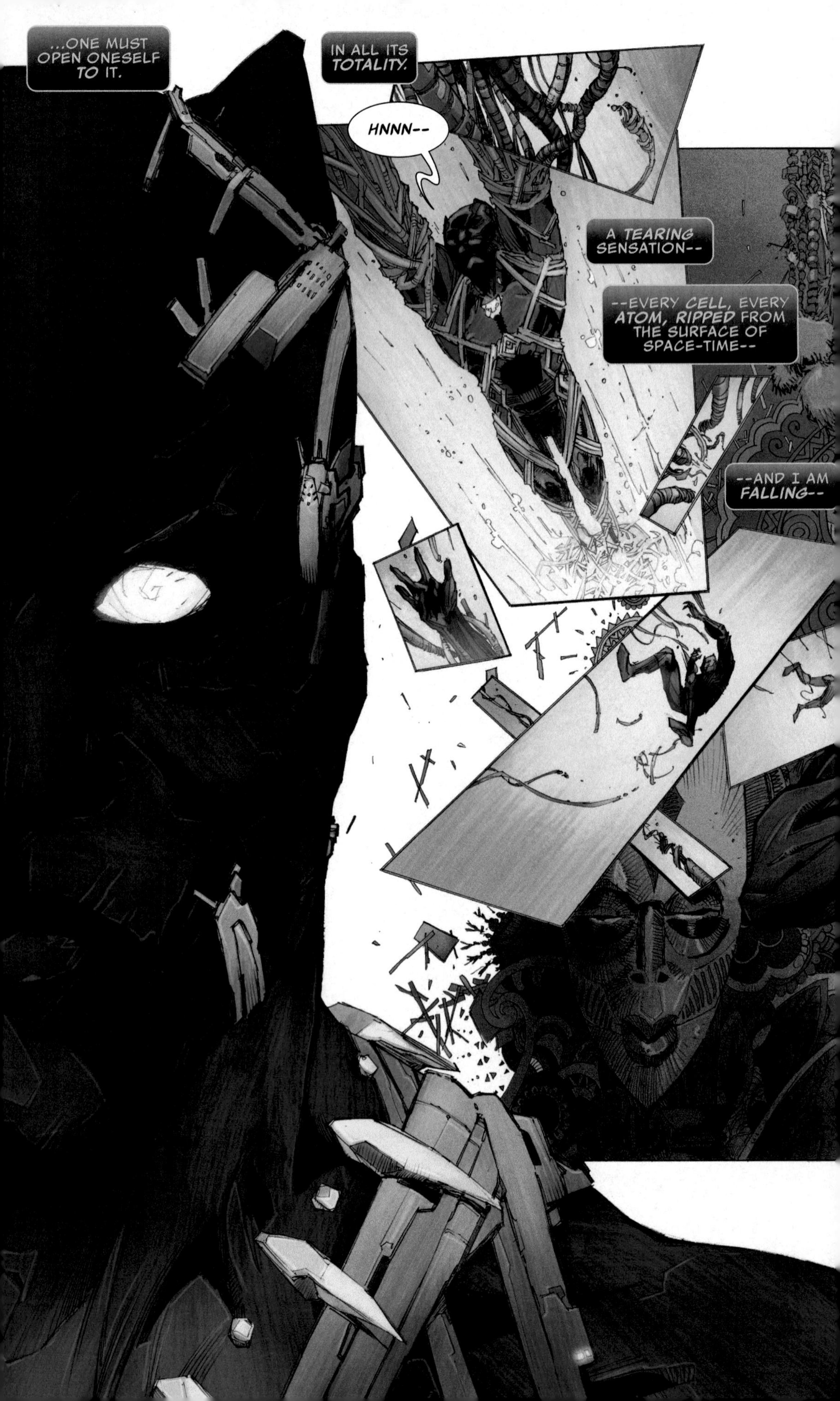
...ONE MUST OPEN ONESELF TO IT.
IN ALL ITS TOTALITY.
HNNN--
A TEARING SENSATION--
--EVERY CELL, EVERY ATOM, RIPPED FROM THE SURFACE OF SPACE-TIME--
--AND I AM FALLING--

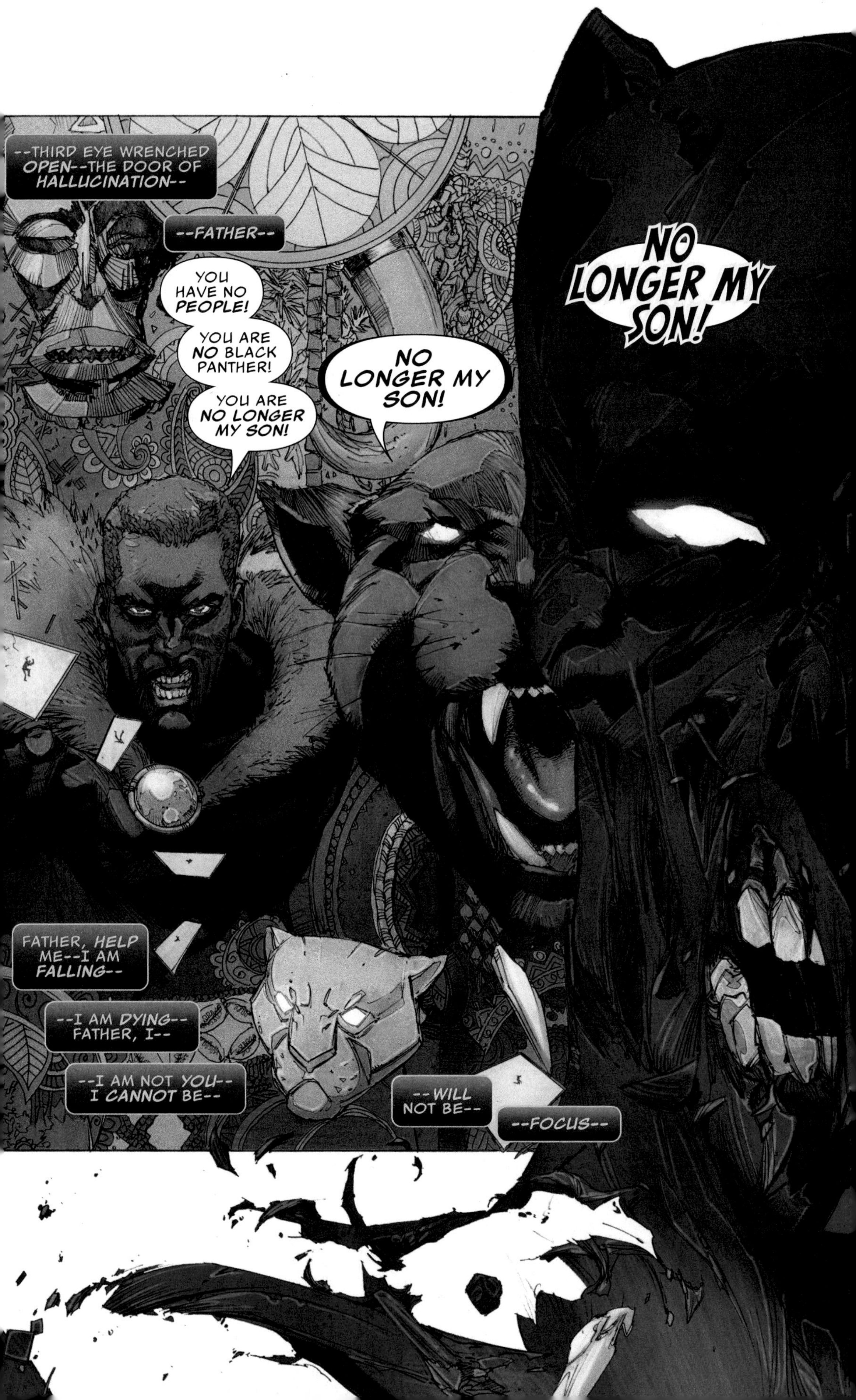

--THIRD EYE WRENCHED OPEN--THE DOOR OF HALLUCINATION--
--FATHER--
YOU HAVE NO PEOPLE!
YOU ARE NO BLACK PANTHER!
YOU ARE NO LONGER MY SON!
NO LONGER MY SON!
NO LONGER MY SON!
FATHER, HELP ME--I AM FALLING--
--I AM DYING--FATHER, I--
--I AM NOT YOU--I CANNOT BE--
--WILL NOT BE--
--FOCUS--

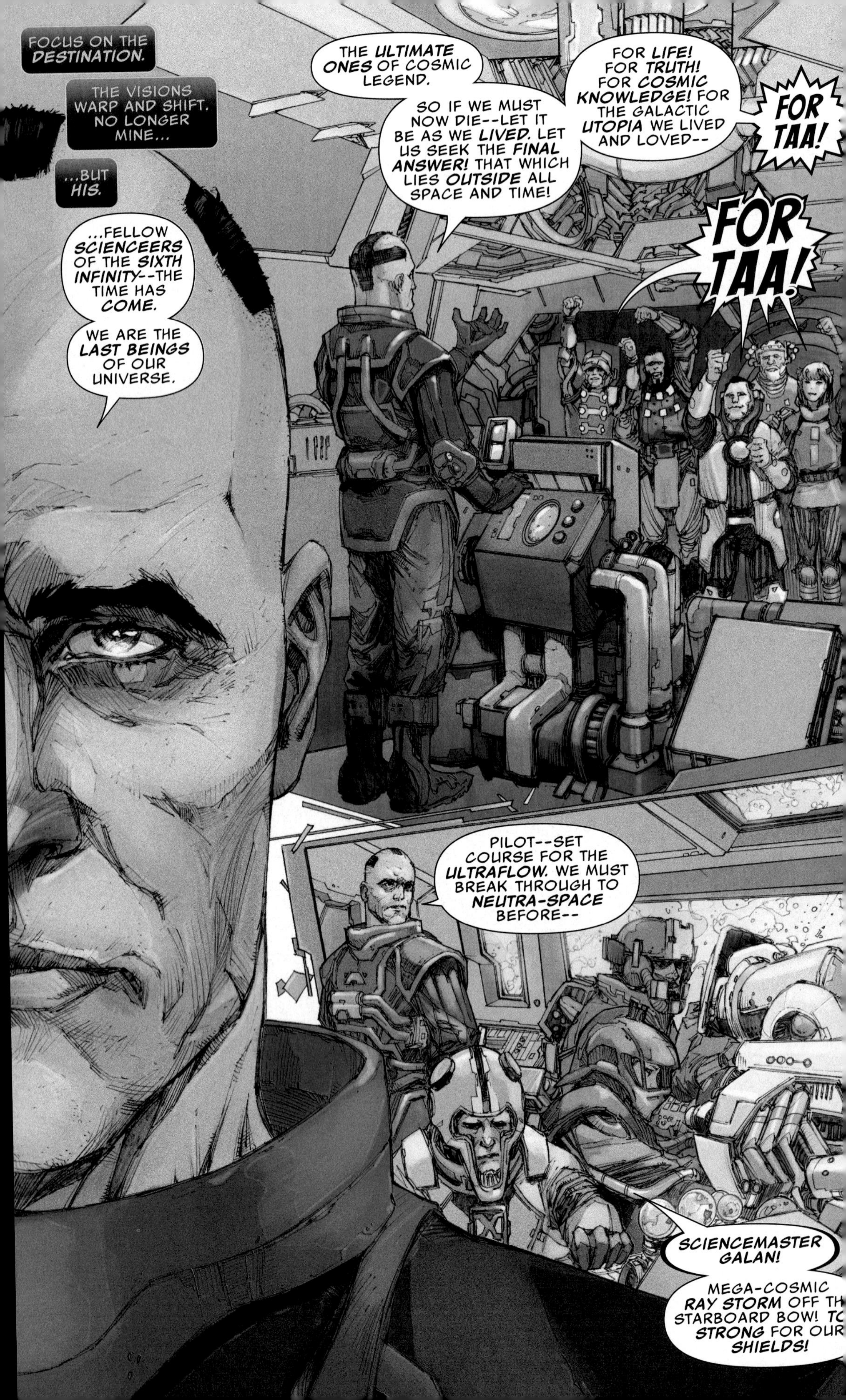
FOCUS ON THE DESTINATION.
THE VISIONS WARP AND SHIFT. NO LONGER MINE...
...BUT HIS.
...FELLOW SCIENCEERS OF THE SIXTH INFINITY--THE TIME HAS COME.
WE ARE THE LAST BEINGS OF OUR UNIVERSE.
THE ULTIMATE ONES OF COSMIC LEGEND.
SO IF WE MUST NOW DIE--LET IT BE AS WE LIVED. LET US SEEK THE FINAL ANSWER! THAT WHICH LIES OUTSIDE ALL SPACE AND TIME!
FOR LIFE! FOR TRUTH! FOR COSMIC KNOWLEDGE! FOR THE GALACTIC UTOPIA WE LIVED AND LOVED--
FOR TAA!
FOR TAA!
PILOT--SET COURSE FOR THE ULTRAFLOW. WE MUST BREAK THROUGH TO NEUTRA-SPACE BEFORE--
SCIENCEMASTER GALAN!
MEGA-COSMIC RAY STORM OFF TH STARBOARD BOW! TO STRONG FOR OUR SHIELDS!

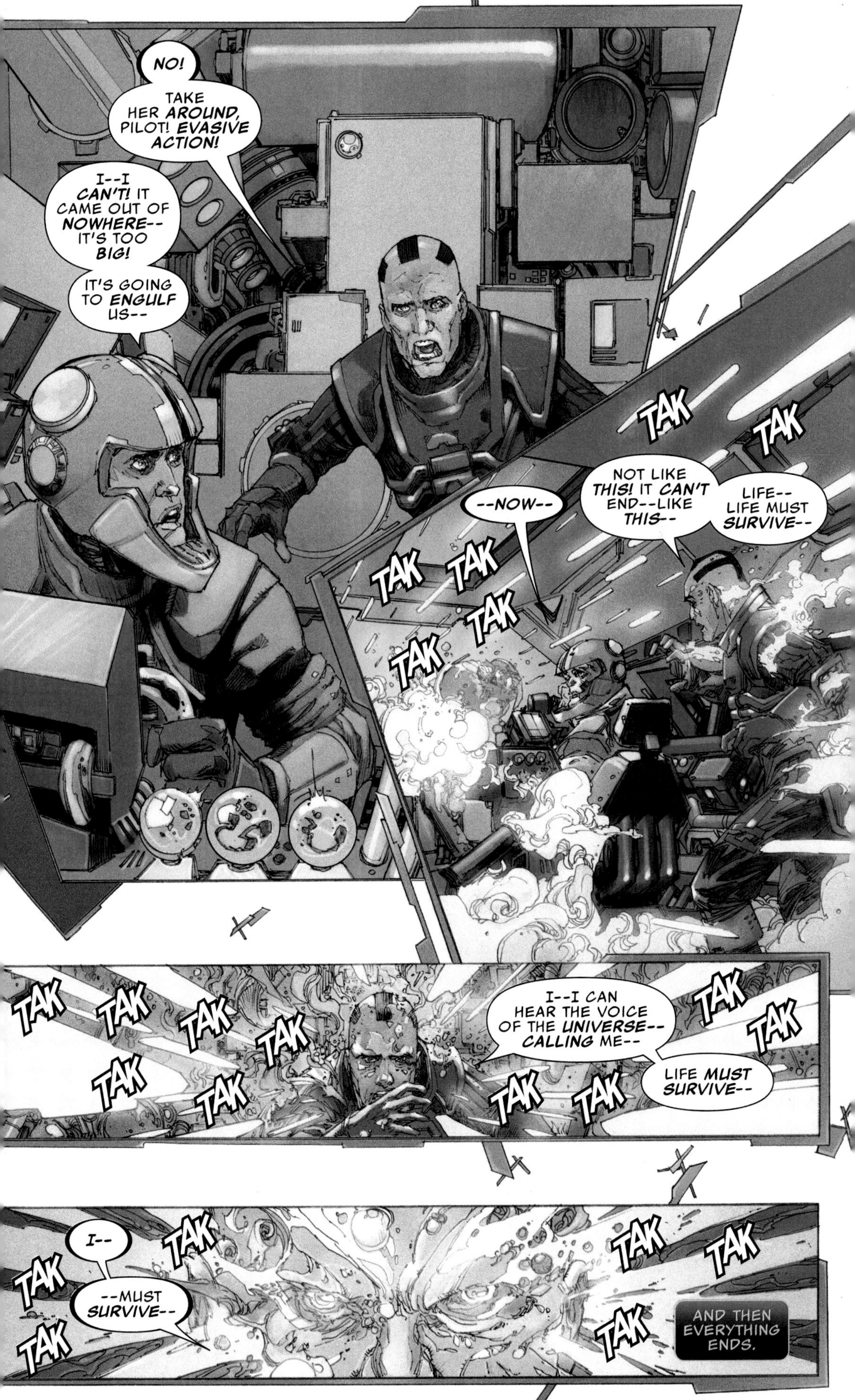
NO!
TAKE HER AROUND, PILOT! EVASIVE ACTION!
I--I CAN'T! IT CAME OUT OF NOWHERE-- IT'S TOO BIG!
IT'S GOING TO ENGULF US--
TAK
TAK
--NOW--
NOT LIKE THIS! IT CAN'T END--LIKE THIS--
LIFE-- LIFE MUST SURVIVE--
TAK
TAK
TAK
TAK
I--I CAN HEAR THE VOICE OF THE UNIVERSE-- CALLING ME--
LIFE MUST SURVIVE--
TAK
TAK
TAK
TAK
TAK
TAK
TAK
TAK
TAK
TAK
I--
--MUST SURVIVE--
TAK
TAK
TAK
TAK
TAK
TAK
AND THEN EVERYTHING ENDS.

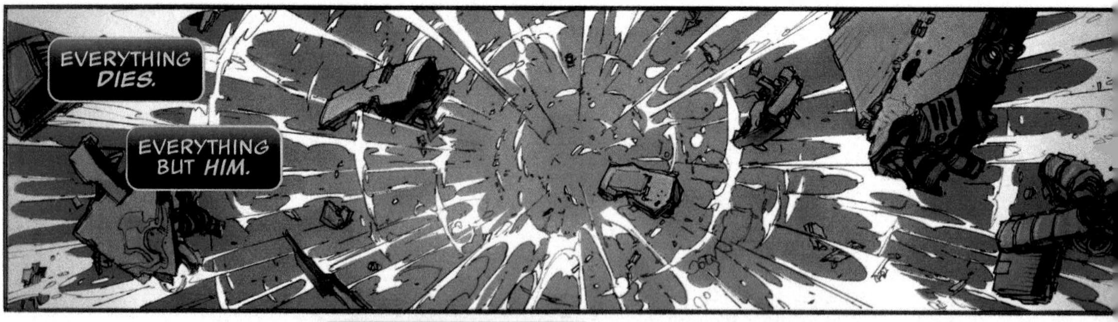

EVERYTHING DIES.
EVERYTHING BUT HIM.

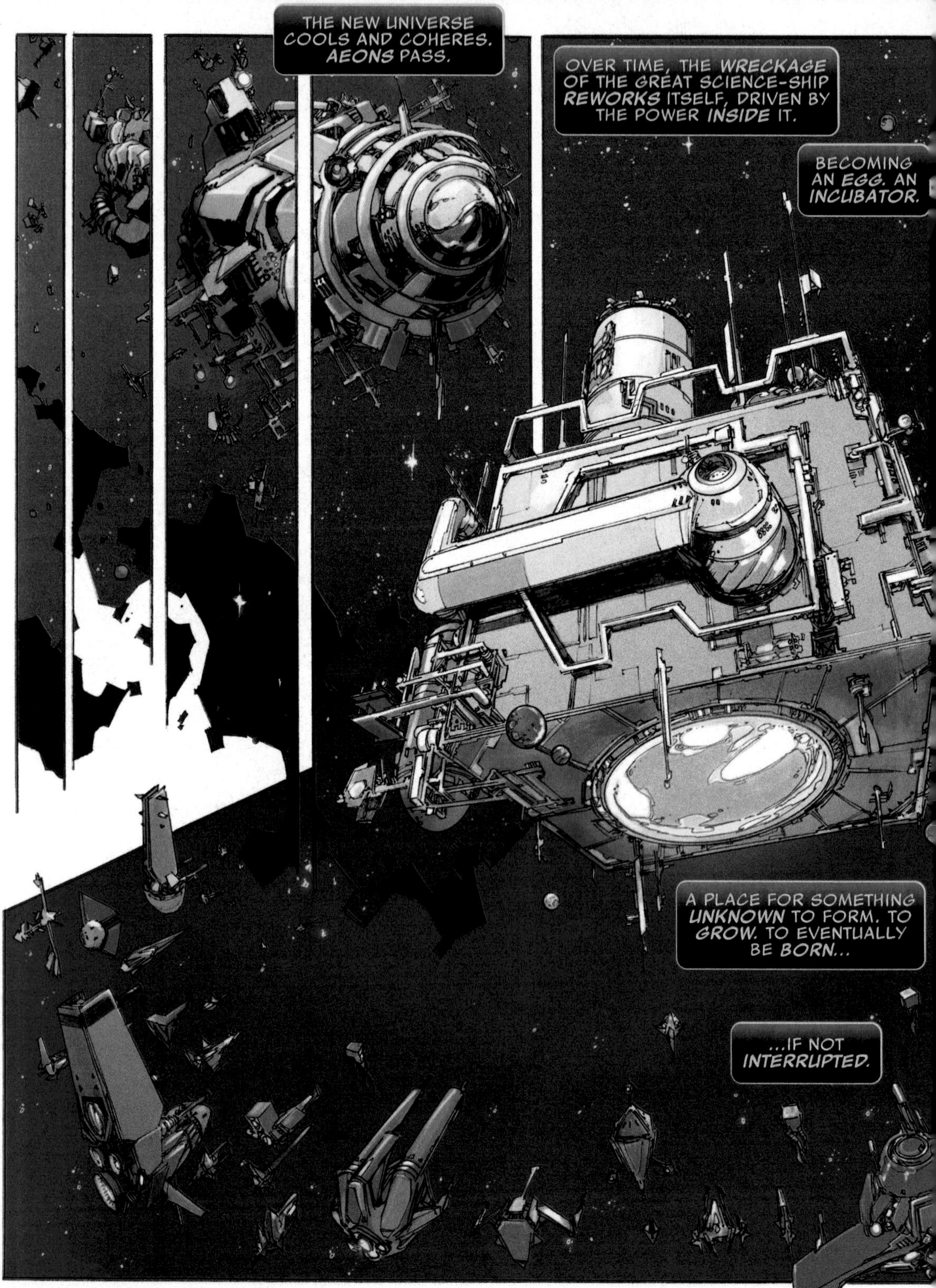

THE NEW UNIVERSE COOLS AND COHERES. AEONS PASS.
OVER TIME, THE WRECKAGE OF THE GREAT SCIENCE-SHIP REWORKS ITSELF, DRIVEN BY THE POWER INSIDE IT.
BECOMING AN EGG. AN INCUBATOR.
A PLACE FOR SOMETHING UNKNOWN TO FORM. TO GROW. TO EVENTUALLY BE BORN...
...IF NOT INTERRUPTED.

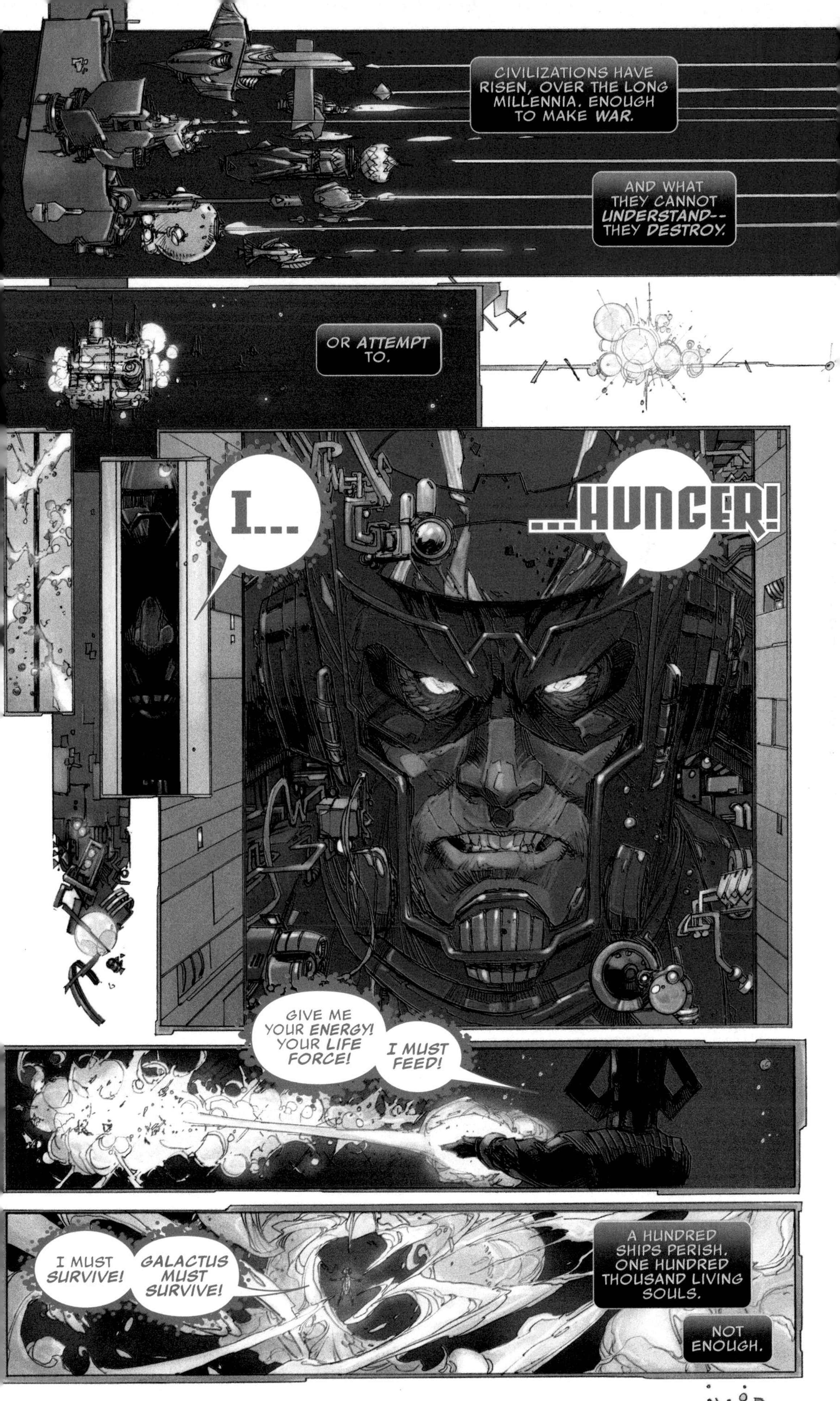

CIVILIZATIONS HAVE RISEN, OVER THE LONG MILLENNIA, ENOUGH TO MAKE WAR.
AND WHAT THEY CANNOT UNDERSTAND-- THEY DESTROY.
OR ATTEMPT TO.
I...
...HUNGER!
GIVE ME YOUR ENERGY! YOUR LIFE FORCE!
I MUST FEED!
I MUST SURVIVE!
GALACTUS MUST SURVIVE!
A HUNDRED SHIPS PERISH. ONE HUNDRED THOUSAND LIVING SOULS.
NOT ENOUGH.

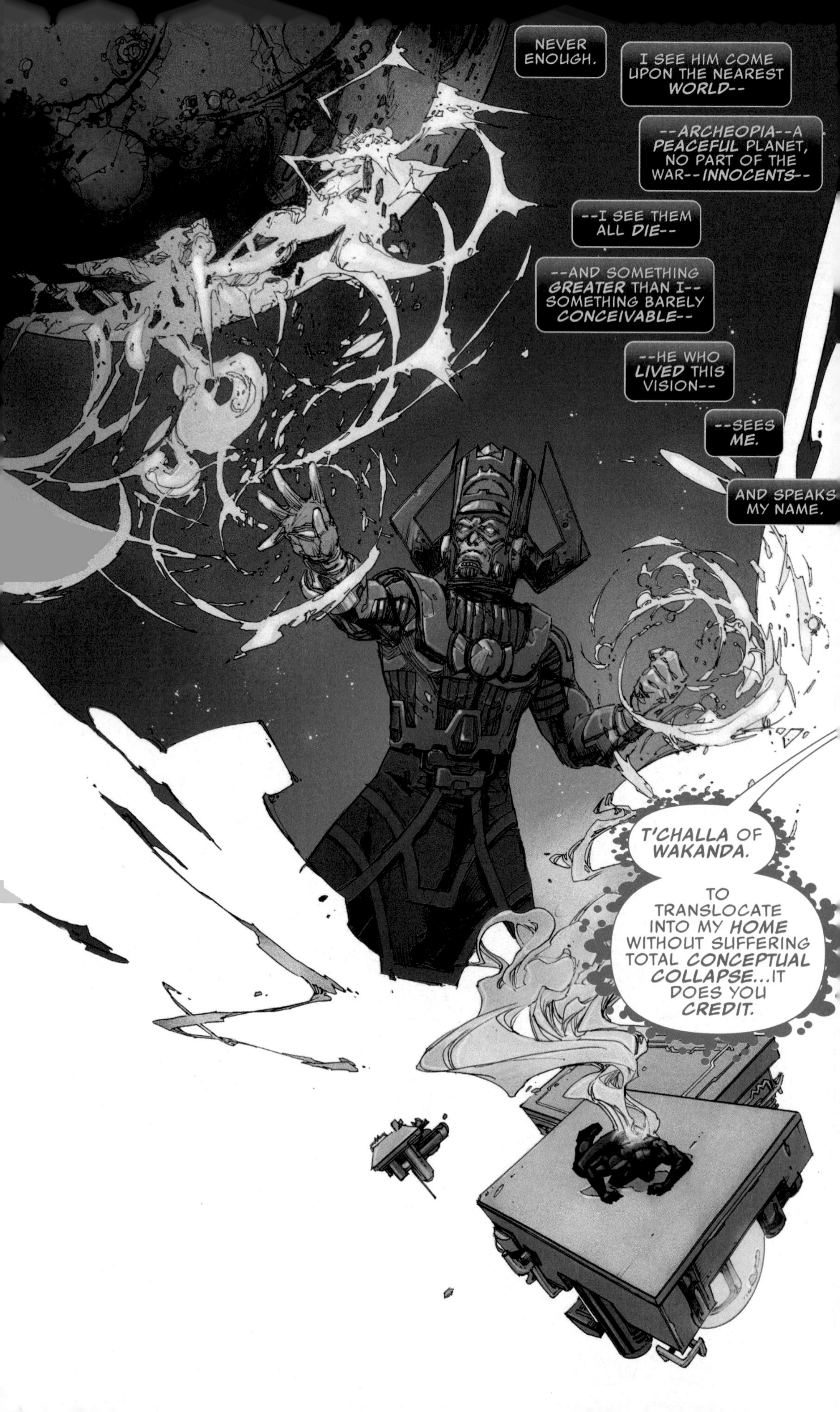
NEVER ENOUGH.
I SEE HIM COME UPON THE NEAREST WORLD--
--ARCHEOPIA--A PEACEFUL PLANET, NO PART OF THE WAR--INNOCENTS--
--I SEE THEM ALL DIE--
--AND SOMETHING GREATER THAN I--SOMETHING BARELY CONCEIVABLE--
--HE WHO LIVED THIS VISION--
--SEES ME.
AND SPEAKS MY NAME.
T'CHALLA OF WAKANDA.
TO TRANSLOCATE INTO MY HOME WITHOUT SUFFERING TOTAL CONCEPTUAL COLLAPSE...IT DOES YOU CREDIT.

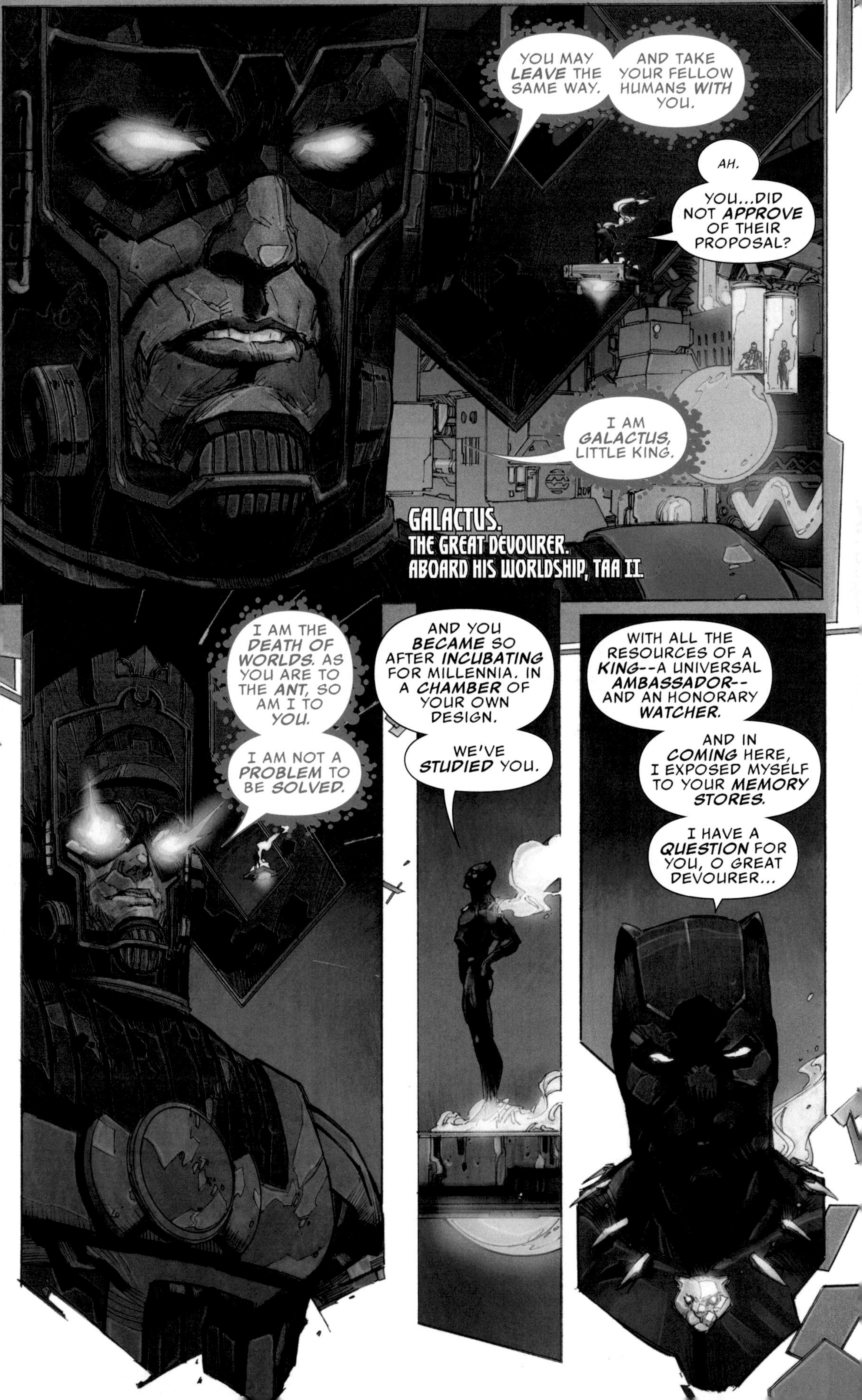
YOU MAY LEAVE THE SAME WAY.
AND TAKE YOUR FELLOW HUMANS WITH YOU.
AH.
YOU...DID NOT APPROVE OF THEIR PROPOSAL?
I AM GALACTUS, LITTLE KING.
GALACTUS.
THE GREAT DEVOURER.
ABOARD HIS WORLDSHIP, TAA II.
I AM THE DEATH OF WORLDS. AS YOU ARE TO THE ANT, SO AM I TO YOU.
I AM NOT A PROBLEM TO BE SOLVED.
AND YOU BECAME SO AFTER INCUBATING FOR MILLENNIA. IN A CHAMBER OF YOUR OWN DESIGN.
WE'VE STUDIED YOU.
WITH ALL THE RESOURCES OF A KING--A UNIVERSAL AMBASSADOR--AND AN HONORARY WATCHER.
AND IN COMING HERE, I EXPOSED MYSELF TO YOUR MEMORY STORES.
I HAVE A QUESTION FOR YOU, O GREAT DEVOURER...

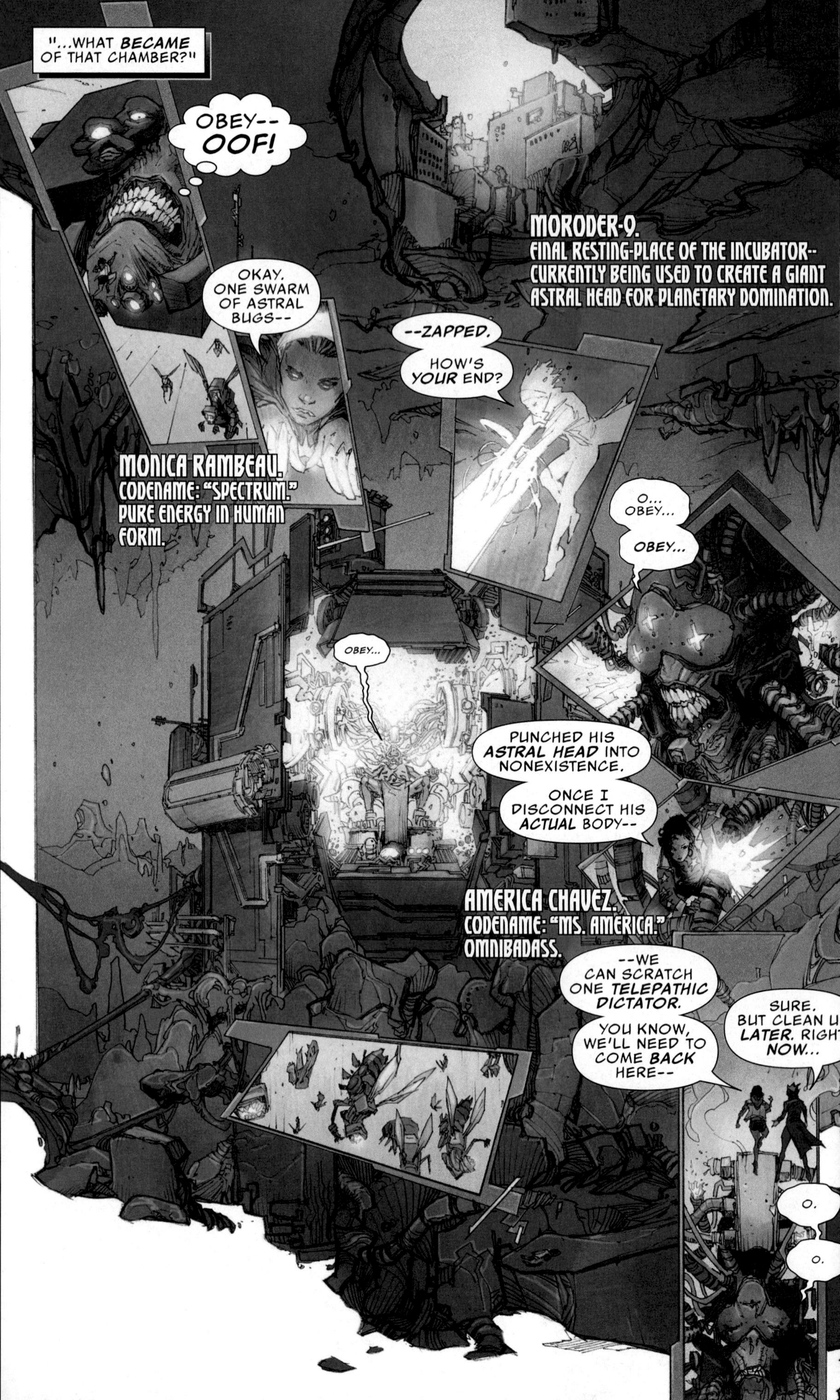
"...WHAT BECAME OF THAT CHAMBER?"
OBEY-- OOF!
MORODER-9.
FINAL RESTING-PLACE OF THE INCUBATOR-- CURRENTLY BEING USED TO CREATE A GIANT ASTRAL HEAD FOR PLANETARY DOMINATION.
OKAY. ONE SWARM OF ASTRAL BUGS--
--ZAPPED.
HOW'S YOUR END?
MONICA RAMBEAU.
CODENAME: "SPECTRUM."
PURE ENERGY IN HUMAN FORM.
O... OBEY...
OBEY...
OBEY...
PUNCHED HIS ASTRAL HEAD INTO NONEXISTENCE.
ONCE I DISCONNECT HIS ACTUAL BODY--
AMERICA CHAVEZ.
CODENAME: "MS. AMERICA."
OMNIBADASS.
--WE CAN SCRATCH ONE TELEPATHIC DICTATOR.
YOU KNOW, WE'LL NEED TO COME BACK HERE--
O.
O.

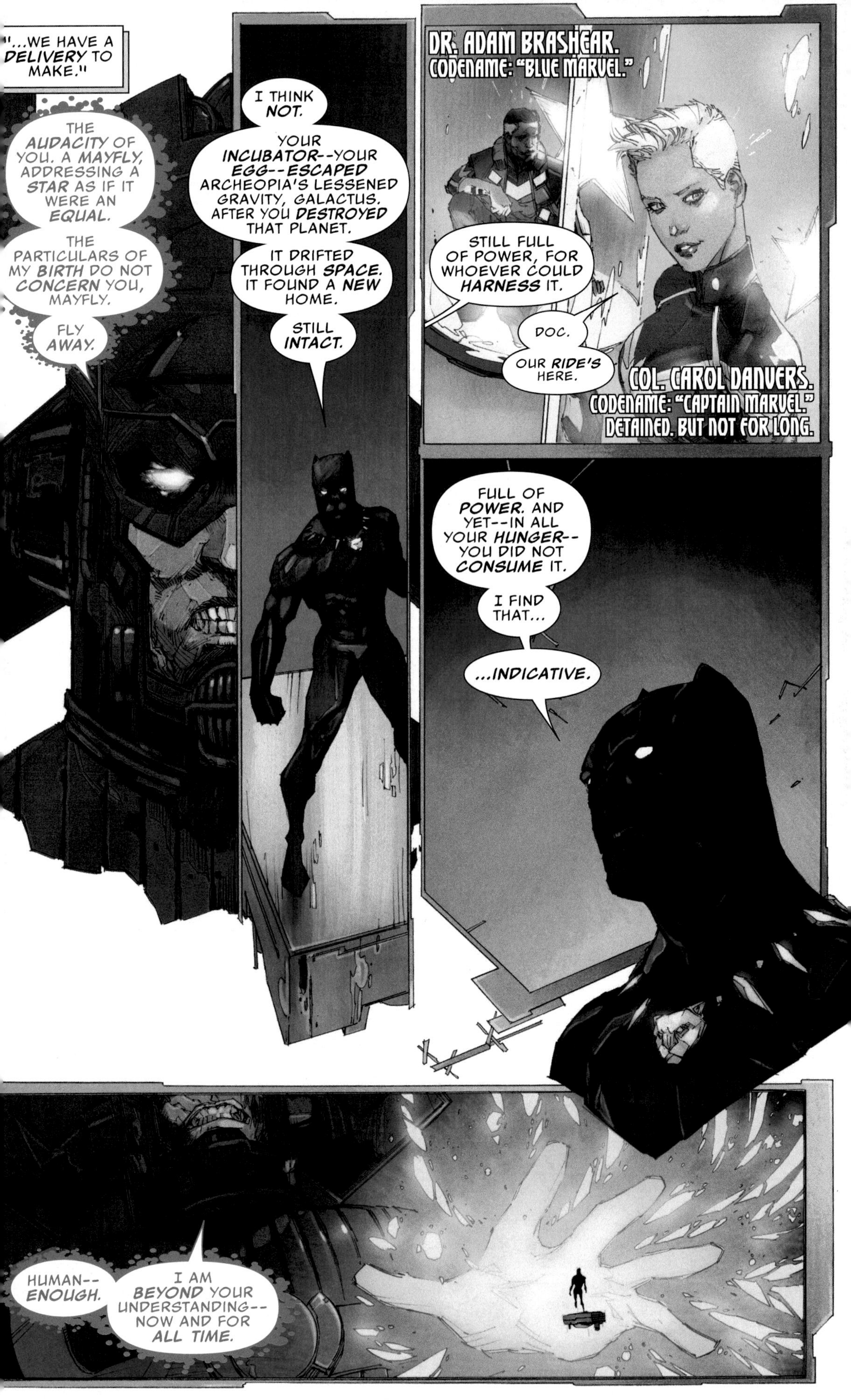
"...WE HAVE A DELIVERY TO MAKE."
THE AUDACITY OF YOU. A MAYFLY, ADDRESSING A STAR AS IF IT WERE AN EQUAL.
THE PARTICULARS OF MY BIRTH DO NOT CONCERN YOU, MAYFLY.
FLY AWAY.
I THINK NOT.
YOUR INCUBATOR--YOUR EGG--ESCAPED ARCHEOPIA'S LESSENED GRAVITY, GALACTUS. AFTER YOU DESTROYED THAT PLANET.
IT DRIFTED THROUGH SPACE. IT FOUND A NEW HOME.
STILL INTACT.
DR. ADAM BRASHEAR. CODENAME: "BLUE MARVEL."
STILL FULL OF POWER, FOR WHOEVER COULD HARNESS IT.
DOC.
OUR RIDE'S HERE.
COL. CAROL DANVERS. CODENAME: "CAPTAIN MARVEL." DETAINED. BUT NOT FOR LONG.
FULL OF POWER. AND YET--IN ALL YOUR HUNGER--YOU DID NOT CONSUME IT.
I FIND THAT...
...INDICATIVE.
HUMAN--ENOUGH.
I AM BEYOND YOUR UNDERSTANDING--NOW AND FOR ALL TIME.

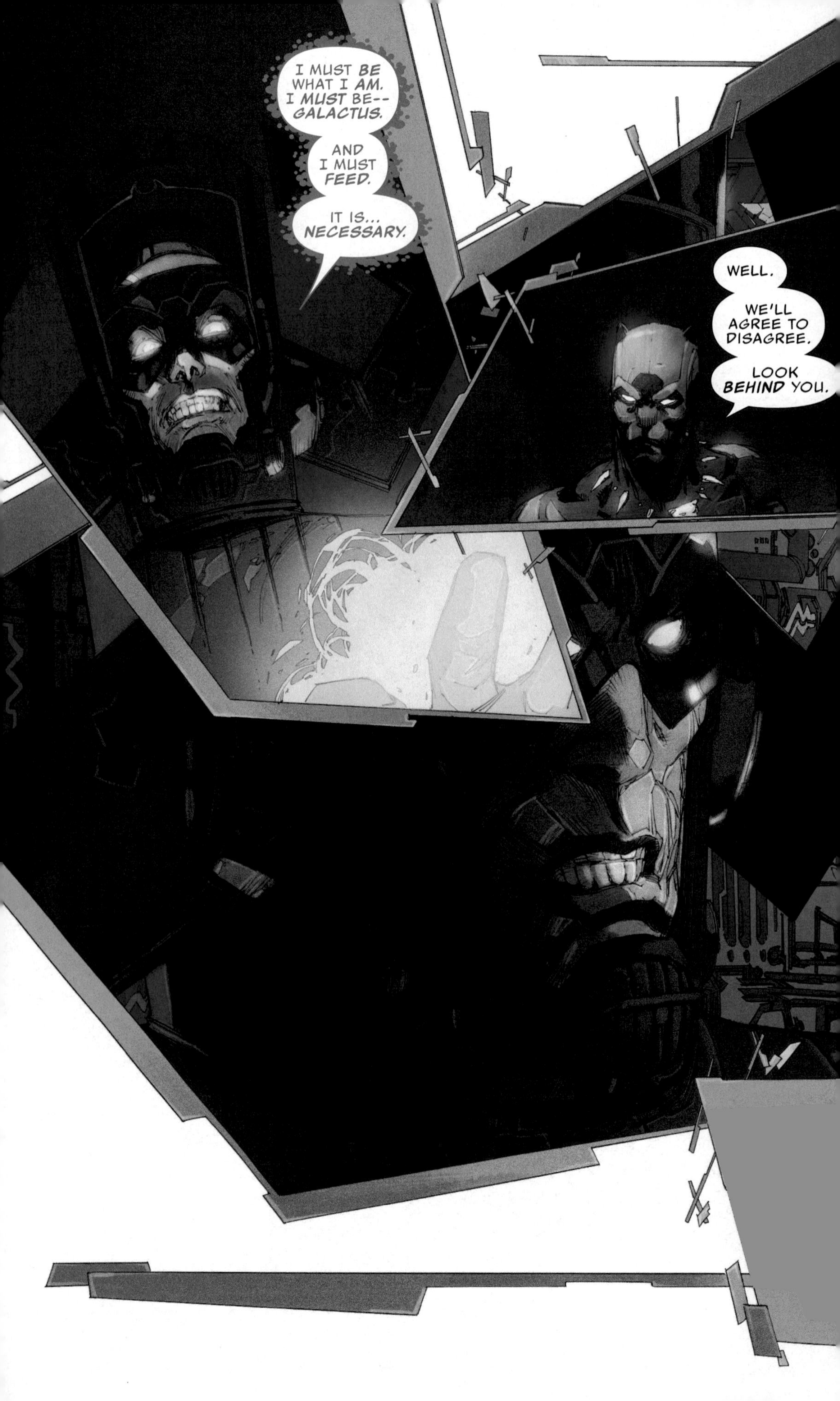
I MUST BE WHAT I AM. I MUST BE-- GALACTUS.
AND I MUST FEED.
IT IS... NECESSARY.
WELL.
WE'LL AGREE TO DISAGREE.
LOOK BEHIND YOU.

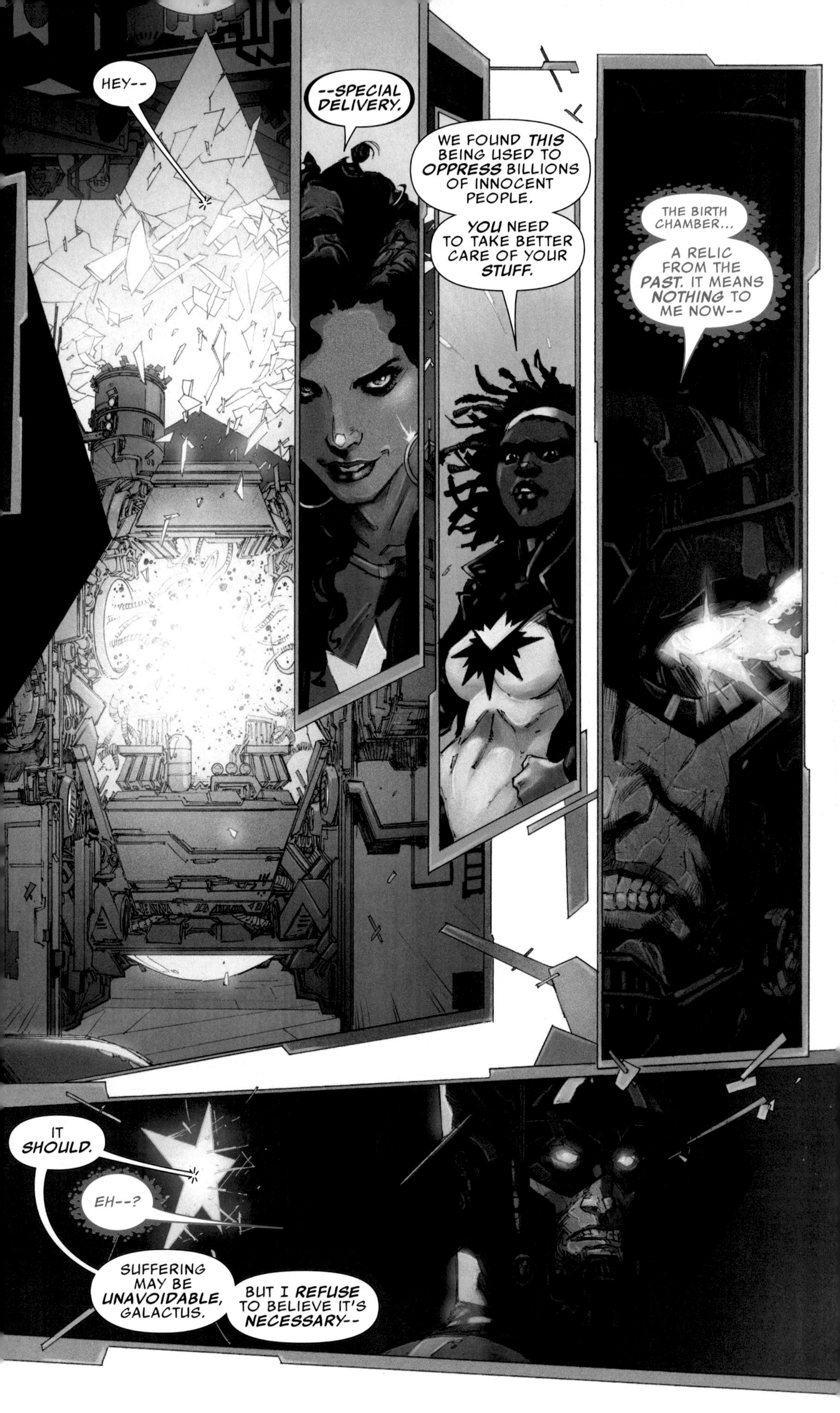
HEY--
--SPECIAL DELIVERY.
WE FOUND THIS BEING USED TO OPPRESS BILLIONS OF INNOCENT PEOPLE.
YOU NEED TO TAKE BETTER CARE OF YOUR STUFF.
THE BIRTH CHAMBER...
A RELIC FROM THE PAST. IT MEANS NOTHING TO ME NOW--
IT SHOULD.
EH--?
SUFFERING MAY BE UNAVOIDABLE, GALACTUS.
BUT I REFUSE TO BELIEVE IT'S NECESSARY--

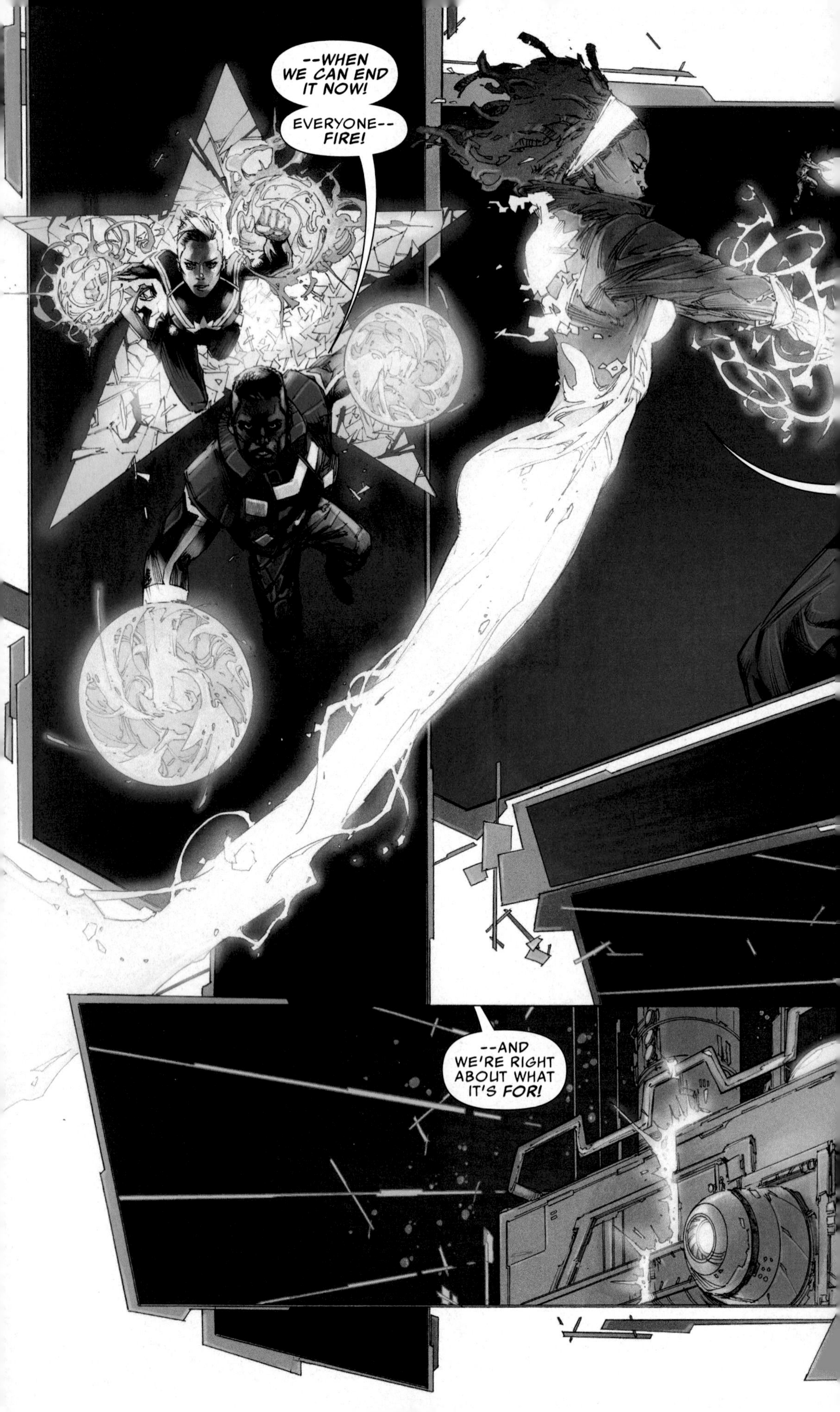
--WHEN WE CAN END IT NOW!
EVERYONE-- FIRE!
--AND WE'RE RIGHT ABOUT WHAT IT'S *FOR!*

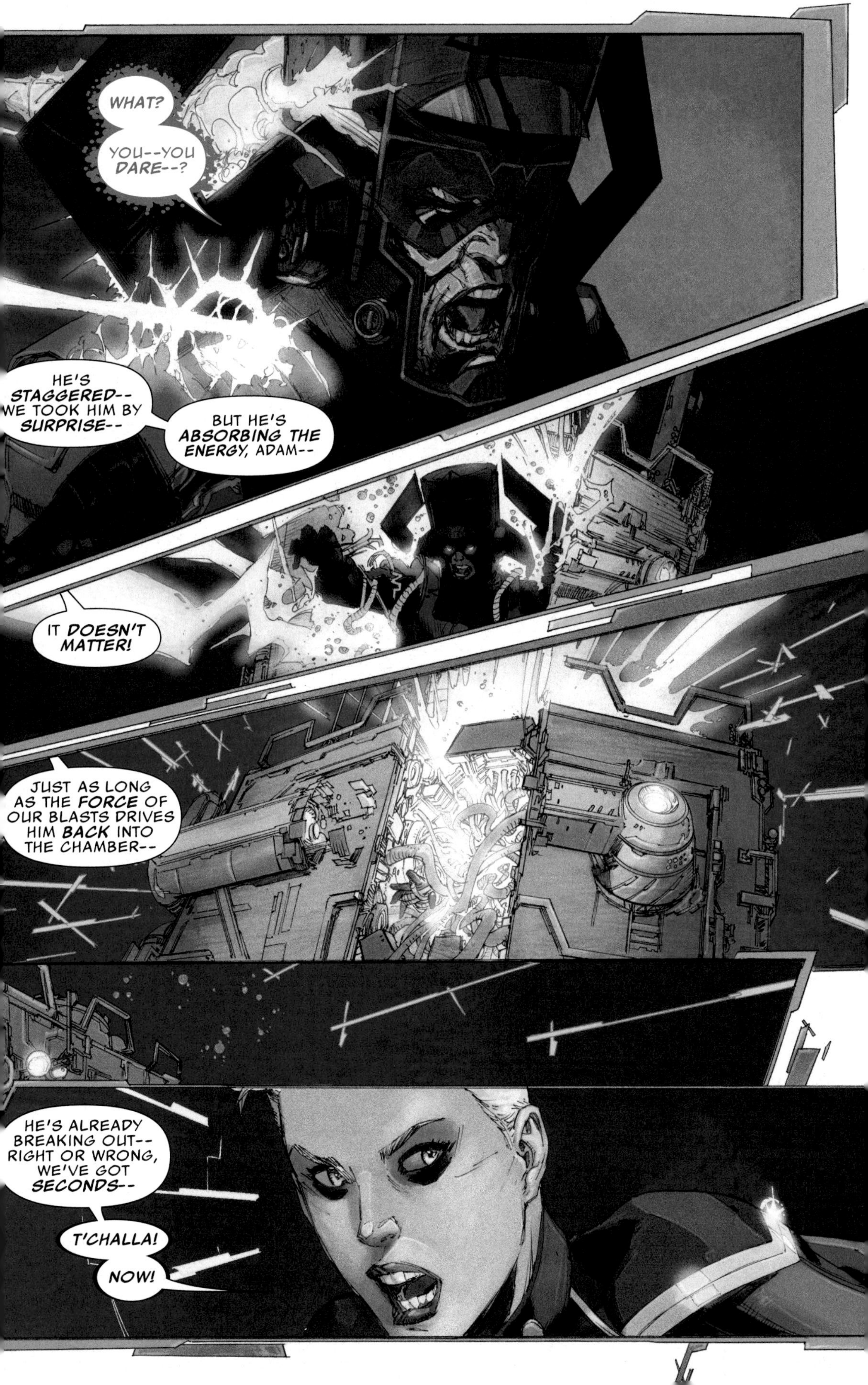
WHAT?
YOU--YOU DARE--?
HE'S STAGGERED--WE TOOK HIM BY SURPRISE--
BUT HE'S ABSORBING THE ENERGY, ADAM--
IT DOESN'T MATTER!
JUST AS LONG AS THE FORCE OF OUR BLASTS DRIVES HIM BACK INTO THE CHAMBER--
HE'S ALREADY BREAKING OUT--RIGHT OR WRONG, WE'VE GOT SECONDS--
T'CHALLA!
NOW!

I HEAR YOU, COLONEL DANVERS.

KIMOYO IS ONLINE--AND ACTIVE.

KIMOYO. NEXT-GEN OPERATING SYSTEM FOR THE WAKANDAN DESIGN GROUP'S WEARABLE SUPERCOMPUTER.

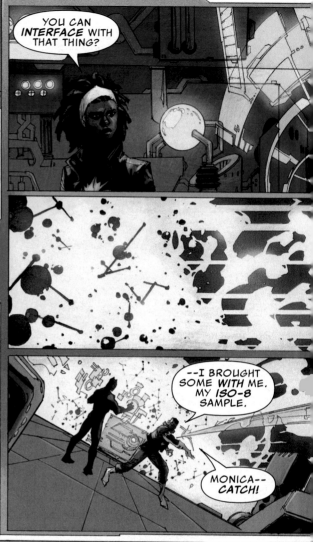

YOU CAN INTERFACE WITH THAT THING?

--I BROUGHT SOME WITH ME. MY ISO-8 SAMPLE.

MONICA-- CATCH!

IF I ABSORB ALL THAT-- TRANSFORM--

--FIND AN ENERGY FREQUENCY THE CHAMBER WILL ACCEPT--

--WE SHOULD--SEE SOME--

--RESULTS!

KIMOYO SINGS IN MY EARS.

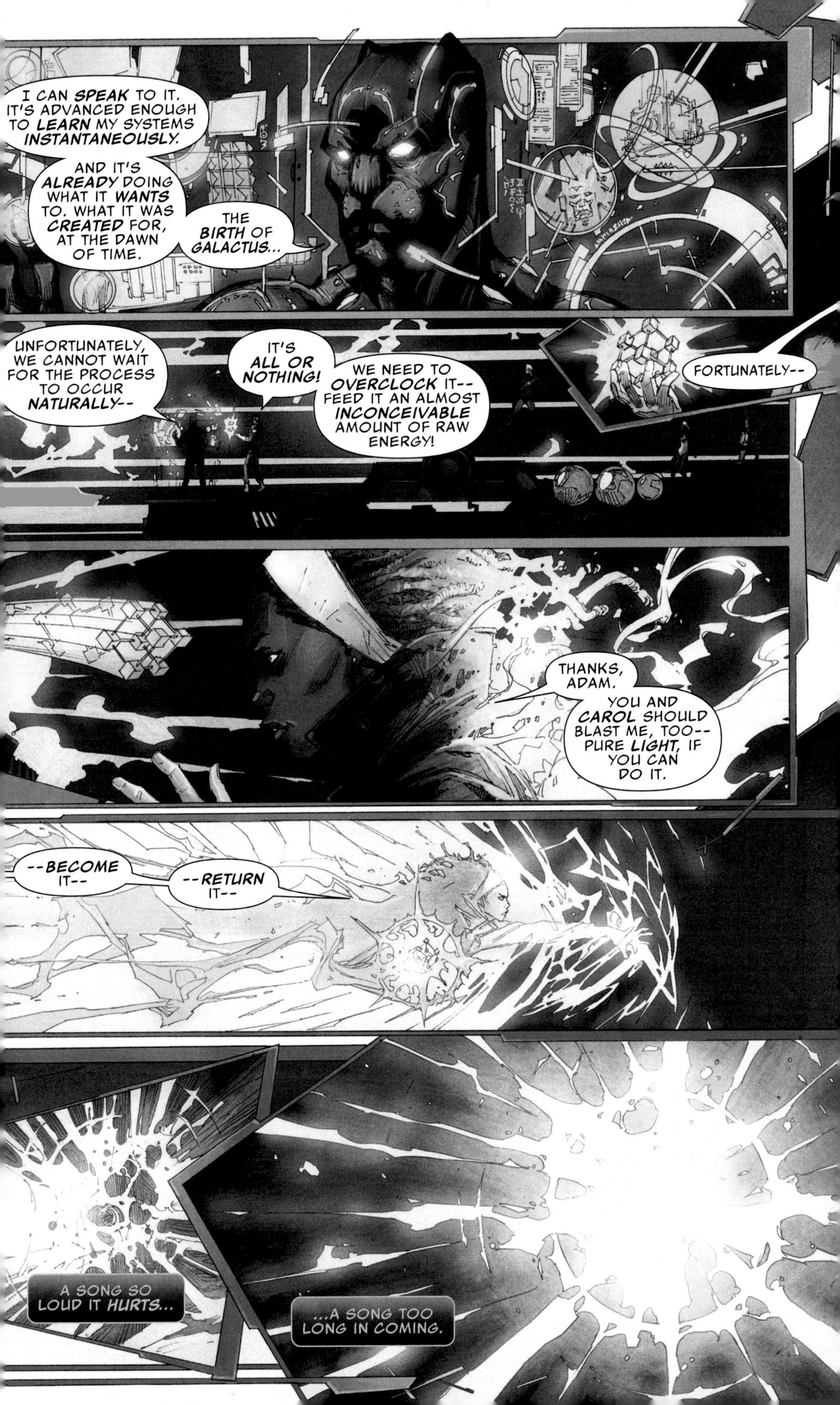

I CAN SPEAK TO IT. IT'S ADVANCED ENOUGH TO LEARN MY SYSTEMS INSTANTANEOUSLY.
AND IT'S ALREADY DOING WHAT IT WANTS TO. WHAT IT WAS CREATED FOR, AT THE DAWN OF TIME.
THE BIRTH OF GALACTUS...
UNFORTUNATELY, WE CANNOT WAIT FOR THE PROCESS TO OCCUR NATURALLY--
IT'S ALL OR NOTHING!
WE NEED TO OVERCLOCK IT-- FEED IT AN ALMOST INCONCEIVABLE AMOUNT OF RAW ENERGY!
FORTUNATELY--
THANKS, ADAM.
YOU AND CAROL SHOULD BLAST ME, TOO-- PURE LIGHT, IF YOU CAN DO IT.
--BECOME IT--
--RETURN IT--
A SONG SO LOUD IT HURTS...
...A SONG TOO LONG IN COMING.

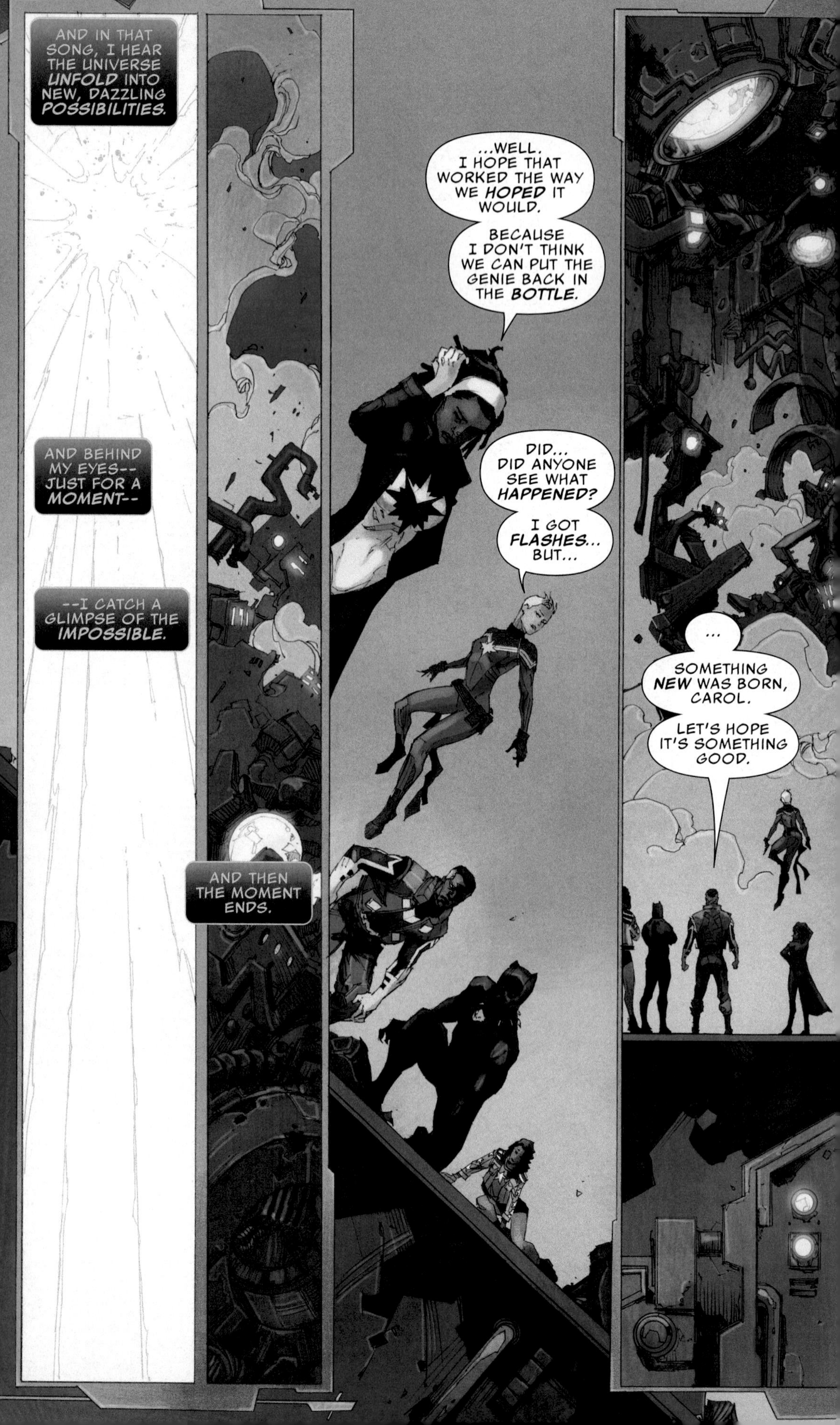

AND IN THAT SONG, I HEAR THE UNIVERSE *UNFOLD* INTO NEW, DAZZLING *POSSIBILITIES.*
AND BEHIND MY EYES-- JUST FOR A *MOMENT*--
--I CATCH A GLIMPSE OF THE *IMPOSSIBLE.*
AND THEN THE MOMENT ENDS.
...WELL. I HOPE THAT WORKED THE WAY WE *HOPED* IT WOULD.
BECAUSE I DON'T THINK WE CAN PUT THE GENIE BACK IN THE *BOTTLE.*
DID... DID ANYONE SEE WHAT *HAPPENED?*
I GOT *FLASHES*... BUT...
...
SOMETHING *NEW* WAS BORN, CAROL.
LET'S HOPE IT'S SOMETHING GOOD.

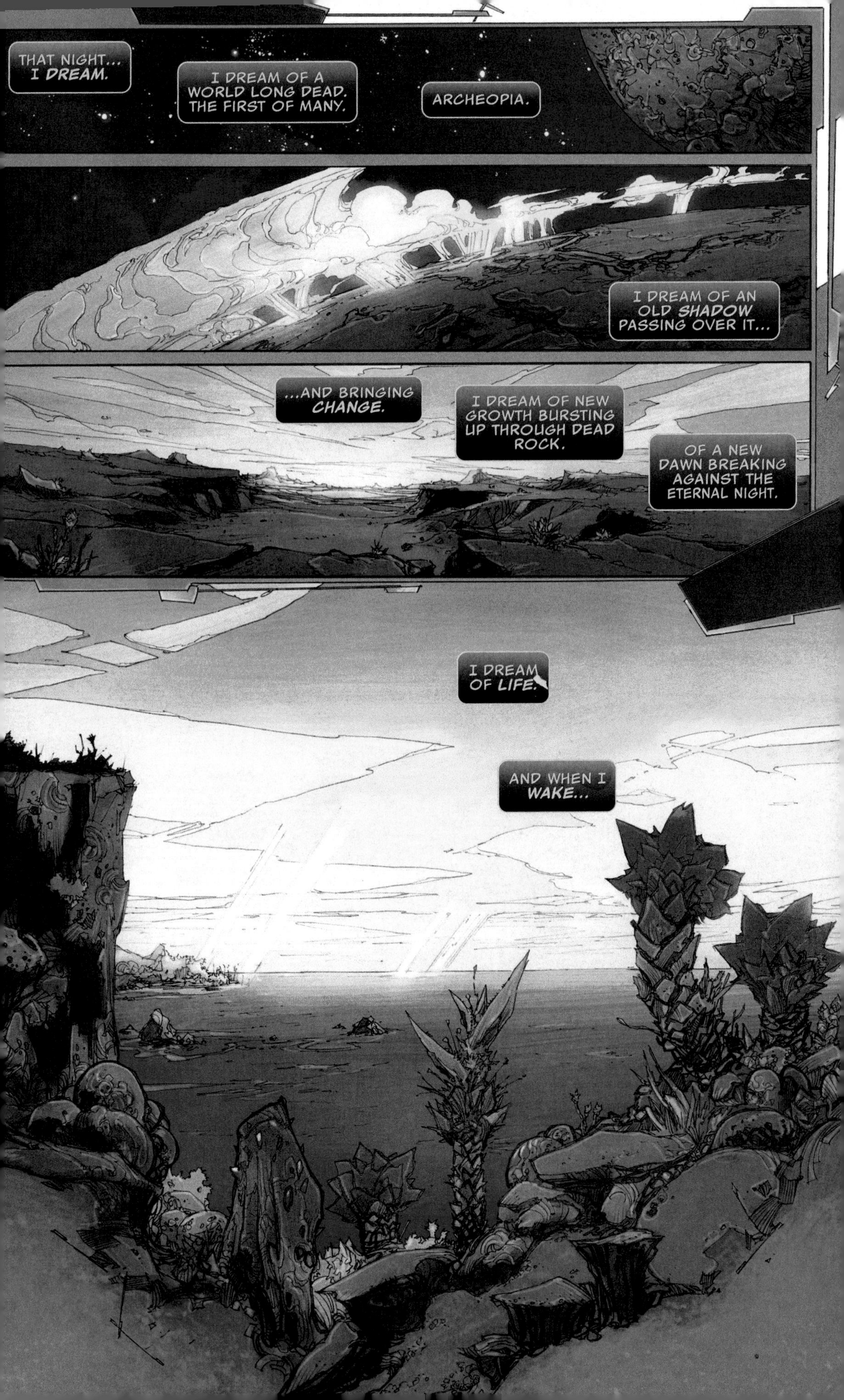
THAT NIGHT... I DREAM.
I DREAM OF A WORLD LONG DEAD. THE FIRST OF MANY.
ARCHEOPIA.
I DREAM OF AN OLD SHADOW PASSING OVER IT...
...AND BRINGING CHANGE.
I DREAM OF NEW GROWTH BURSTING UP THROUGH DEAD ROCK.
OF A NEW DAWN BREAKING AGAINST THE ETERNAL NIGHT.
I DREAM OF LIFE.
AND WHEN I WAKE...

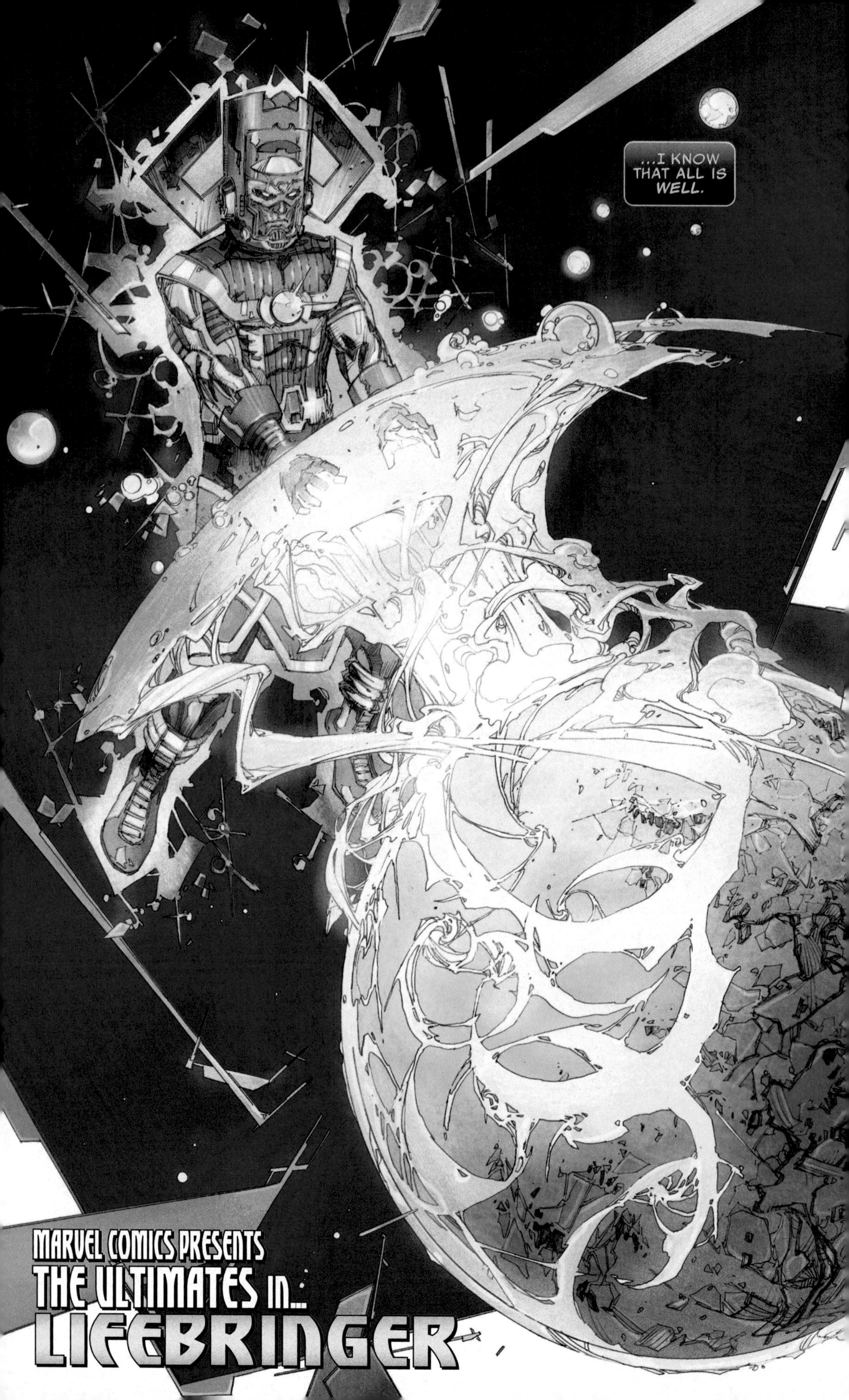
...I KNOW THAT ALL IS WELL.
MARVEL COMICS PRESENTS
THE ULTIMATES IN...
LIFEBRINGER

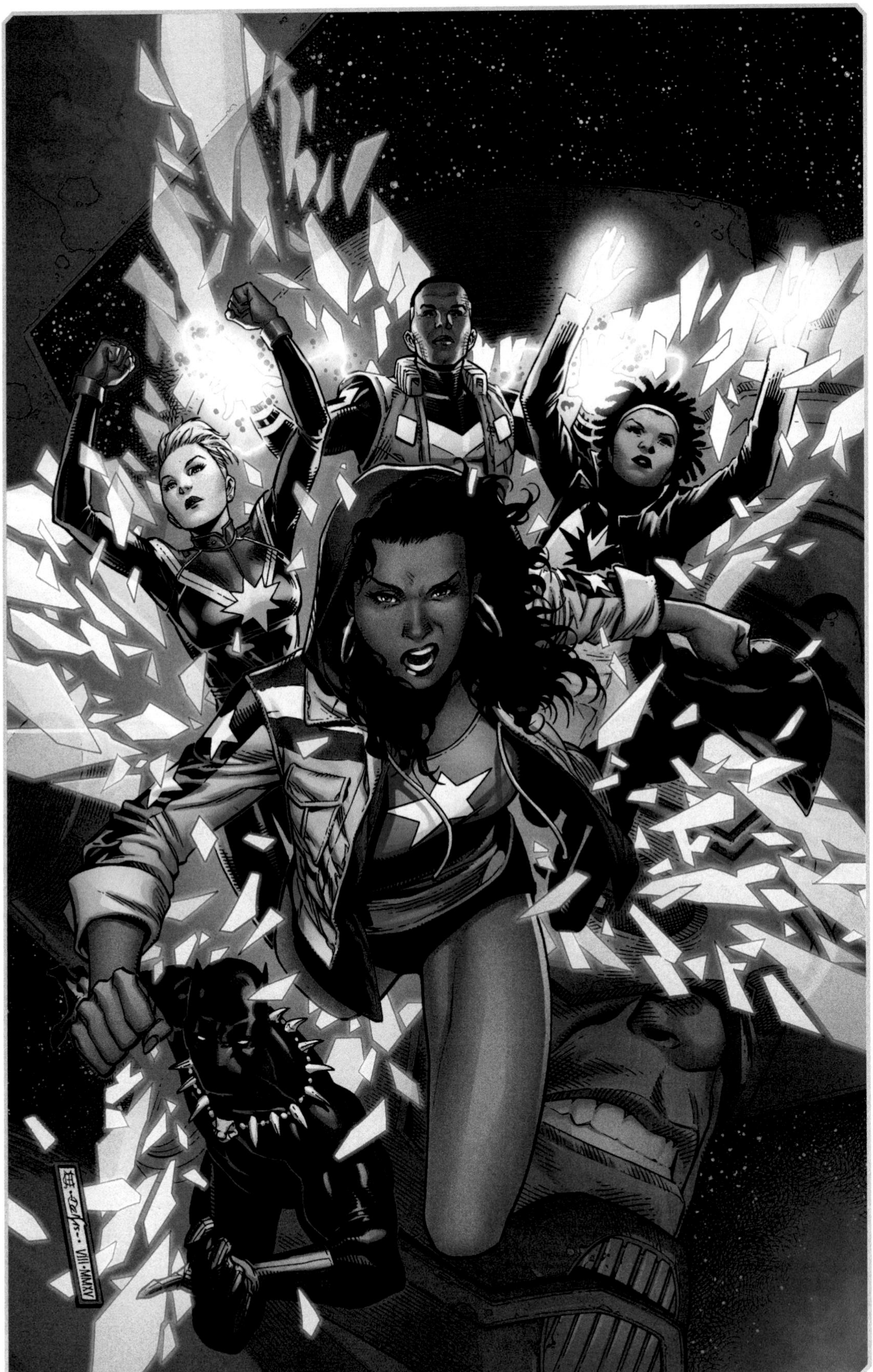

#2 VARIANT BY JIM CHEUNG, JOHN DELL & LAURA MARTIN

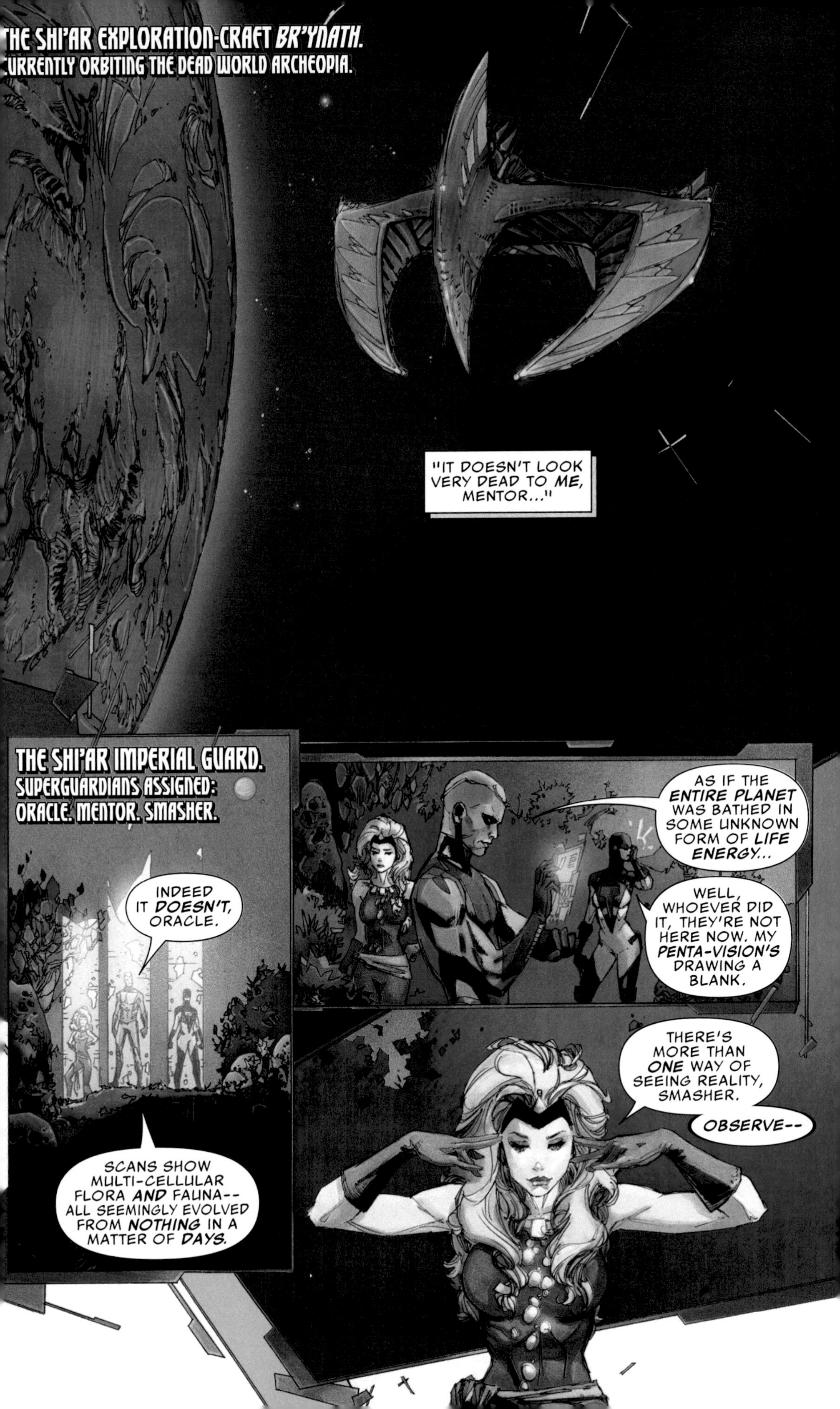
THE SHI'AR EXPLORATION-CRAFT BR'YNATH.
CURRENTLY ORBITING THE DEAD WORLD ARCHEOPIA.
"IT DOESN'T LOOK VERY DEAD TO ME, MENTOR..."
THE SHI'AR IMPERIAL GUARD. SUPERGUARDIANS ASSIGNED: ORACLE. MENTOR. SMASHER.
INDEED IT DOESN'T, ORACLE.
SCANS SHOW MULTI-CELLULAR FLORA AND FAUNA--ALL SEEMINGLY EVOLVED FROM NOTHING IN A MATTER OF DAYS.
AS IF THE ENTIRE PLANET WAS BATHED IN SOME UNKNOWN FORM OF LIFE ENERGY...
WELL, WHOEVER DID IT, THEY'RE NOT HERE NOW. MY PENTA-VISION'S DRAWING A BLANK.
THERE'S MORE THAN ONE WAY OF SEEING REALITY, SMASHER.
OBSERVE--

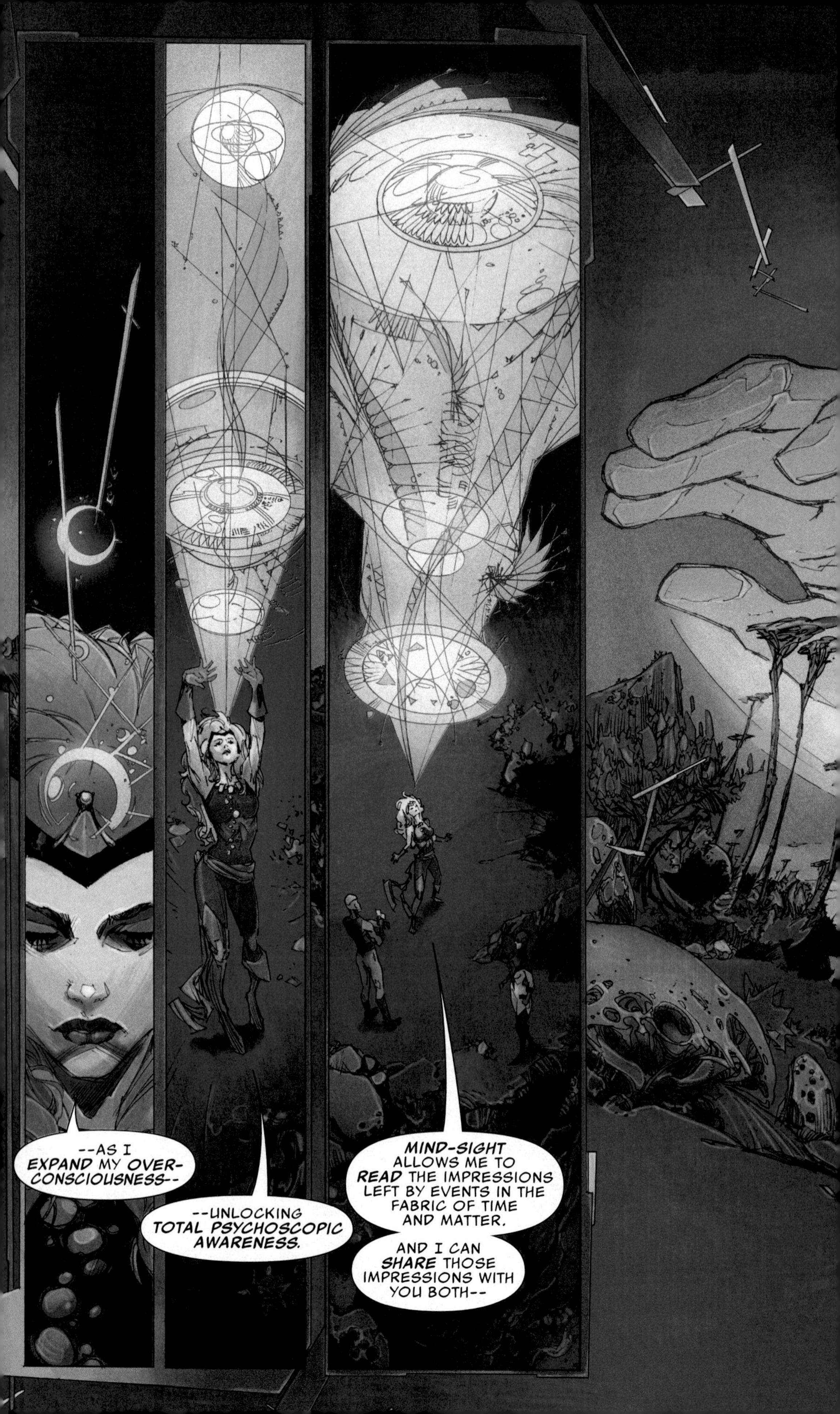
--AS I EXPAND MY OVER-CONSCIOUSNESS--
--UNLOCKING TOTAL PSYCHOSCOPIC AWARENESS.
MIND-SIGHT ALLOWS ME TO READ THE IMPRESSIONS LEFT BY EVENTS IN THE FABRIC OF TIME AND MATTER.
AND I CAN SHARE THOSE IMPRESSIONS WITH YOU BOTH--

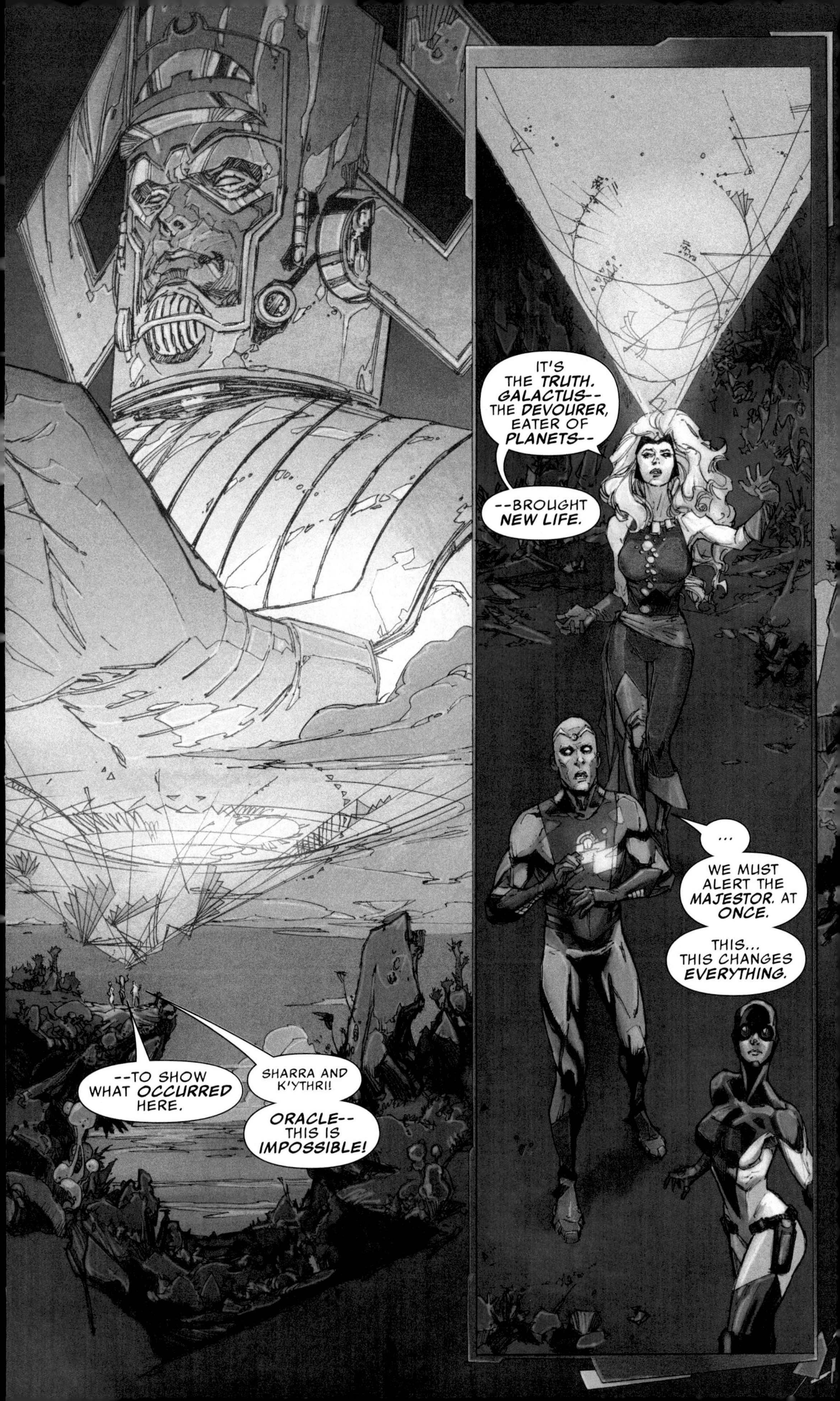

IT'S THE TRUTH. GALACTUS-- THE DEVOURER, EATER OF PLANETS--
--BROUGHT NEW LIFE.
...
WE MUST ALERT THE MAJESTOR. AT ONCE.
THIS... THIS CHANGES EVERYTHING.
--TO SHOW WHAT OCCURRED HERE.
SHARRA AND K'YTHRI!
ORACLE-- THIS IS IMPOSSIBLE!

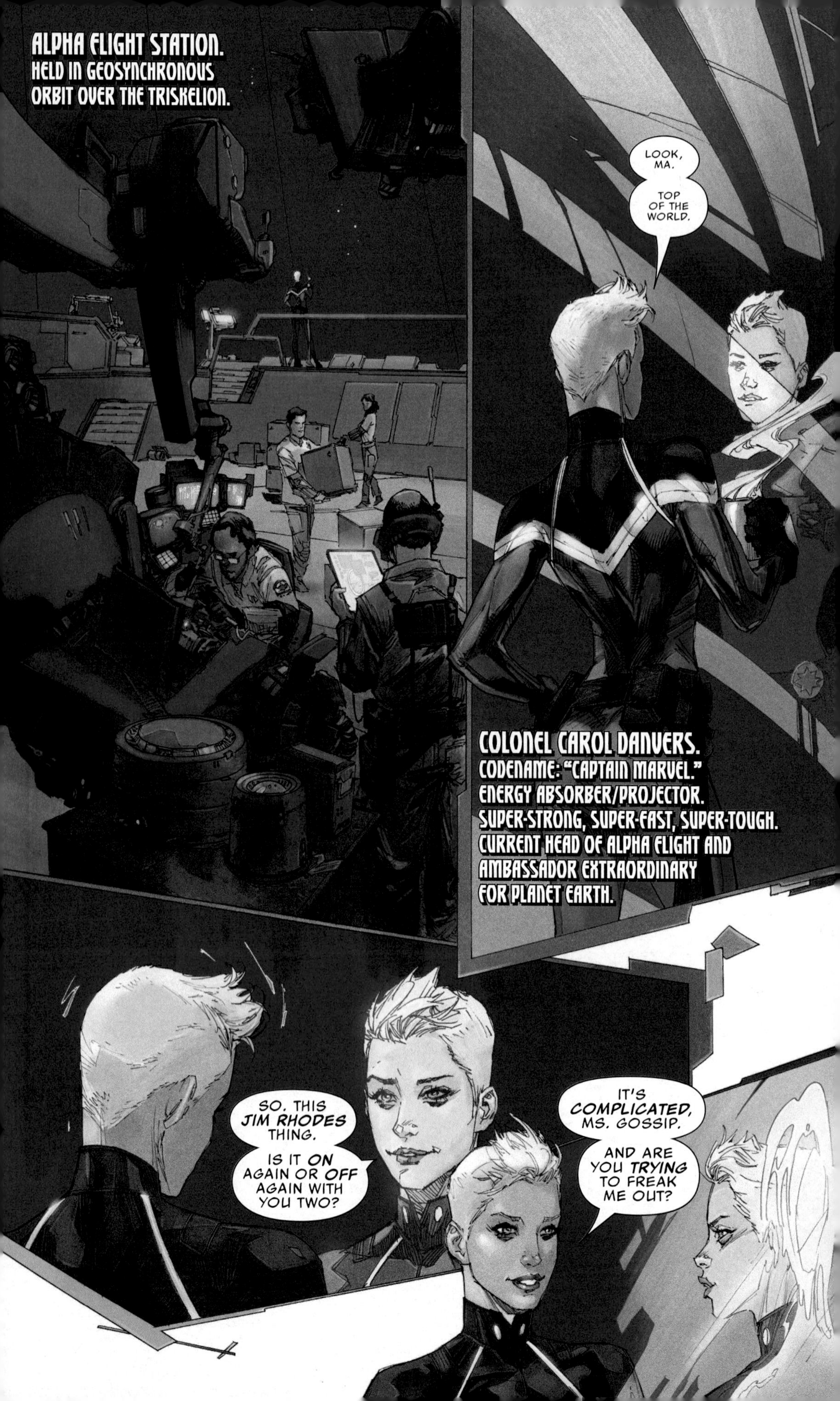
ALPHA FLIGHT STATION.
HELD IN GEOSYNCHRONOUS ORBIT OVER THE TRISKELION.
LOOK, MA.
TOP OF THE WORLD.
COLONEL CAROL DANVERS.
CODENAME: "CAPTAIN MARVEL."
ENERGY ABSORBER/PROJECTOR.
SUPER-STRONG, SUPER-FAST, SUPER-TOUGH.
CURRENT HEAD OF ALPHA FLIGHT AND AMBASSADOR EXTRAORDINARY FOR PLANET EARTH.
SO. THIS JIM RHODES THING.
IS IT ON AGAIN OR OFF AGAIN WITH YOU TWO?
IT'S COMPLICATED, MS. GOSSIP.
AND ARE YOU TRYING TO FREAK ME OUT?

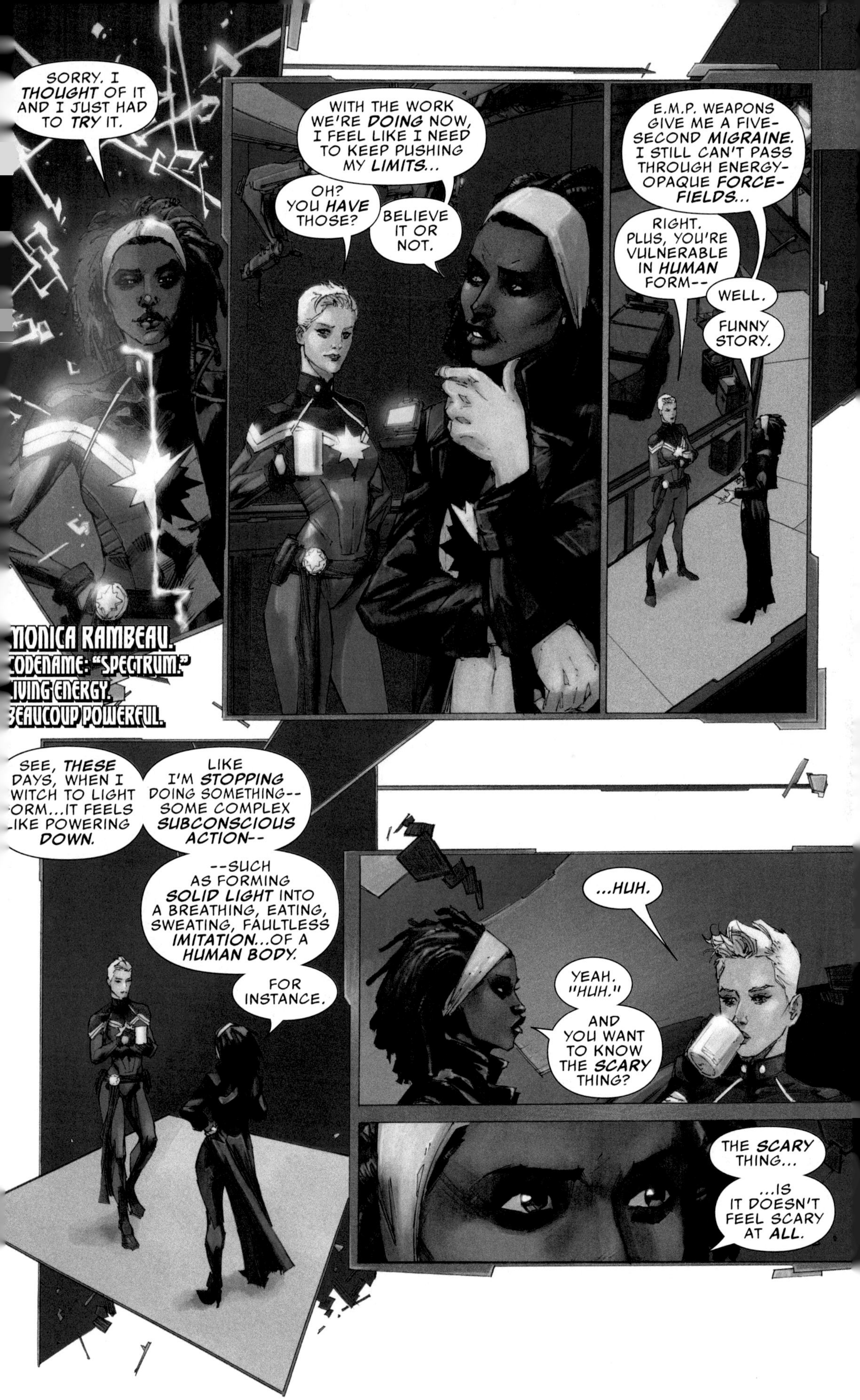
SORRY. I THOUGHT OF IT AND I JUST HAD TO TRY IT.
WITH THE WORK WE'RE DOING NOW, I FEEL LIKE I NEED TO KEEP PUSHING MY LIMITS...
OH? YOU HAVE THOSE?
BELIEVE IT OR NOT.
E.M.P. WEAPONS GIVE ME A FIVE-SECOND MIGRAINE. I STILL CAN'T PASS THROUGH ENERGY-OPAQUE FORCE-FIELDS...
RIGHT. PLUS, YOU'RE VULNERABLE IN HUMAN FORM--
WELL.
FUNNY STORY.
MONICA RAMBEAU. CODENAME: "SPECTRUM." LIVING ENERGY. BEAUCOUP POWERFUL.
SEE, THESE DAYS, WHEN I SWITCH TO LIGHT FORM...IT FEELS LIKE POWERING DOWN.
LIKE I'M STOPPING DOING SOMETHING-- SOME COMPLEX SUBCONSCIOUS ACTION--
--SUCH AS FORMING SOLID LIGHT INTO A BREATHING, EATING, SWEATING, FAULTLESS IMITATION...OF A HUMAN BODY.
FOR INSTANCE.
...HUH.
YEAH. "HUH."
AND YOU WANT TO KNOW THE SCARY THING?
THE SCARY THING...
...IS IT DOESN'T FEEL SCARY AT ALL.

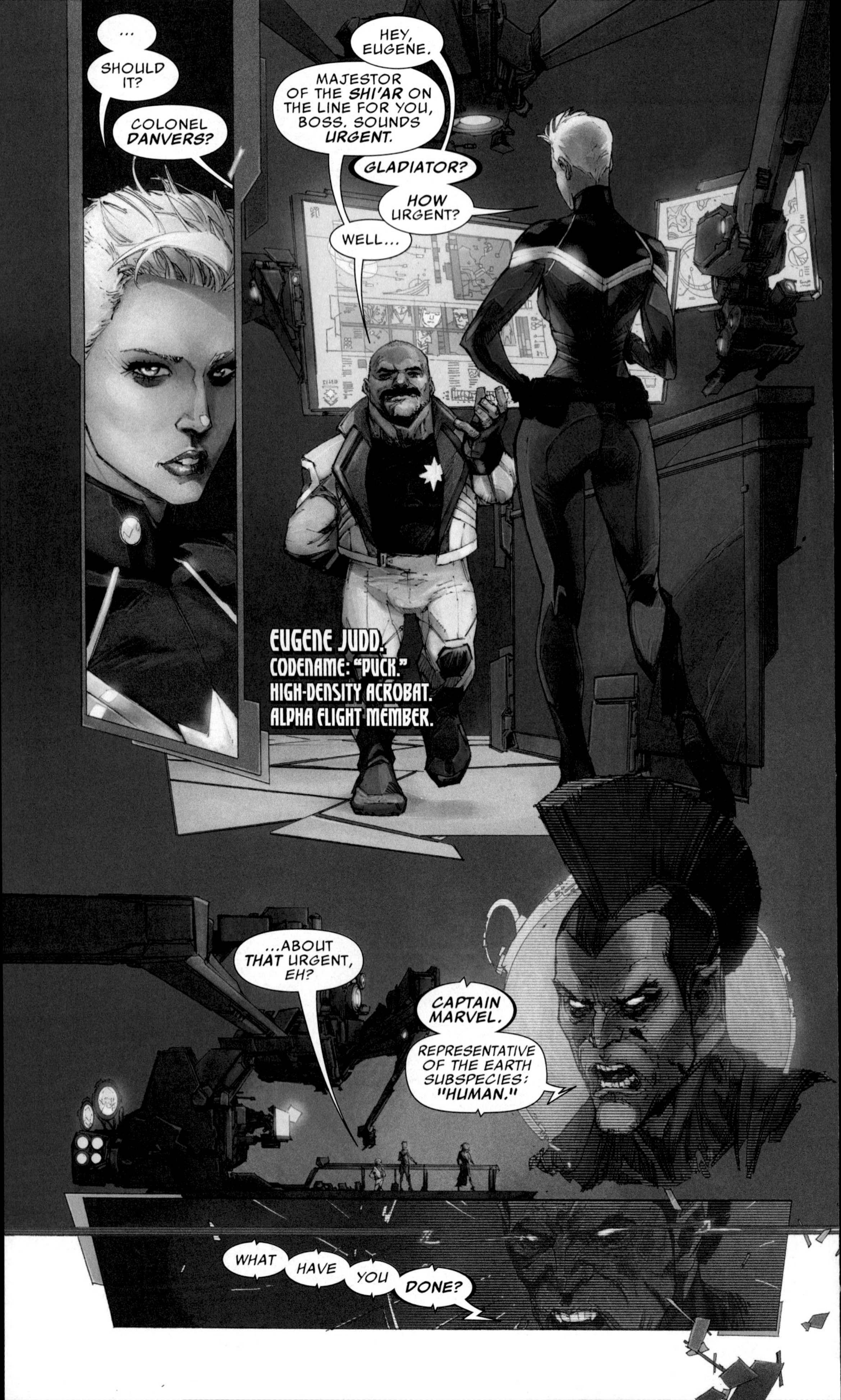
...
SHOULD IT?
COLONEL DANVERS?
HEY, EUGENE.
MAJESTOR OF THE SHI'AR ON THE LINE FOR YOU, BOSS. SOUNDS URGENT.
GLADIATOR?
HOW URGENT?
WELL...
EUGENE JUDD.
CODENAME: "PUCK."
HIGH-DENSITY ACROBAT.
ALPHA FLIGHT MEMBER.
...ABOUT THAT URGENT, EH?
CAPTAIN MARVEL.
REPRESENTATIVE OF THE EARTH SUBSPECIES: "HUMAN."
WHAT HAVE YOU DONE?

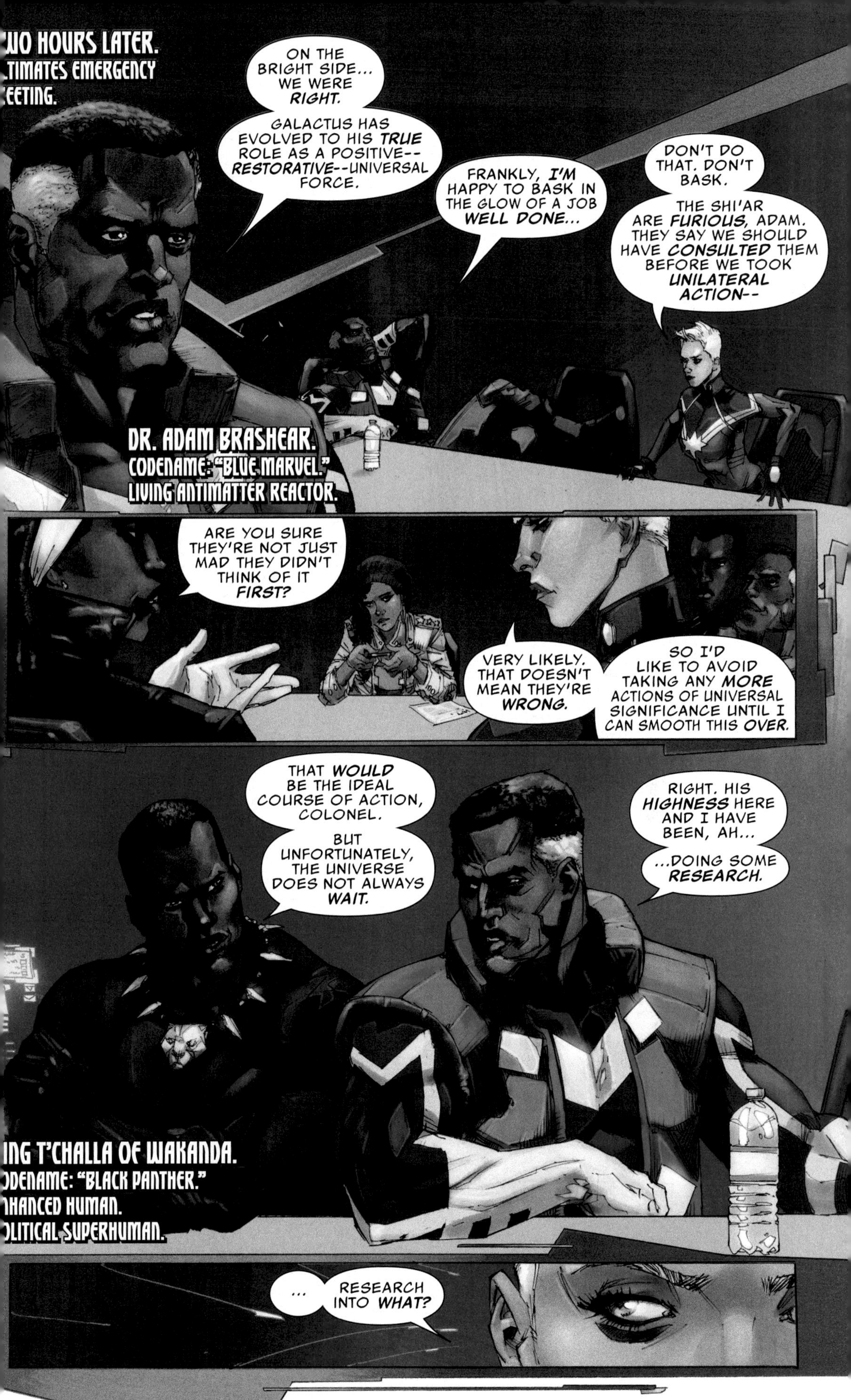

WO HOURS LATER.
TIMATES EMERGENCY
EETING.
ON THE BRIGHT SIDE... WE WERE RIGHT.
GALACTUS HAS EVOLVED TO HIS TRUE ROLE AS A POSITIVE--RESTORATIVE--UNIVERSAL FORCE.
FRANKLY, I'M HAPPY TO BASK IN THE GLOW OF A JOB WELL DONE...
DON'T DO THAT. DON'T BASK.
THE SHI'AR ARE FURIOUS, ADAM. THEY SAY WE SHOULD HAVE CONSULTED THEM BEFORE WE TOOK UNILATERAL ACTION--
DR. ADAM BRASHEAR.
CODENAME: "BLUE MARVEL."
LIVING ANTIMATTER REACTOR.
ARE YOU SURE THEY'RE NOT JUST MAD THEY DIDN'T THINK OF IT FIRST?
VERY LIKELY. THAT DOESN'T MEAN THEY'RE WRONG.
SO I'D LIKE TO AVOID TAKING ANY MORE ACTIONS OF UNIVERSAL SIGNIFICANCE UNTIL I CAN SMOOTH THIS OVER.
THAT WOULD BE THE IDEAL COURSE OF ACTION, COLONEL.
BUT UNFORTUNATELY, THE UNIVERSE DOES NOT ALWAYS WAIT.
RIGHT. HIS HIGHNESS HERE AND I HAVE BEEN, AH...
...DOING SOME RESEARCH.
ING T'CHALLA OF WAKANDA.
ODENAME: "BLACK PANTHER."
HANCED HUMAN.
OLITICAL SUPERHUMAN.
...
RESEARCH INTO WHAT?

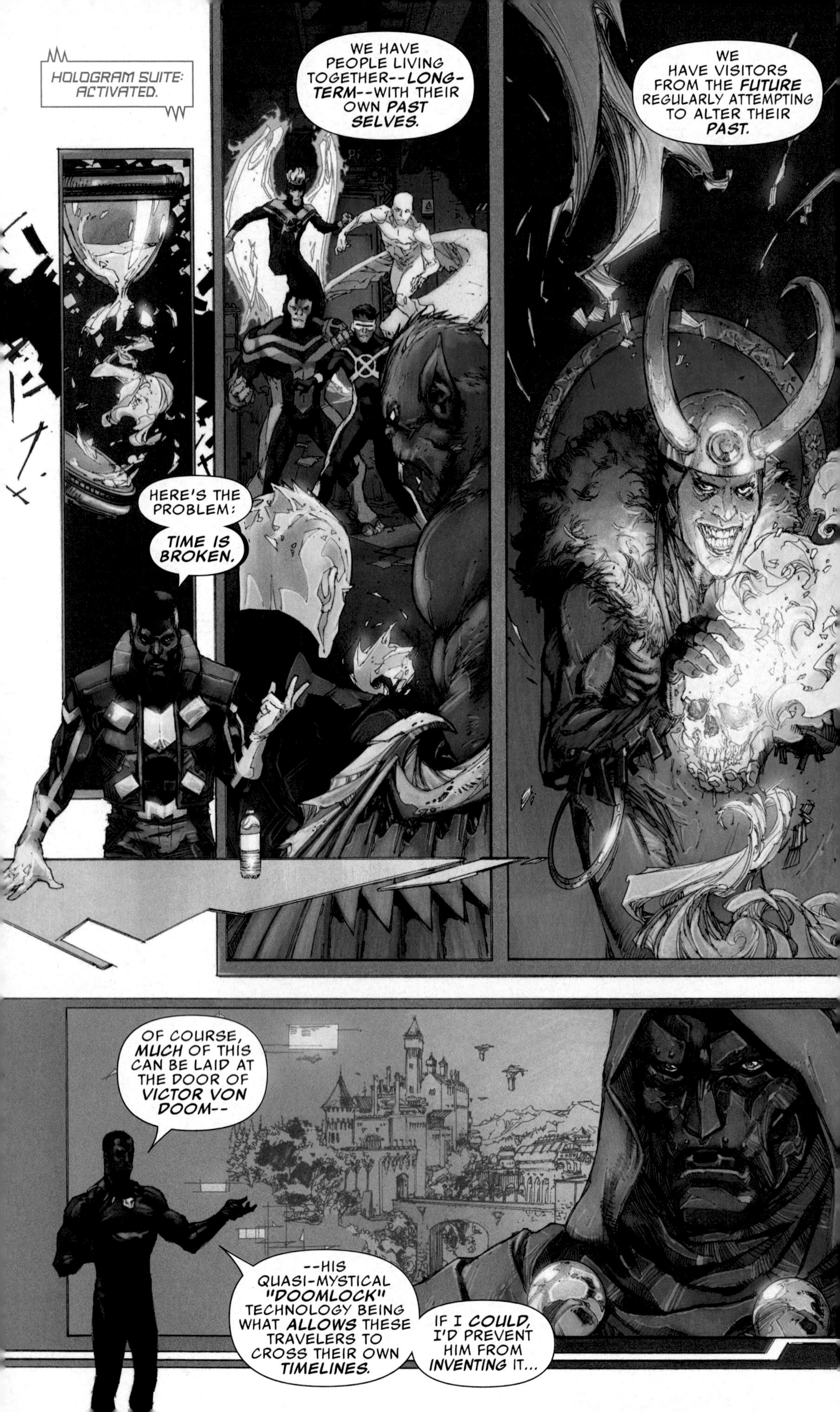
HOLOGRAM SUITE: ACTIVATED.
WE HAVE PEOPLE LIVING TOGETHER--LONG-TERM--WITH THEIR OWN PAST SELVES.
WE HAVE VISITORS FROM THE FUTURE REGULARLY ATTEMPTING TO ALTER THEIR PAST.
HERE'S THE PROBLEM:
TIME IS BROKEN.
OF COURSE, MUCH OF THIS CAN BE LAID AT THE DOOR OF VICTOR VON DOOM--
--HIS QUASI-MYSTICAL "DOOMLOCK" TECHNOLOGY BEING WHAT ALLOWS THESE TRAVELERS TO CROSS THEIR OWN TIMELINES.
IF I COULD, I'D PREVENT HIM FROM INVENTING IT...

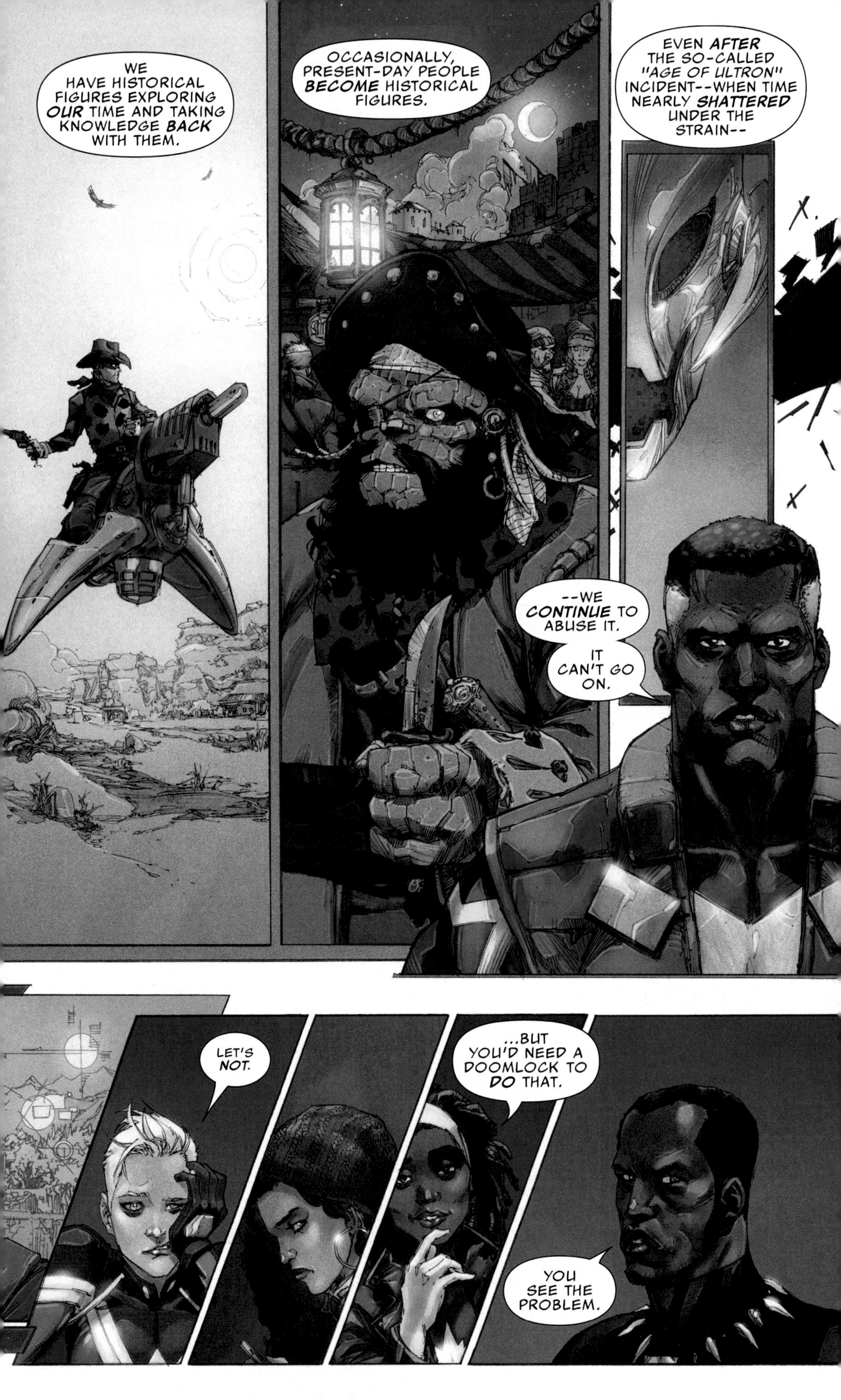
WE HAVE HISTORICAL FIGURES EXPLORING OUR TIME AND TAKING KNOWLEDGE BACK WITH THEM.
OCCASIONALLY, PRESENT-DAY PEOPLE BECOME HISTORICAL FIGURES.
EVEN AFTER THE SO-CALLED "AGE OF ULTRON" INCIDENT--WHEN TIME NEARLY SHATTERED UNDER THE STRAIN--
--WE CONTINUE TO ABUSE IT.
IT CAN'T GO ON.
LET'S NOT.
...BUT YOU'D NEED A DOOMLOCK TO DO THAT.
YOU SEE THE PROBLEM.

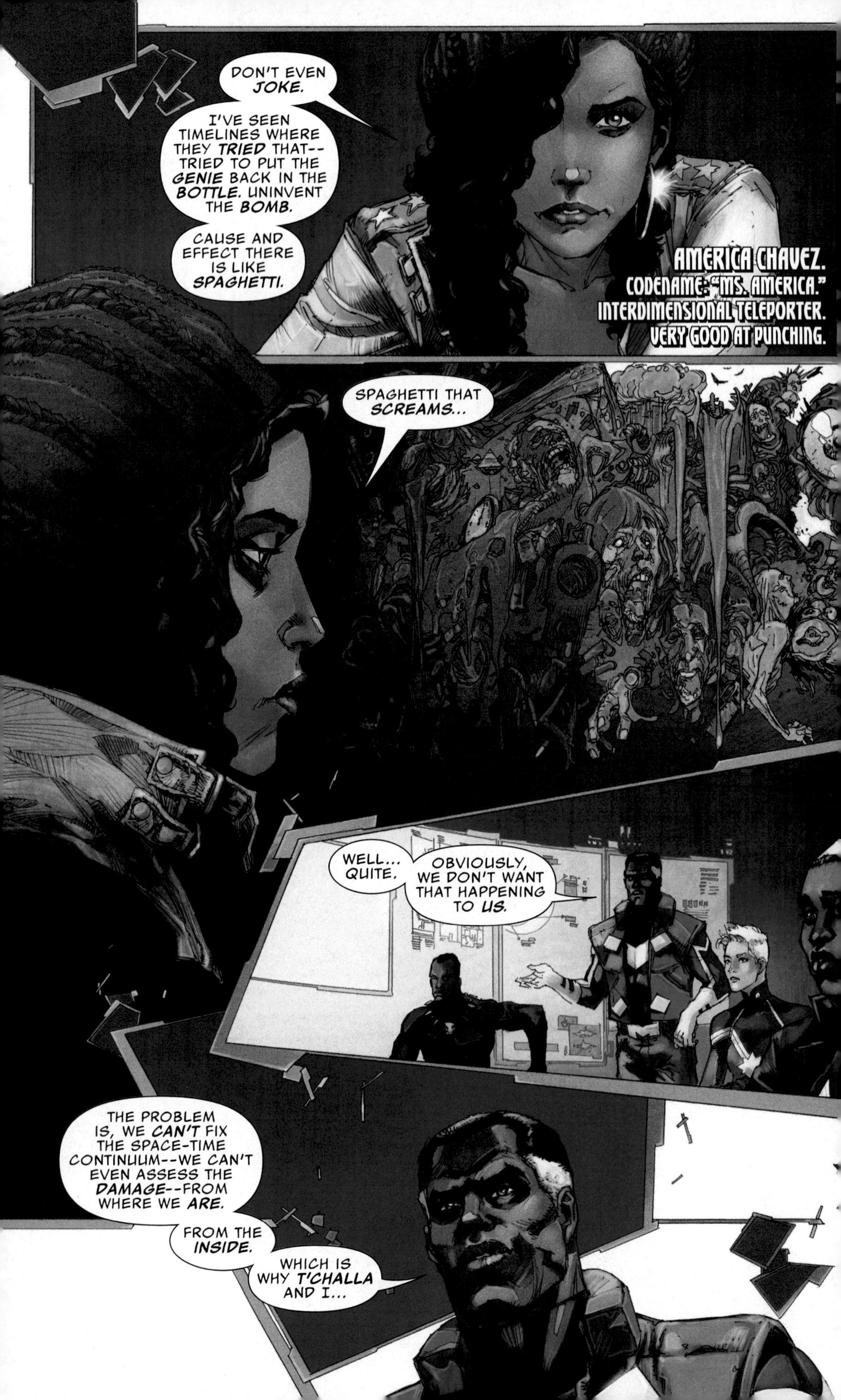

DON'T EVEN JOKE.
I'VE SEEN TIMELINES WHERE THEY TRIED THAT--TRIED TO PUT THE GENIE BACK IN THE BOTTLE. UNINVENT THE BOMB.
CAUSE AND EFFECT THERE IS LIKE SPAGHETTI.
AMERICA CHAVEZ.
CODENAME: "MS. AMERICA."
INTERDIMENSIONAL TELEPORTER.
VERY GOOD AT PUNCHING.
SPAGHETTI THAT SCREAMS...
WELL... QUITE.
OBVIOUSLY, WE DON'T WANT THAT HAPPENING TO US.
THE PROBLEM IS, WE CAN'T FIX THE SPACE-TIME CONTINUUM--WE CAN'T EVEN ASSESS THE DAMAGE--FROM WHERE WE ARE.
FROM THE INSIDE.
WHICH IS WHY T'CHALLA AND I...

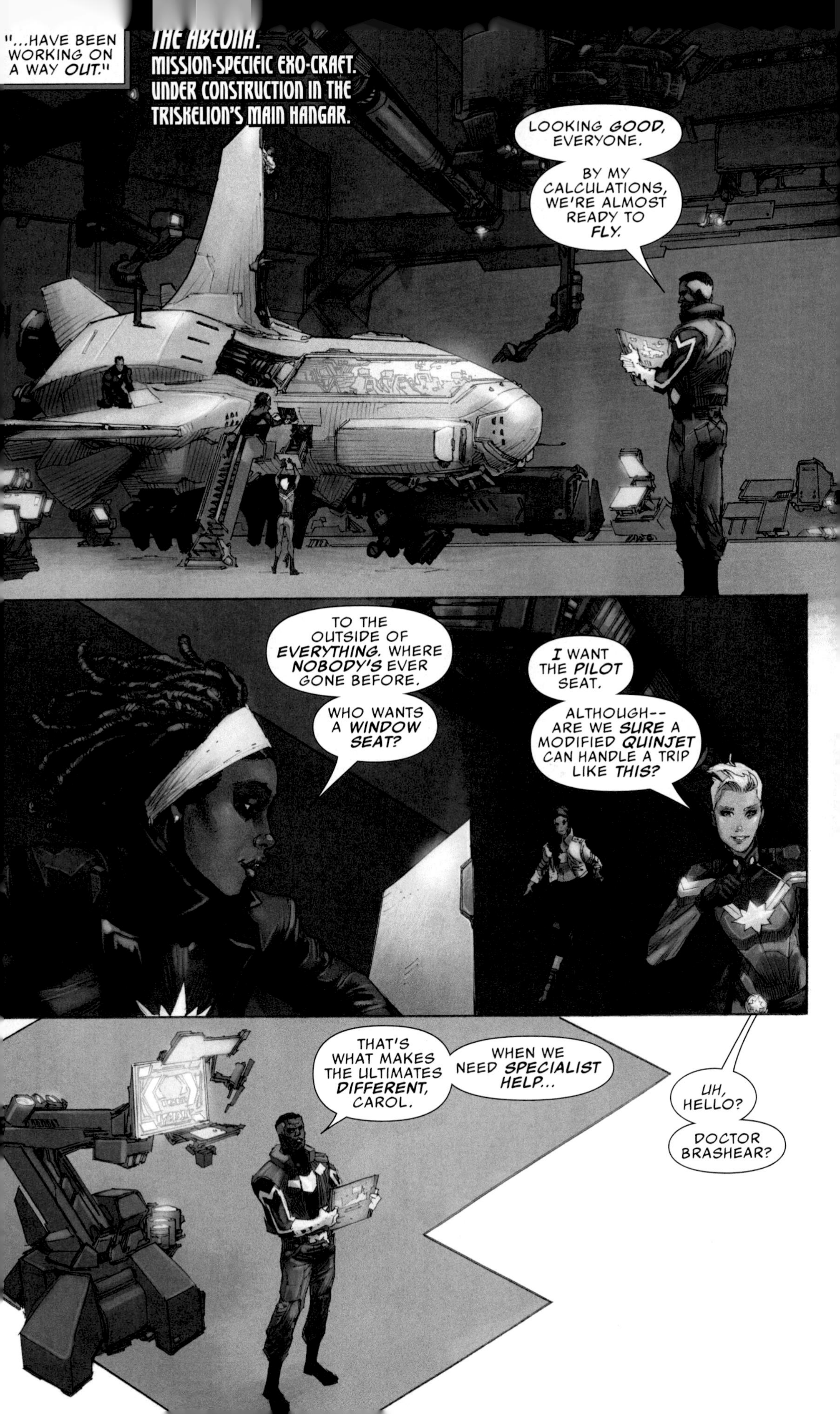
"...HAVE BEEN WORKING ON A WAY OUT."
THE ABEONA.
MISSION-SPECIFIC EXO-CRAFT. UNDER CONSTRUCTION IN THE TRISKELION'S MAIN HANGAR.
LOOKING GOOD, EVERYONE.
BY MY CALCULATIONS, WE'RE ALMOST READY TO FLY.
TO THE OUTSIDE OF EVERYTHING. WHERE NOBODY'S EVER GONE BEFORE.
WHO WANTS A WINDOW SEAT?
I WANT THE PILOT SEAT.
ALTHOUGH-- ARE WE SURE A MODIFIED QUINJET CAN HANDLE A TRIP LIKE THIS?
THAT'S WHAT MAKES THE ULTIMATES DIFFERENT, CAROL.
WHEN WE NEED SPECIALIST HELP...
UH, HELLO?
DOCTOR BRASHEAR?

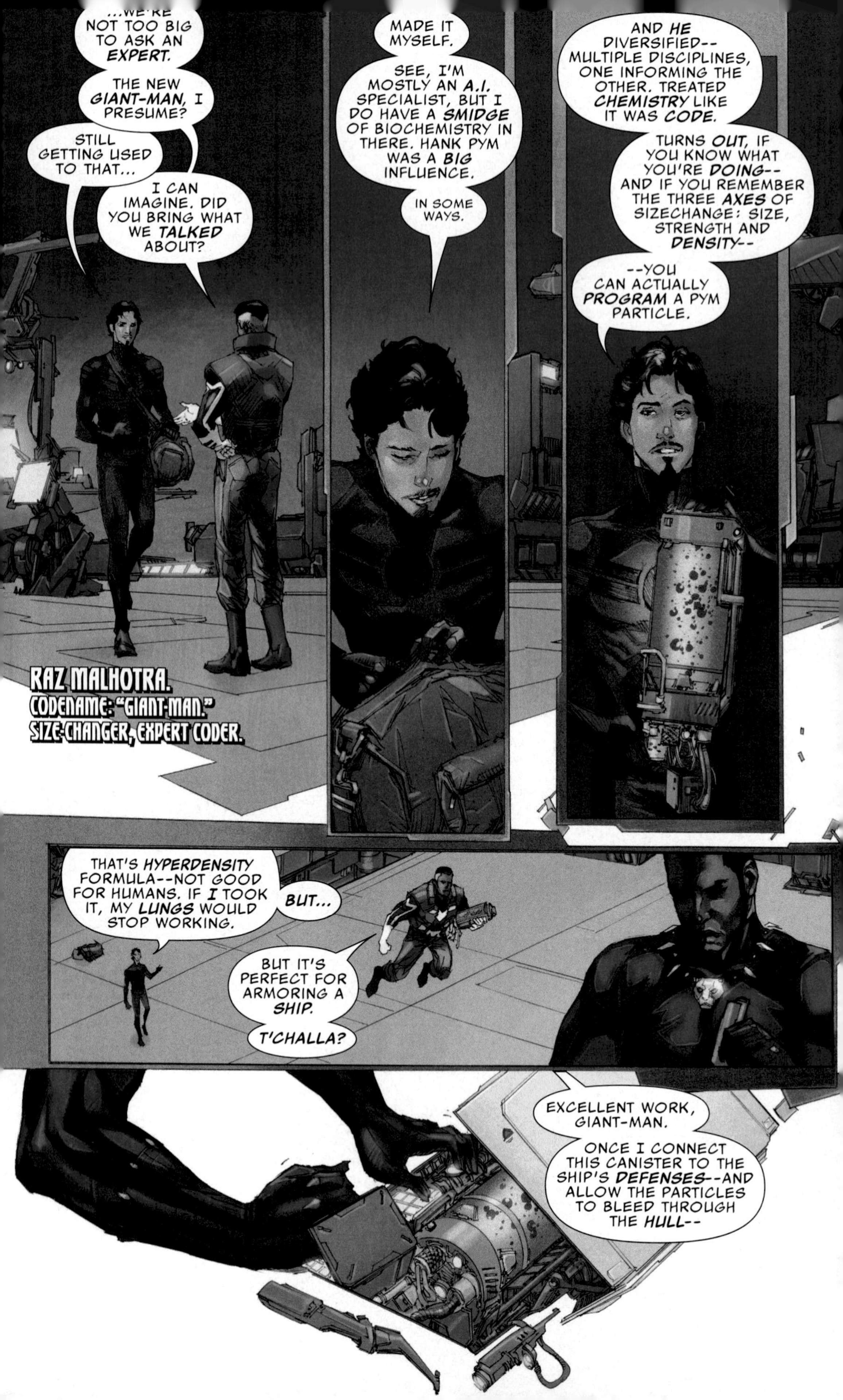
...WE'RE NOT TOO BIG TO ASK AN EXPERT.
THE NEW GIANT-MAN, I PRESUME?
STILL GETTING USED TO THAT...
I CAN IMAGINE. DID YOU BRING WHAT WE TALKED ABOUT?
RAZ MALHOTRA.
CODENAME: "GIANT-MAN."
SIZE-CHANGER, EXPERT CODER.
MADE IT MYSELF.
SEE, I'M MOSTLY AN A.I. SPECIALIST, BUT I DO HAVE A SMIDGE OF BIOCHEMISTRY IN THERE. HANK PYM WAS A BIG INFLUENCE.
IN SOME WAYS.
AND HE DIVERSIFIED-- MULTIPLE DISCIPLINES, ONE INFORMING THE OTHER. TREATED CHEMISTRY LIKE IT WAS CODE.
TURNS OUT, IF YOU KNOW WHAT YOU'RE DOING-- AND IF YOU REMEMBER THE THREE AXES OF SIZECHANGE: SIZE, STRENGTH AND DENSITY--
--YOU CAN ACTUALLY PROGRAM A PYM PARTICLE.
THAT'S HYPERDENSITY FORMULA--NOT GOOD FOR HUMANS. IF I TOOK IT, MY LUNGS WOULD STOP WORKING.
BUT...
BUT IT'S PERFECT FOR ARMORING A SHIP.
T'CHALLA?
EXCELLENT WORK, GIANT-MAN.
ONCE I CONNECT THIS CANISTER TO THE SHIP'S DEFENSES--AND ALLOW THE PARTICLES TO BLEED THROUGH THE HULL--

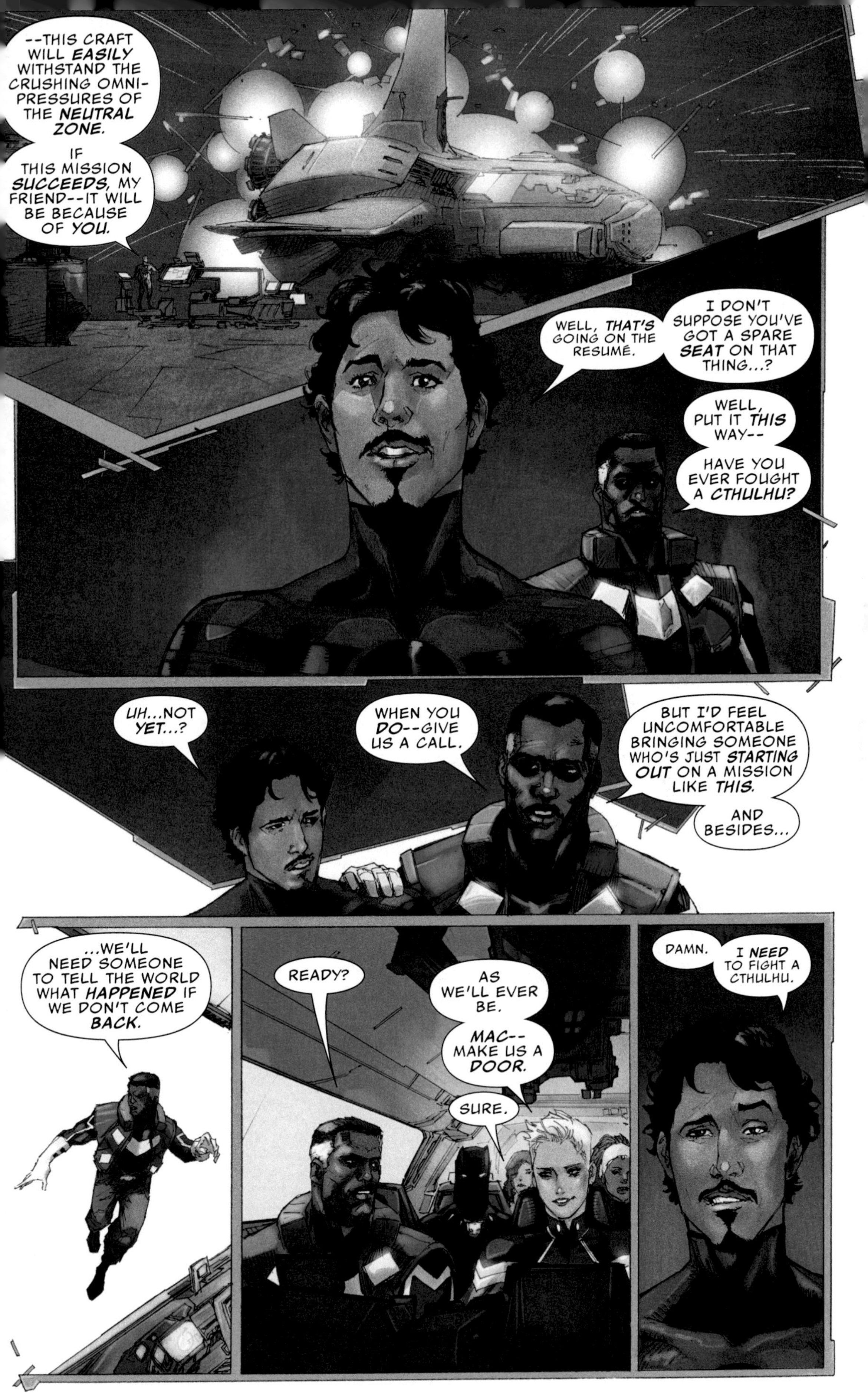

--THIS CRAFT WILL EASILY WITHSTAND THE CRUSHING OMNI-PRESSURES OF THE NEUTRAL ZONE.
IF THIS MISSION SUCCEEDS, MY FRIEND--IT WILL BE BECAUSE OF YOU.
WELL, THAT'S GOING ON THE RESUMÉ.
I DON'T SUPPOSE YOU'VE GOT A SPARE SEAT ON THAT THING...?
WELL, PUT IT THIS WAY--
HAVE YOU EVER FOUGHT A CTHULHU?
UH...NOT YET...?
WHEN YOU DO--GIVE US A CALL.
BUT I'D FEEL UNCOMFORTABLE BRINGING SOMEONE WHO'S JUST STARTING OUT ON A MISSION LIKE THIS.
AND BESIDES...
...WE'LL NEED SOMEONE TO TELL THE WORLD WHAT HAPPENED IF WE DON'T COME BACK.
READY?
AS WE'LL EVER BE.
MAC--MAKE US A DOOR.
SURE.
DAMN.
I NEED TO FIGHT A CTHULHU.

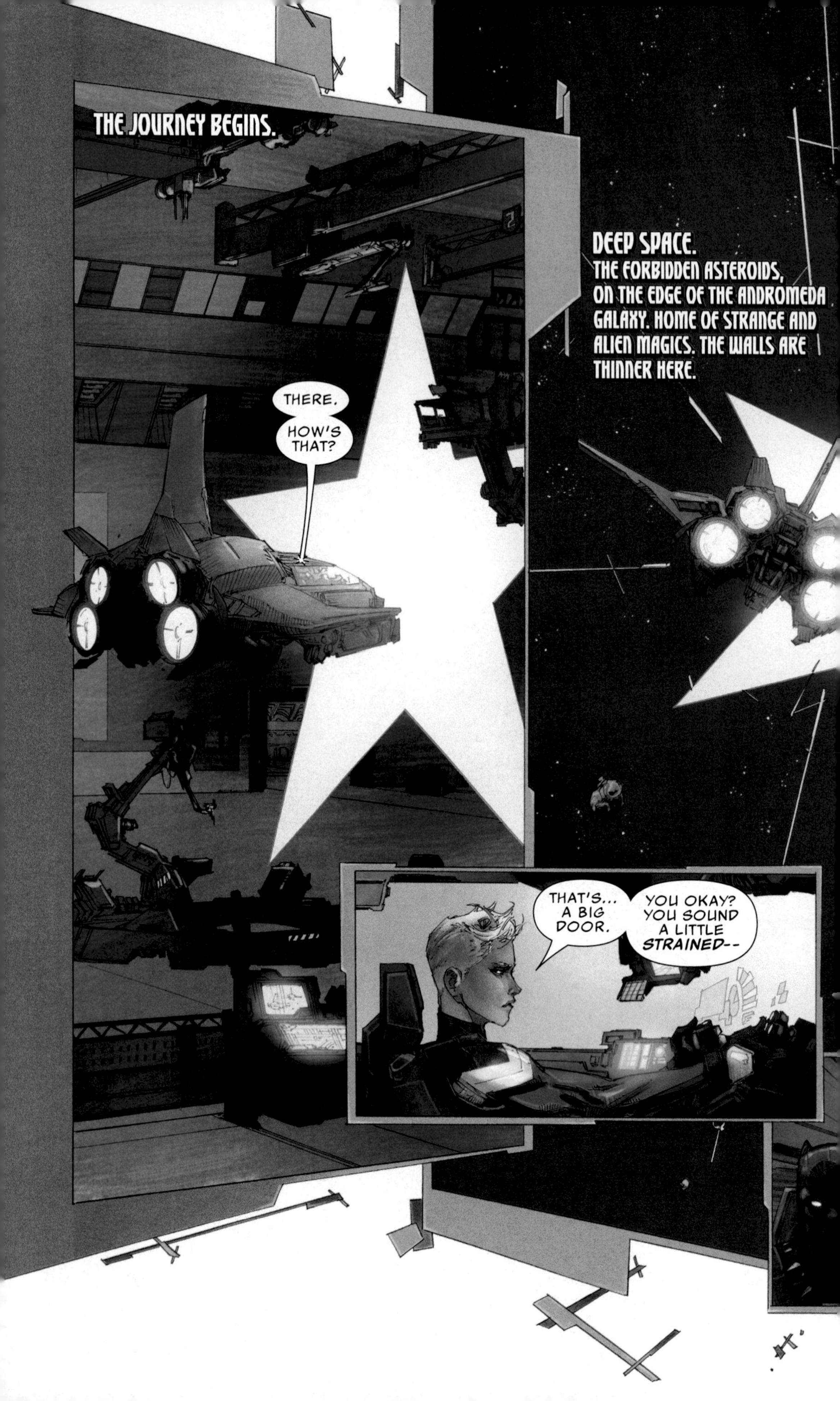
THE JOURNEY BEGINS.
THERE.
HOW'S THAT?
DEEP SPACE.
THE FORBIDDEN ASTEROIDS, ON THE EDGE OF THE ANDROMEDA GALAXY. HOME OF STRANGE AND ALIEN MAGICS. THE WALLS ARE THINNER HERE.
THAT'S... A BIG DOOR.
YOU OKAY? YOU SOUND A LITTLE STRAINED--

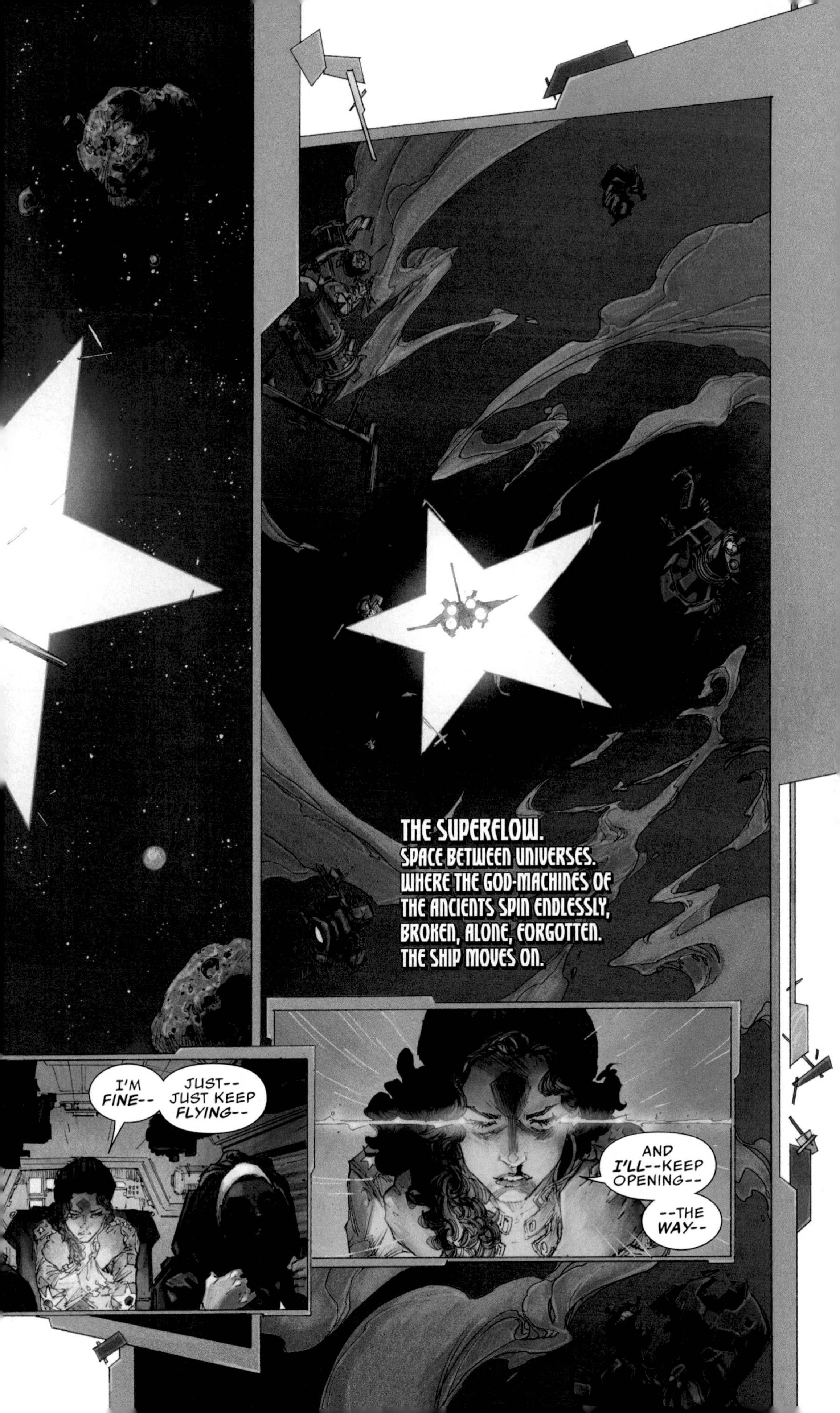
THE SUPERFLOW.
SPACE BETWEEN UNIVERSES.
WHERE THE GOD-MACHINES OF
THE ANCIENTS SPIN ENDLESSLY,
BROKEN, ALONE, FORGOTTEN.
THE SHIP MOVES ON.
I'M FINE--
JUST-- JUST KEEP FLYING--
AND I'LL--KEEP OPENING--
--THE WAY--

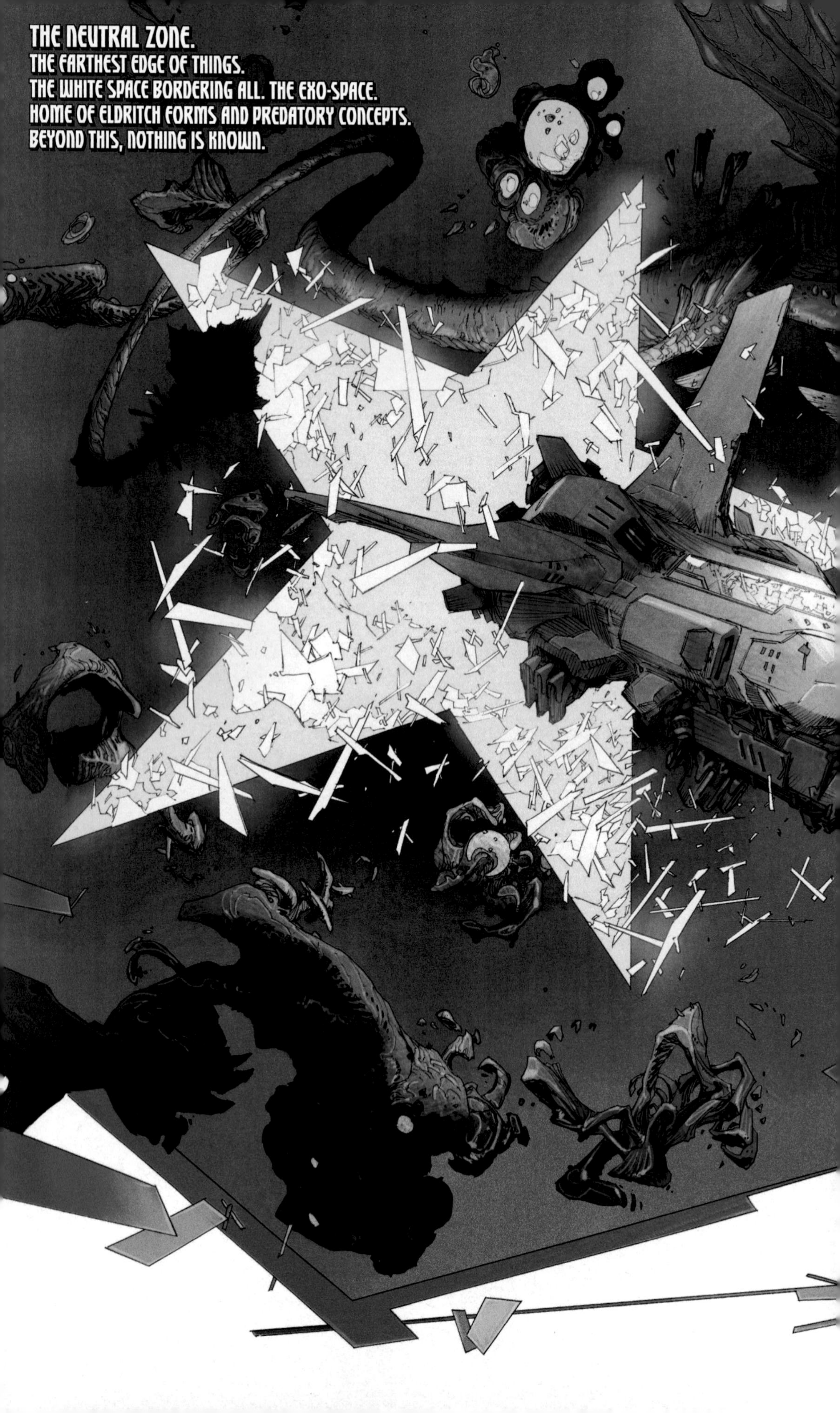
THE NEUTRAL ZONE.
THE FARTHEST EDGE OF THINGS.
THE WHITE SPACE BORDERING ALL. THE EXO-SPACE.
HOME OF ELDRITCH FORMS AND PREDATORY CONCEPTS.
BEYOND THIS, NOTHING IS KNOWN.

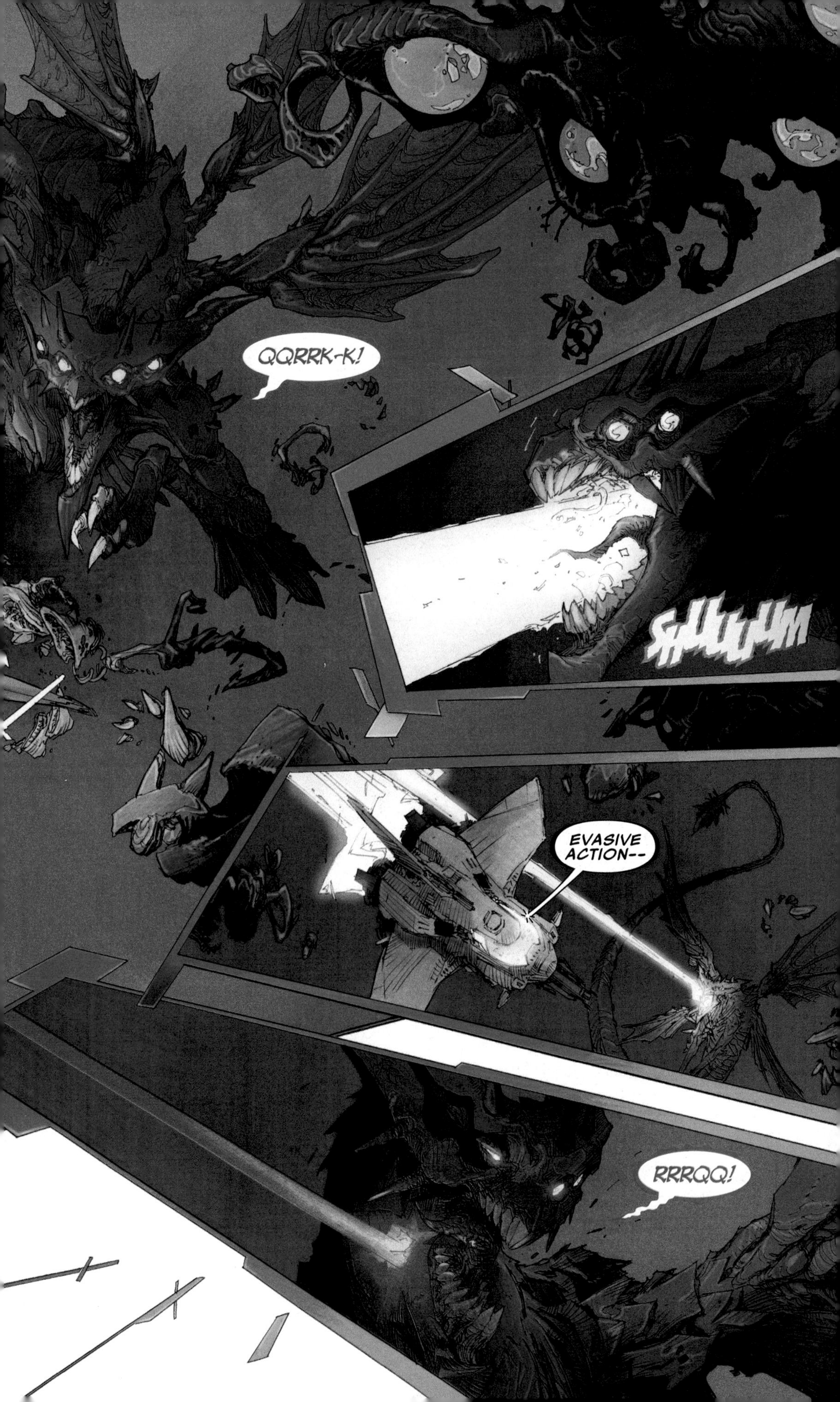
QQRRK-K!
SHUUUM
EVASIVE ACTION--
RRRQQ!

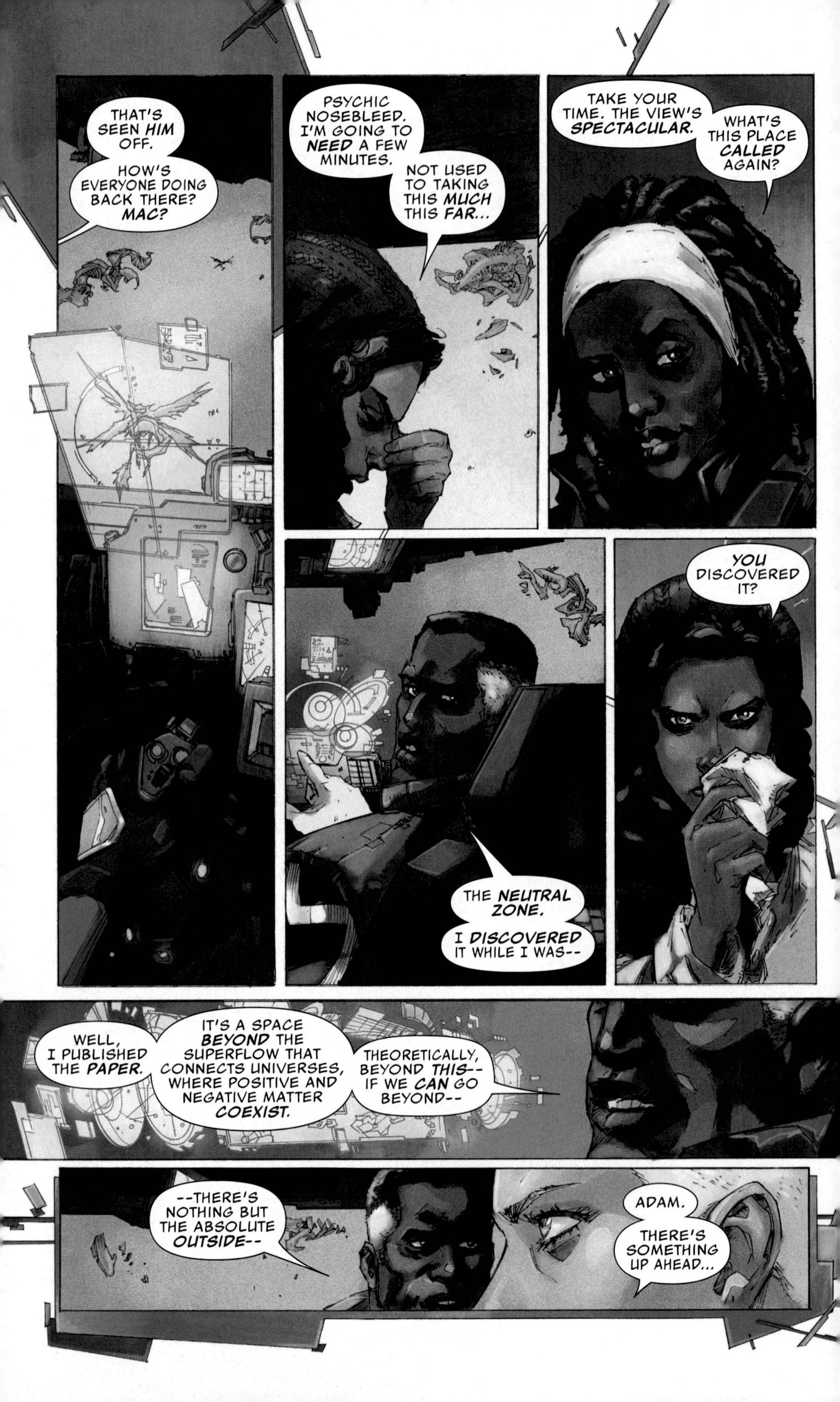

THAT'S SEEN HIM OFF.
HOW'S EVERYONE DOING BACK THERE? MAC?
PSYCHIC NOSEBLEED. I'M GOING TO NEED A FEW MINUTES.
NOT USED TO TAKING THIS MUCH THIS FAR...
TAKE YOUR TIME. THE VIEW'S SPECTACULAR.
WHAT'S THIS PLACE CALLED AGAIN?
THE NEUTRAL ZONE.
I DISCOVERED IT WHILE I WAS--
YOU DISCOVERED IT?
WELL, I PUBLISHED THE PAPER.
IT'S A SPACE BEYOND THE SUPERFLOW THAT CONNECTS UNIVERSES, WHERE POSITIVE AND NEGATIVE MATTER COEXIST.
THEORETICALLY, BEYOND THIS-- IF WE CAN GO BEYOND--
--THERE'S NOTHING BUT THE ABSOLUTE OUTSIDE--
ADAM.
THERE'S SOMETHING UP AHEAD...

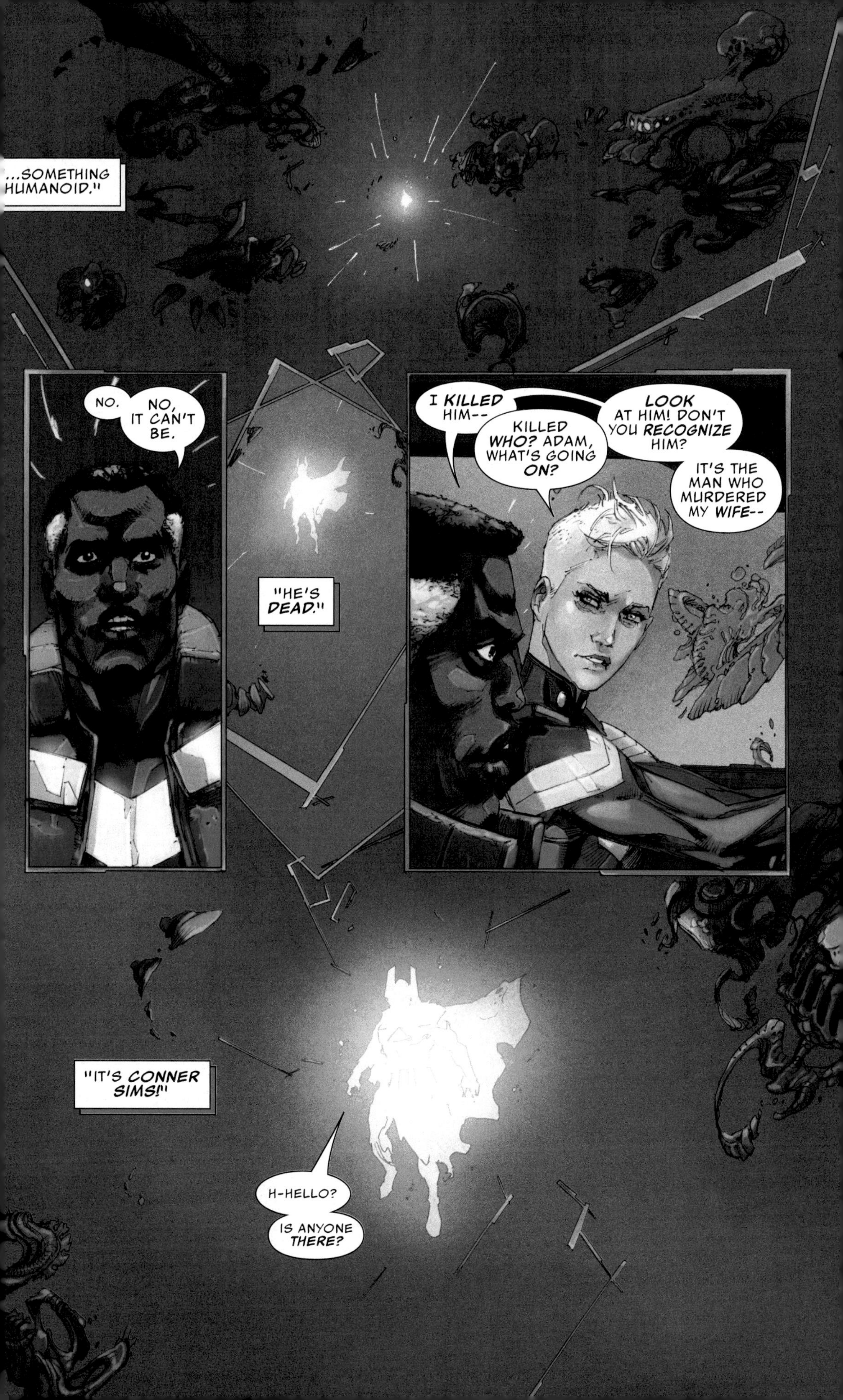

"...SOMETHING HUMANOID."
NO.
NO, IT CAN'T BE.
"HE'S DEAD."
I KILLED HIM--
KILLED WHO? ADAM, WHAT'S GOING ON?
LOOK AT HIM! DON'T YOU RECOGNIZE HIM?
IT'S THE MAN WHO MURDERED MY WIFE--
"IT'S CONNER SIMS!"
H-HELLO?
IS ANYONE THERE?

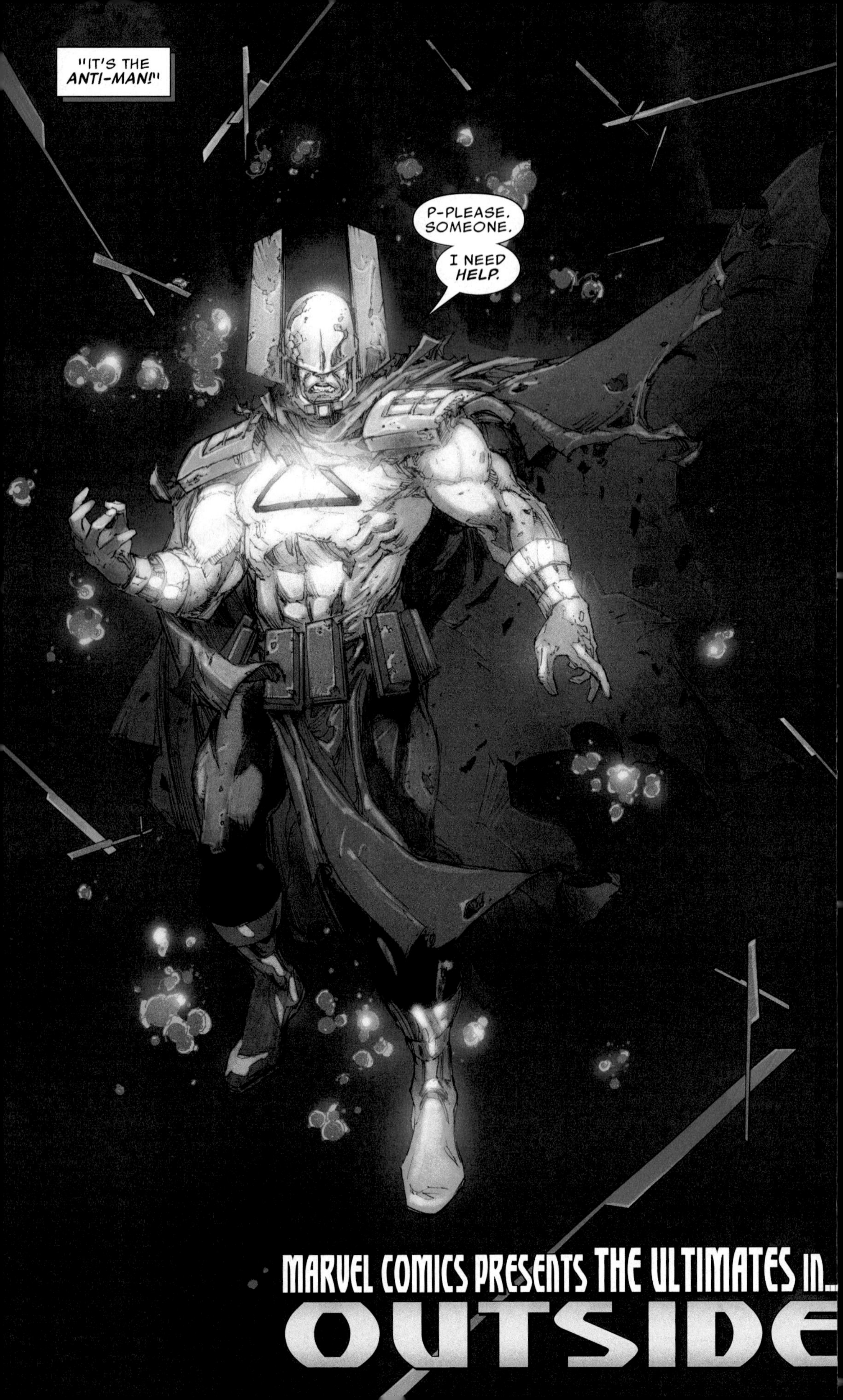
"IT'S THE ANTI-MAN!"
P-PLEASE. SOMEONE.
I NEED HELP.
MARVEL COMICS PRESENTS THE ULTIMATES IN...
OUTSIDE

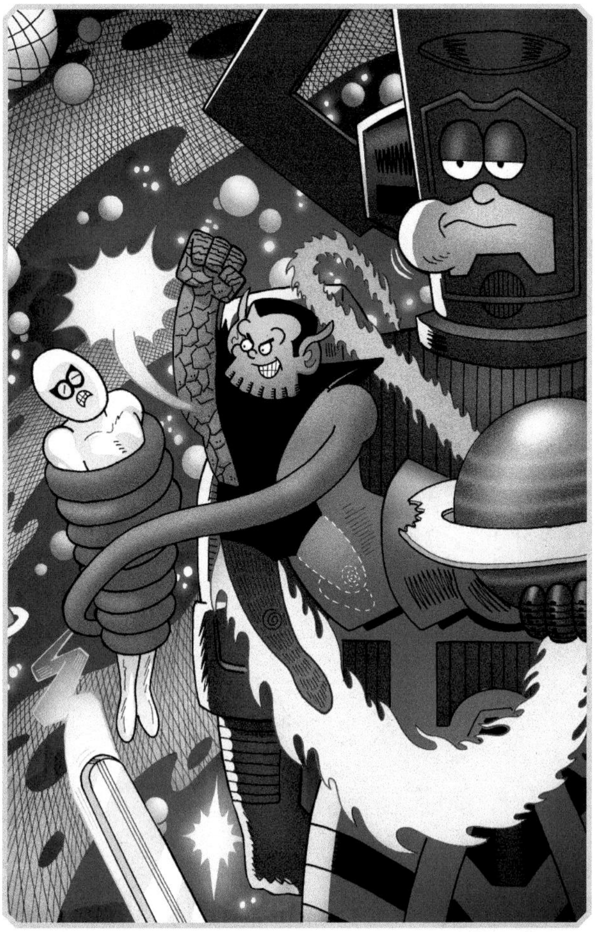

#2 VARIANT BY
FRED HEMBECK &
EDGAR DELGADO

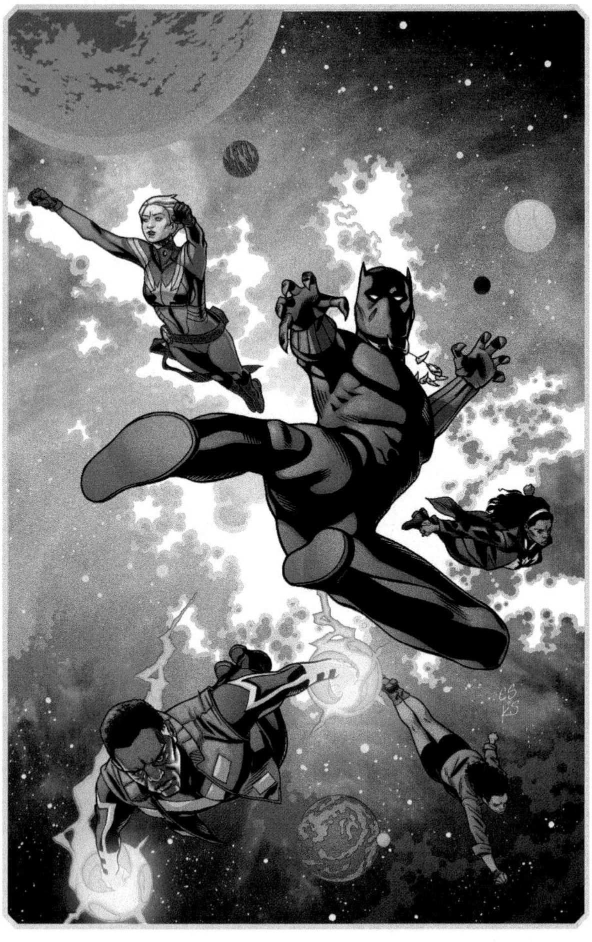

#3 VARIANT BY
CHRIS SPROUSE,
KARL STORY
& DAVE MCCAIG

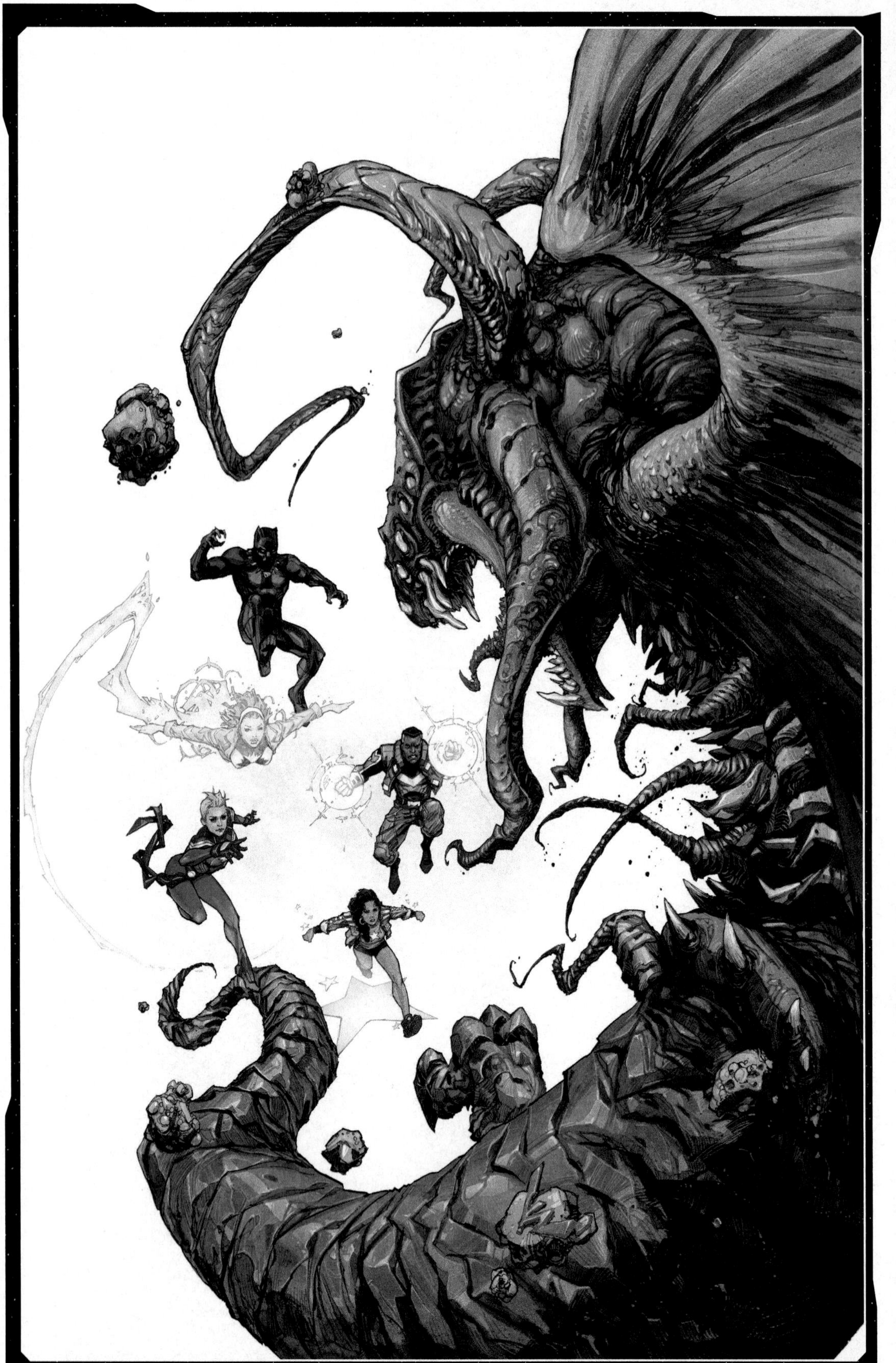

4

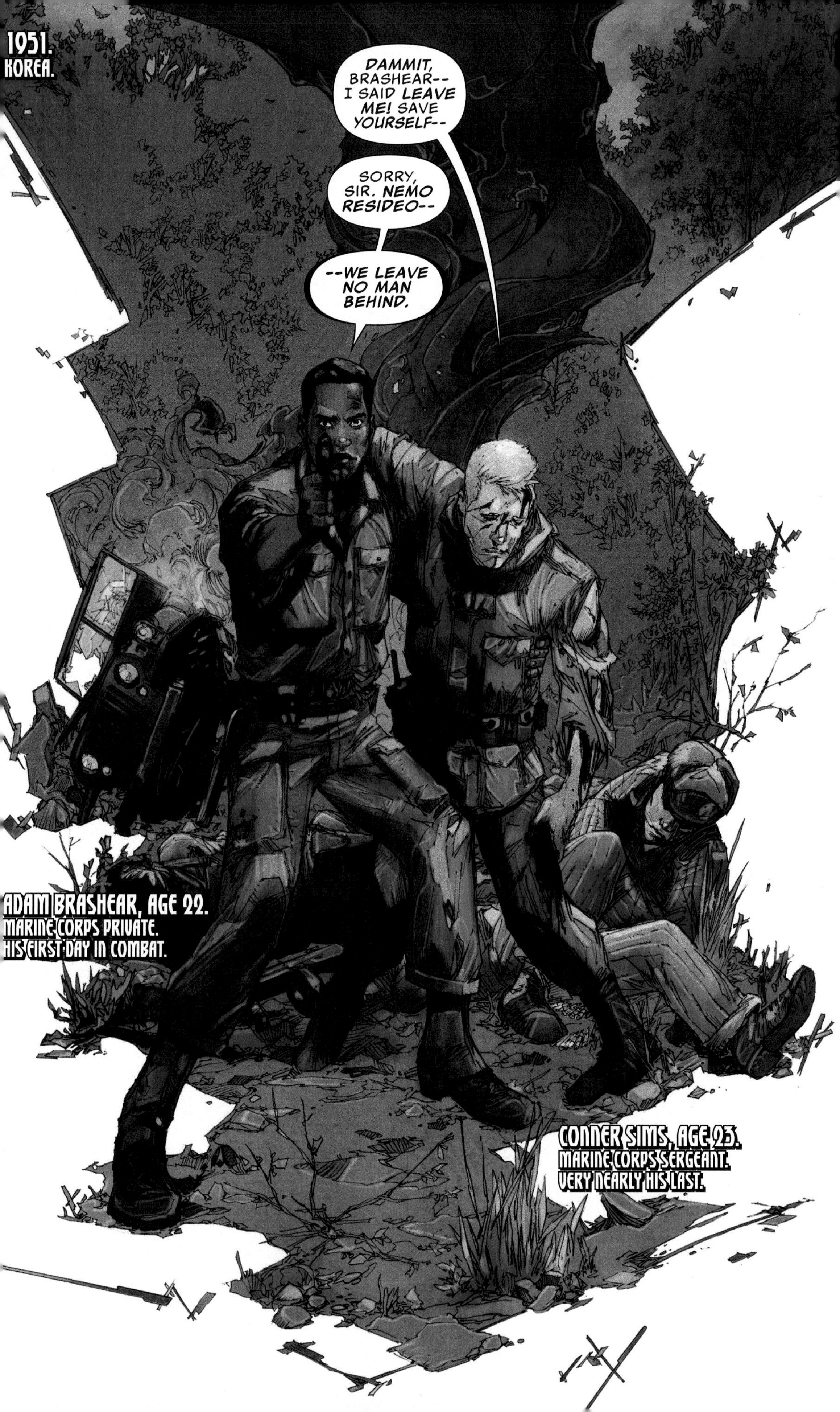
1951.
KOREA.
DAMMIT, BRASHEAR-- I SAID LEAVE ME! SAVE YOURSELF--
SORRY, SIR. NEMO RESIDEO--
--WE LEAVE NO MAN BEHIND.
ADAM BRASHEAR, AGE 22.
MARINE CORPS PRIVATE.
HIS FIRST DAY IN COMBAT.
CONNER SIMS, AGE 23.
MARINE CORPS SERGEANT.
VERY NEARLY HIS LAST.

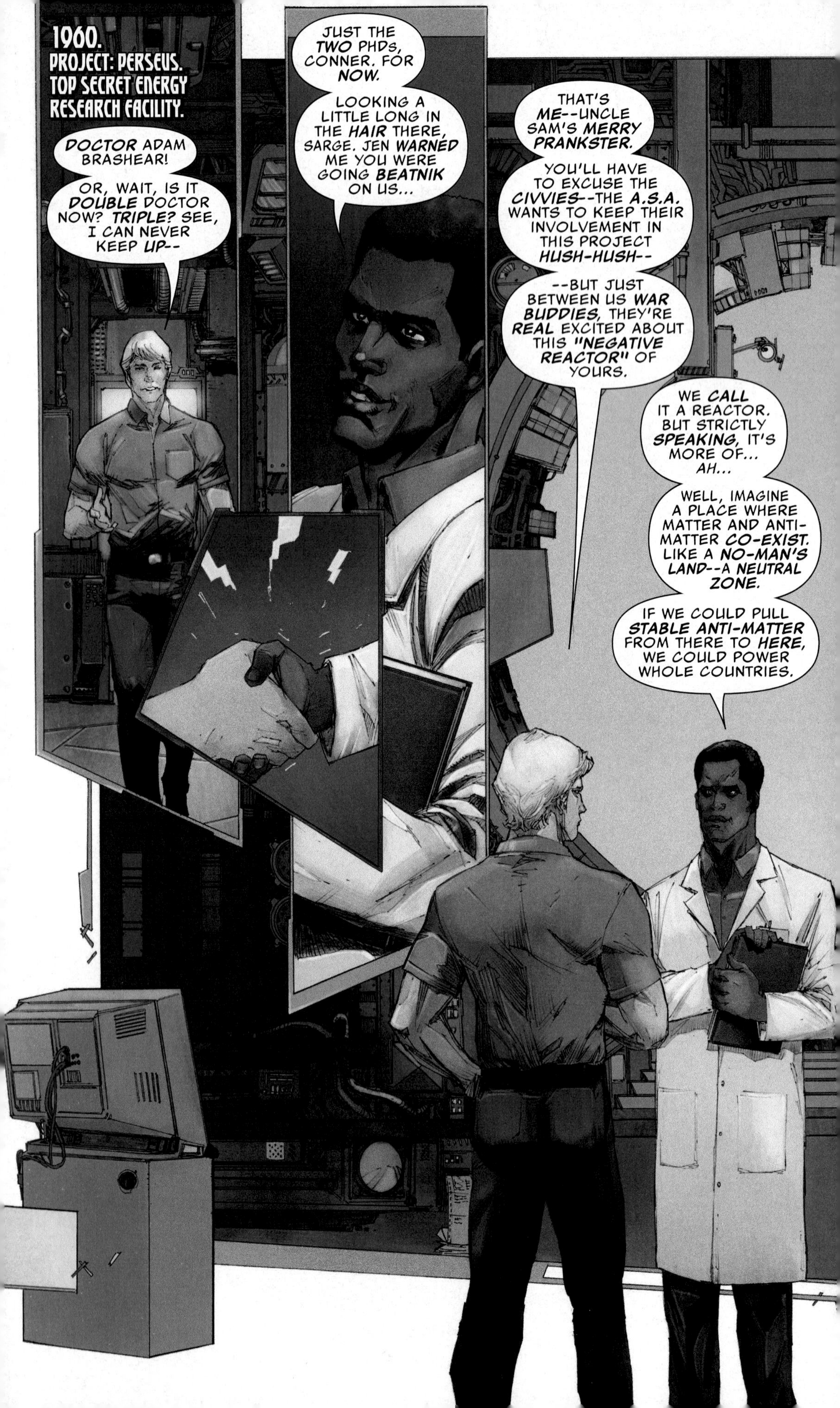

1960.
PROJECT: PERSEUS.
TOP SECRET ENERGY RESEARCH FACILITY.
DOCTOR ADAM BRASHEAR!
OR, WAIT, IS IT DOUBLE DOCTOR NOW? TRIPLE? SEE, I CAN NEVER KEEP UP--
JUST THE TWO PHDs, CONNER. FOR NOW.
LOOKING A LITTLE LONG IN THE HAIR THERE, SARGE. JEN WARNED ME YOU WERE GOING BEATNIK ON US...
THAT'S ME--UNCLE SAM'S MERRY PRANKSTER.
YOU'LL HAVE TO EXCUSE THE CIVVIES--THE A.S.A. WANTS TO KEEP THEIR INVOLVEMENT IN THIS PROJECT HUSH-HUSH--
--BUT JUST BETWEEN US WAR BUDDIES, THEY'RE REAL EXCITED ABOUT THIS "NEGATIVE REACTOR" OF YOURS.
WE CALL IT A REACTOR. BUT STRICTLY SPEAKING, IT'S MORE OF... AH...
WELL, IMAGINE A PLACE WHERE MATTER AND ANTI-MATTER CO-EXIST. LIKE A NO-MAN'S LAND--A NEUTRAL ZONE.
IF WE COULD PULL STABLE ANTI-MATTER FROM THERE TO HERE, WE COULD POWER WHOLE COUNTRIES.

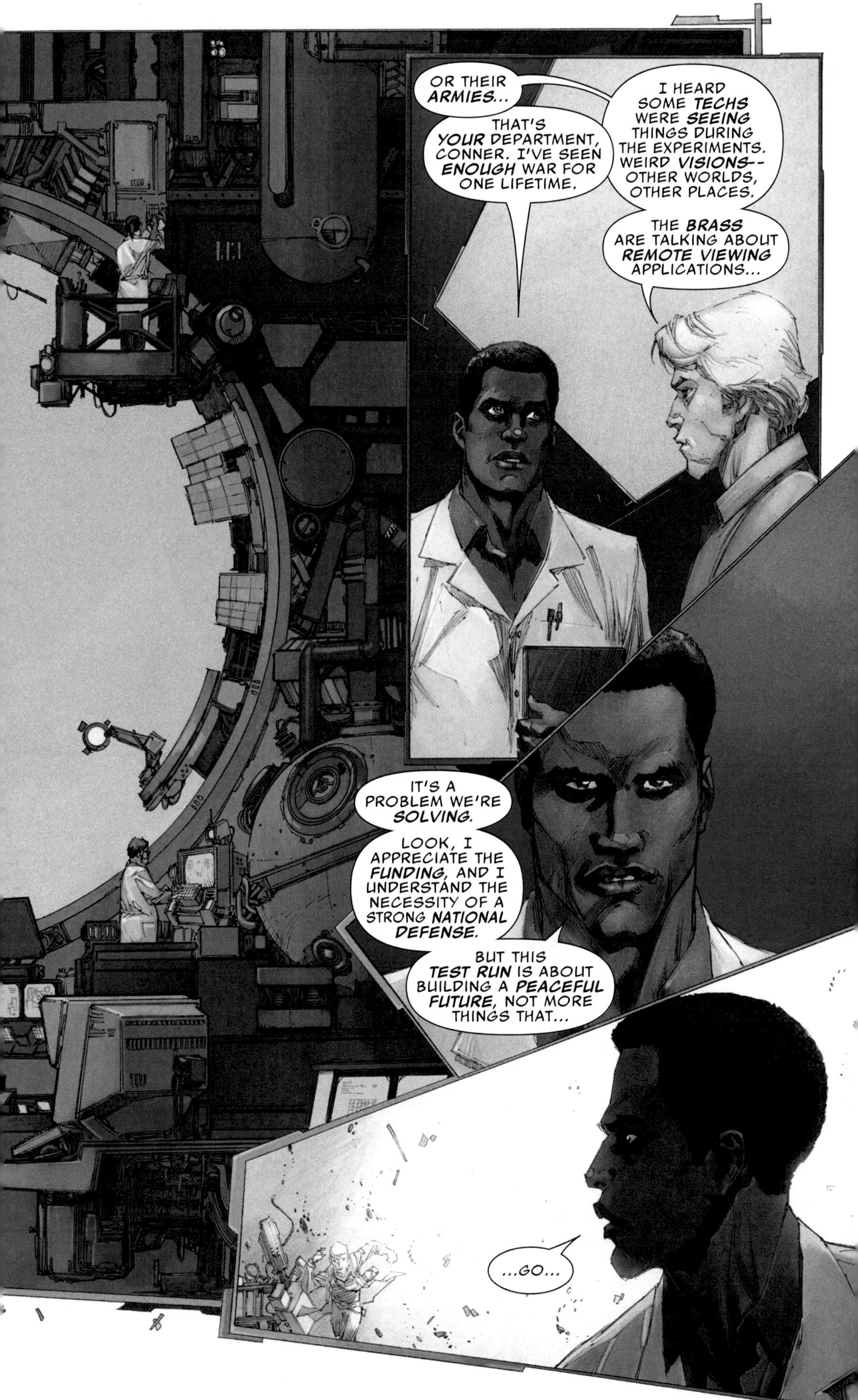
OR THEIR ARMIES...
I HEARD SOME TECHS WERE SEEING THINGS DURING THE EXPERIMENTS. WEIRD VISIONS--OTHER WORLDS, OTHER PLACES.
THE BRASS ARE TALKING ABOUT REMOTE VIEWING APPLICATIONS...
THAT'S YOUR DEPARTMENT, CONNER. I'VE SEEN ENOUGH WAR FOR ONE LIFETIME.
IT'S A PROBLEM WE'RE SOLVING.
LOOK, I APPRECIATE THE FUNDING, AND I UNDERSTAND THE NECESSITY OF A STRONG NATIONAL DEFENSE.
BUT THIS TEST RUN IS ABOUT BUILDING A PEACEFUL FUTURE, NOT MORE THINGS THAT...
...GO...

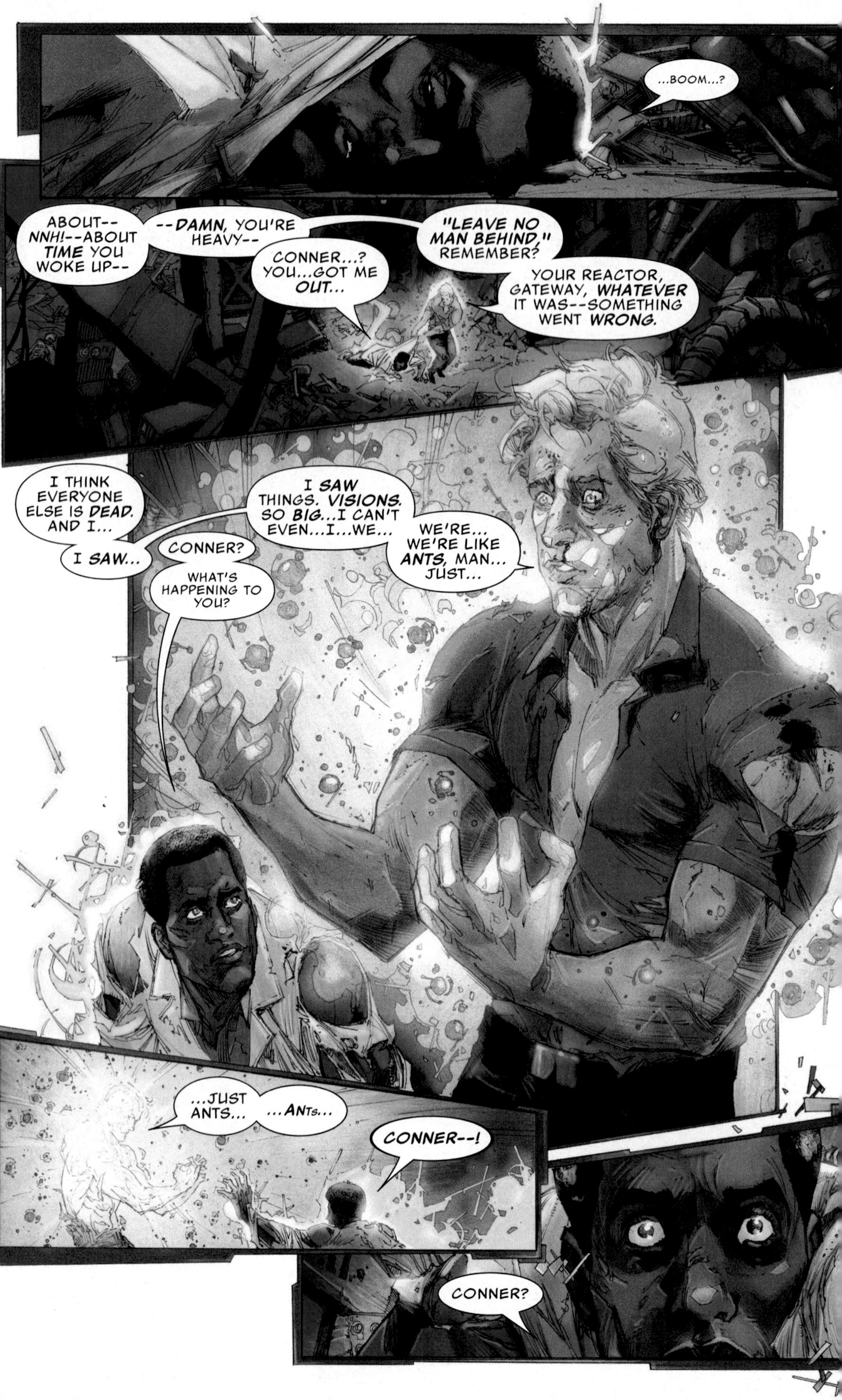
...BOOM...?
ABOUT-- NNH!--ABOUT TIME YOU WOKE UP--
--DAMN, YOU'RE HEAVY--
"LEAVE NO MAN BEHIND," REMEMBER?
CONNER...? YOU...GOT ME OUT...
YOUR REACTOR, GATEWAY, WHATEVER IT WAS--SOMETHING WENT WRONG.
I THINK EVERYONE ELSE IS DEAD. AND I...
I SAW...
I SAW THINGS. VISIONS. SO BIG...I CAN'T EVEN...I...WE...
WE'RE... WE'RE LIKE ANTS, MAN... JUST...
CONNER?
WHAT'S HAPPENING TO YOU?
...JUST ANTS...
...ANTS...
CONNER--!
CONNER?

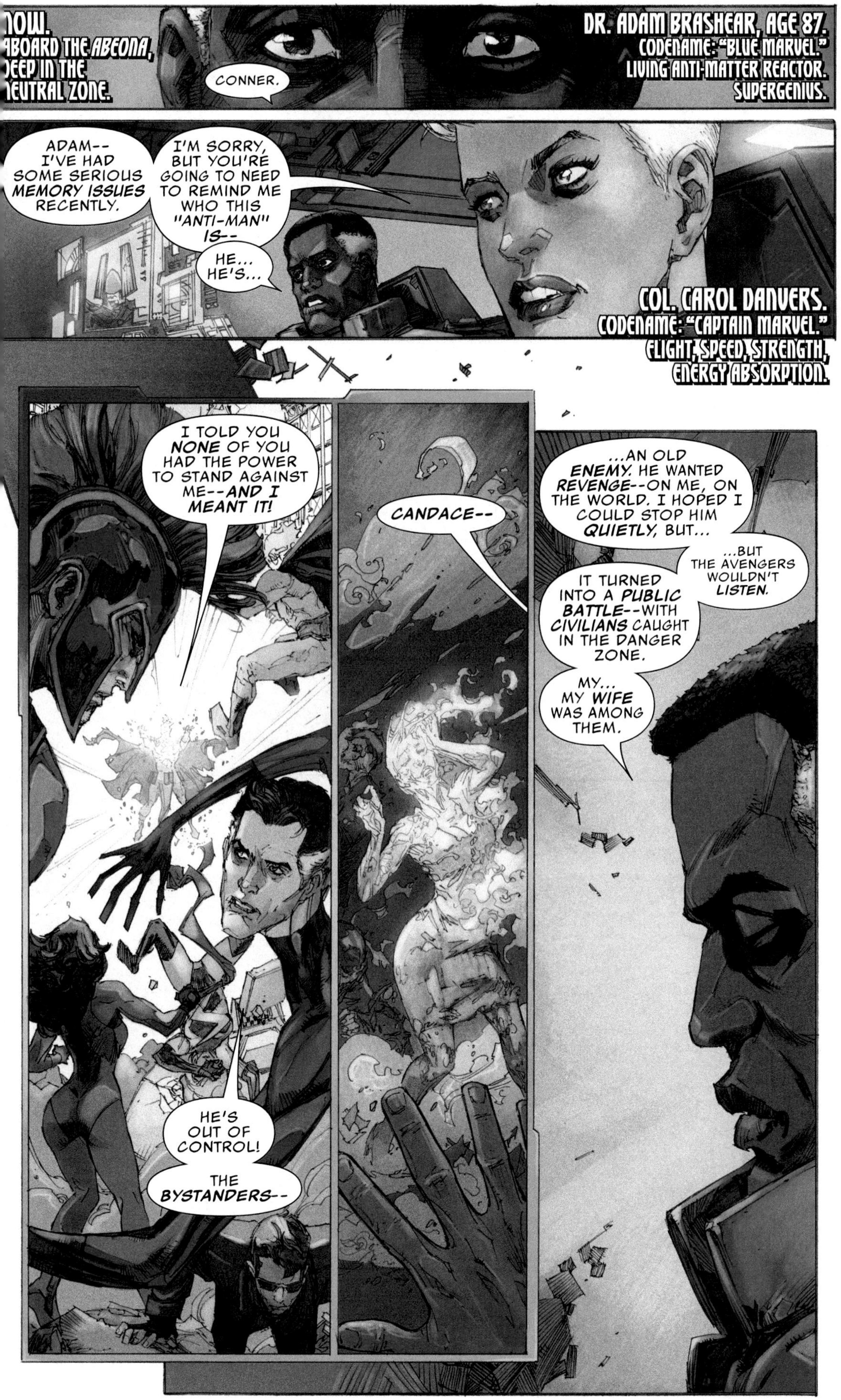

NOW.
ABOARD THE ABEONA,
DEEP IN THE
NEUTRAL ZONE.
CONNER.
DR. ADAM BRASHEAR, AGE 87.
CODENAME: "BLUE MARVEL."
LIVING ANTI-MATTER REACTOR.
SUPERGENIUS.
ADAM-- I'VE HAD SOME SERIOUS MEMORY ISSUES RECENTLY.
I'M SORRY, BUT YOU'RE GOING TO NEED TO REMIND ME WHO THIS "ANTI-MAN" IS--
HE... HE'S...
COL. CAROL DANVERS.
CODENAME: "CAPTAIN MARVEL."
FLIGHT, SPEED, STRENGTH,
ENERGY ABSORPTION.
I TOLD YOU NONE OF YOU HAD THE POWER TO STAND AGAINST ME--AND I MEANT IT!
HE'S OUT OF CONTROL!
THE BYSTANDERS--
CANDACE--
...AN OLD ENEMY. HE WANTED REVENGE--ON ME, ON THE WORLD. I HOPED I COULD STOP HIM QUIETLY, BUT...
...BUT THE AVENGERS WOULDN'T LISTEN.
IT TURNED INTO A PUBLIC BATTLE--WITH CIVILIANS CAUGHT IN THE DANGER ZONE.
MY... MY WIFE WAS AMONG THEM.

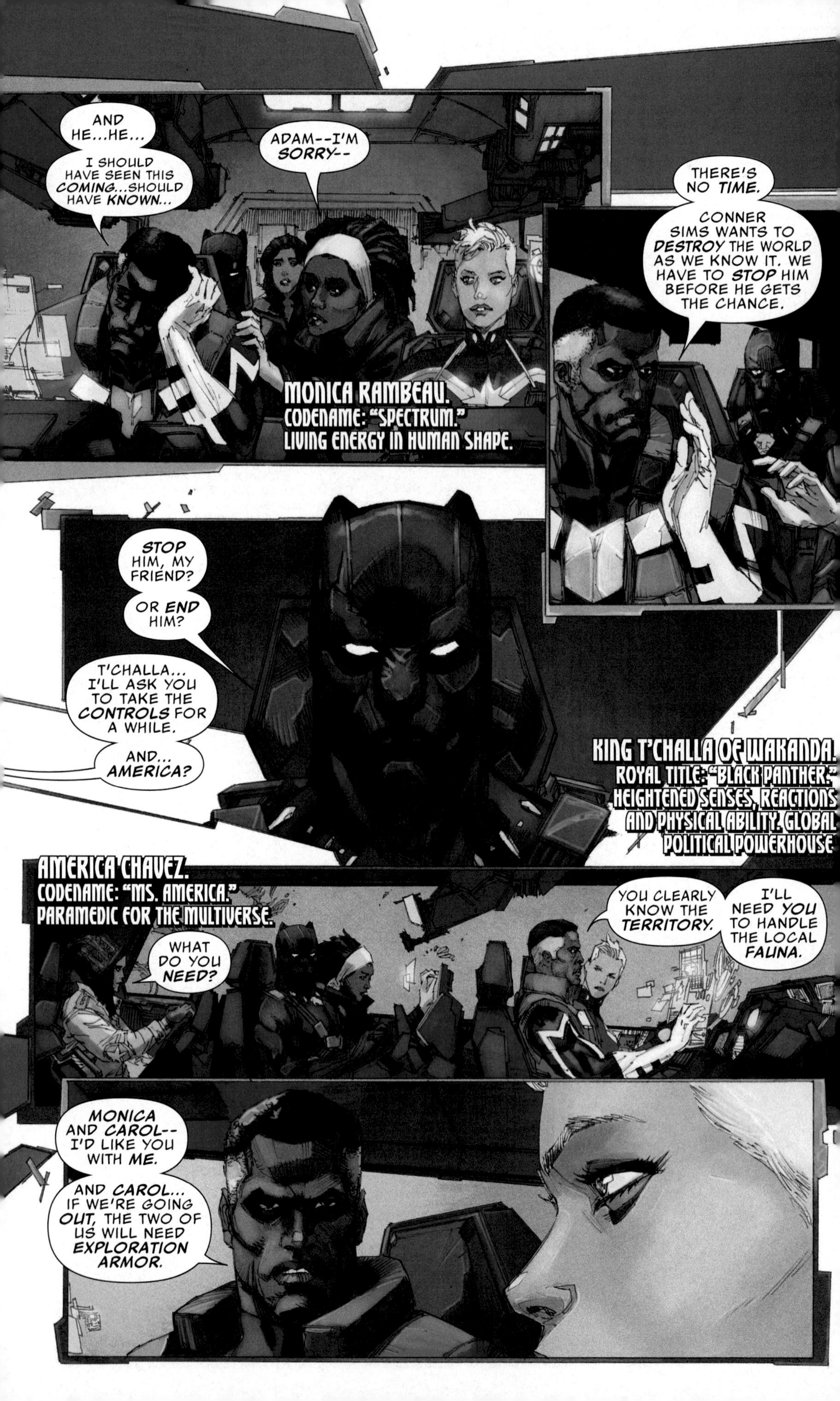

AND HE...HE...
I SHOULD HAVE SEEN THIS COMING...SHOULD HAVE KNOWN...
ADAM--I'M SORRY--
MONICA RAMBEAU. CODENAME: "SPECTRUM." LIVING ENERGY IN HUMAN SHAPE.
THERE'S NO TIME.
CONNER SIMS WANTS TO DESTROY THE WORLD AS WE KNOW IT. WE HAVE TO STOP HIM BEFORE HE GETS THE CHANCE.
STOP HIM, MY FRIEND?
OR END HIM?
T'CHALLA... I'LL ASK YOU TO TAKE THE CONTROLS FOR A WHILE.
AND... AMERICA?
KING T'CHALLA OF WAKANDA. ROYAL TITLE: "BLACK PANTHER." HEIGHTENED SENSES, REACTIONS AND PHYSICAL ABILITY. GLOBAL POLITICAL POWERHOUSE
AMERICA CHAVEZ. CODENAME: "MS. AMERICA." PARAMEDIC FOR THE MULTIVERSE.
WHAT DO YOU NEED?
YOU CLEARLY KNOW THE TERRITORY.
I'LL NEED YOU TO HANDLE THE LOCAL FAUNA.
MONICA AND CAROL-- I'D LIKE YOU WITH ME.
AND CAROL... IF WE'RE GOING OUT, THE TWO OF US WILL NEED EXPLORATION ARMOR.

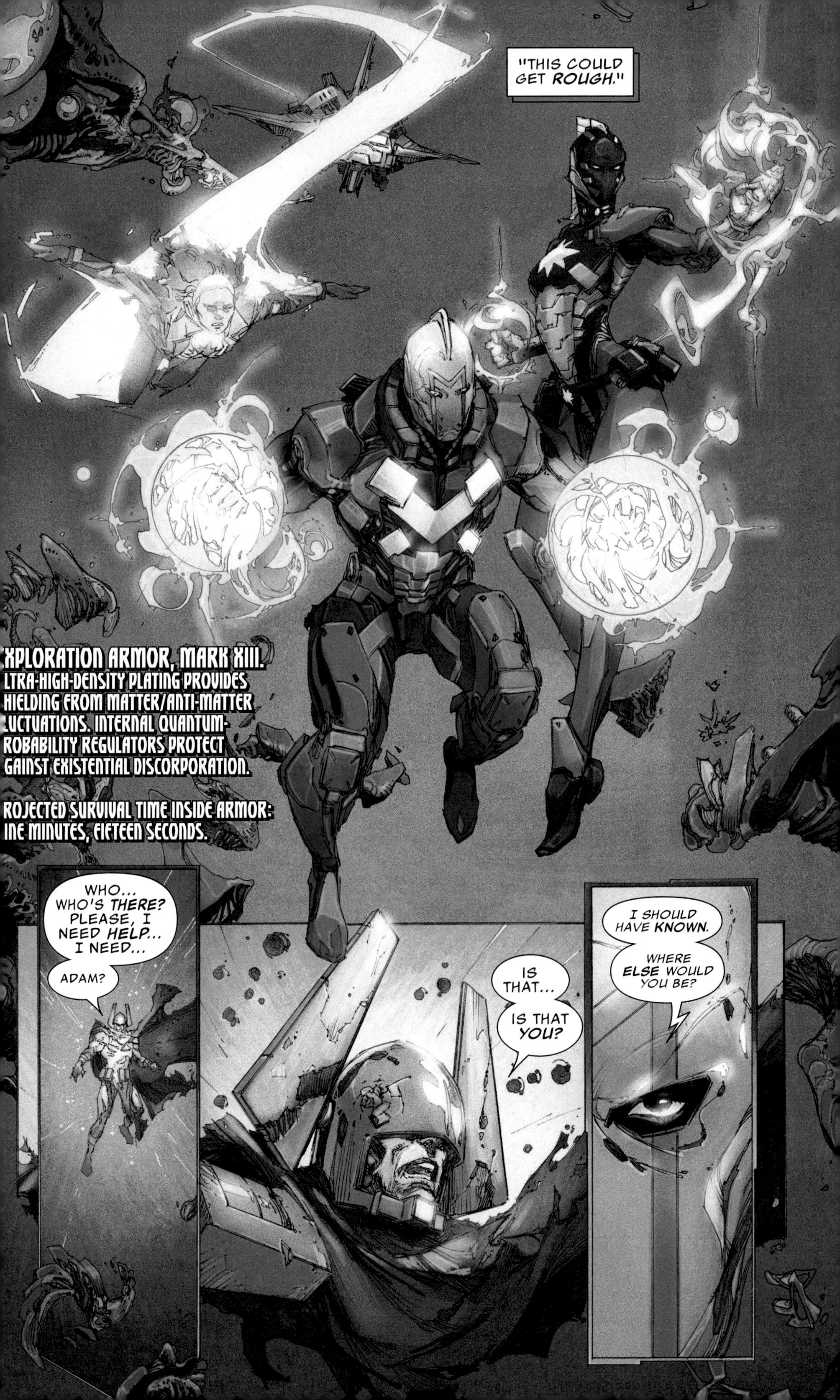

"THIS COULD GET ROUGH."
XPLORATION ARMOR, MARK XIII.
LTRA-HIGH-DENSITY PLATING PROVIDES HIELDING FROM MATTER/ANTI-MATTER LUCTUATIONS. INTERNAL QUANTUM-ROBABILITY REGULATORS PROTECT GAINST EXISTENTIAL DISCORPORATION.
ROJECTED SURVIVAL TIME INSIDE ARMOR: INE MINUTES, FIFTEEN SECONDS.
WHO... WHO'S THERE? PLEASE, I NEED HELP... I NEED...
ADAM?
IS THAT...
IS THAT YOU?
I SHOULD HAVE KNOWN.
WHERE ELSE WOULD YOU BE?

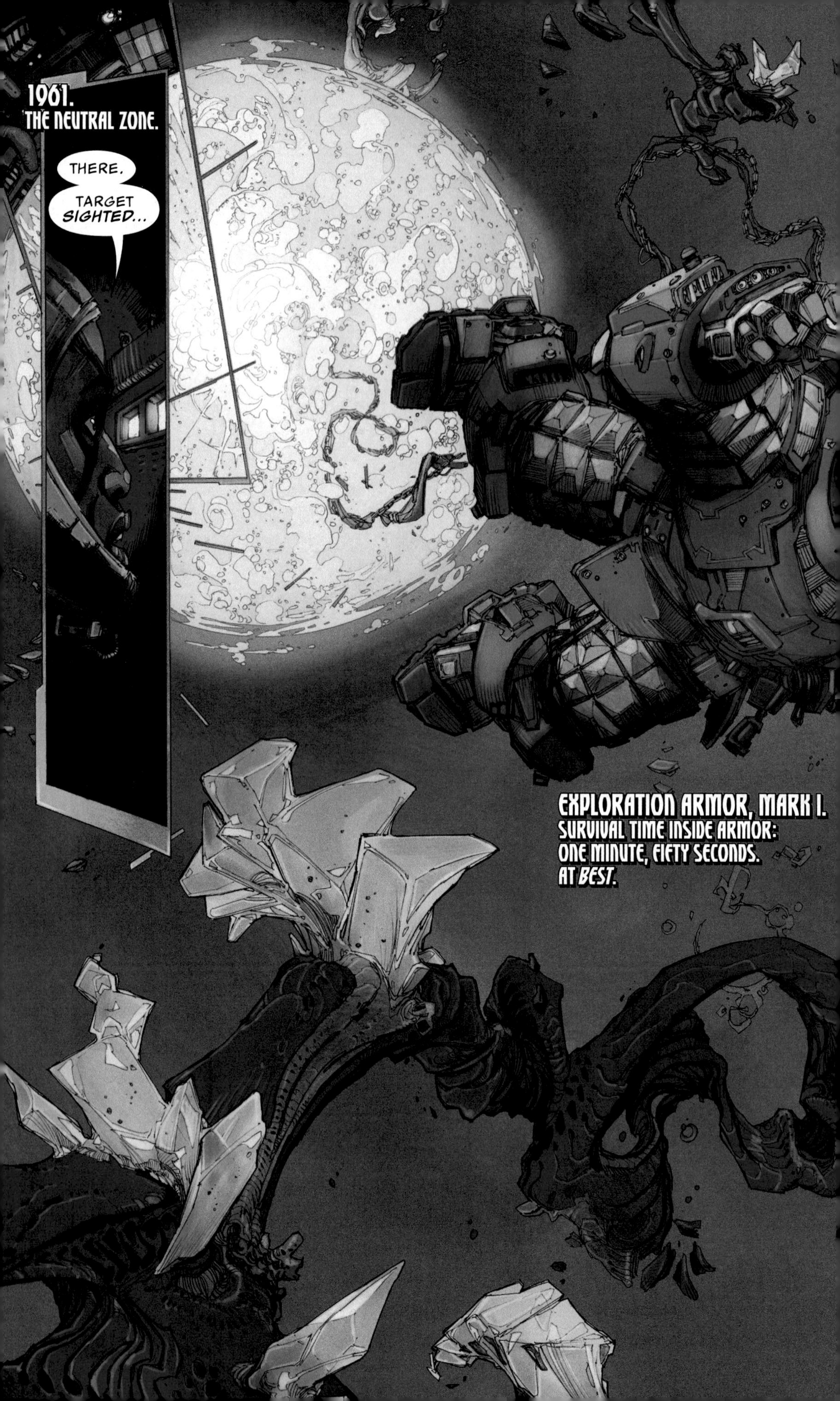

1961.
THE NEUTRAL ZONE.
THERE.
TARGET SIGHTED...
EXPLORATION ARMOR, MARK I.
SURVIVAL TIME INSIDE ARMOR:
ONE MINUTE, FIFTY SECONDS.
AT BEST.

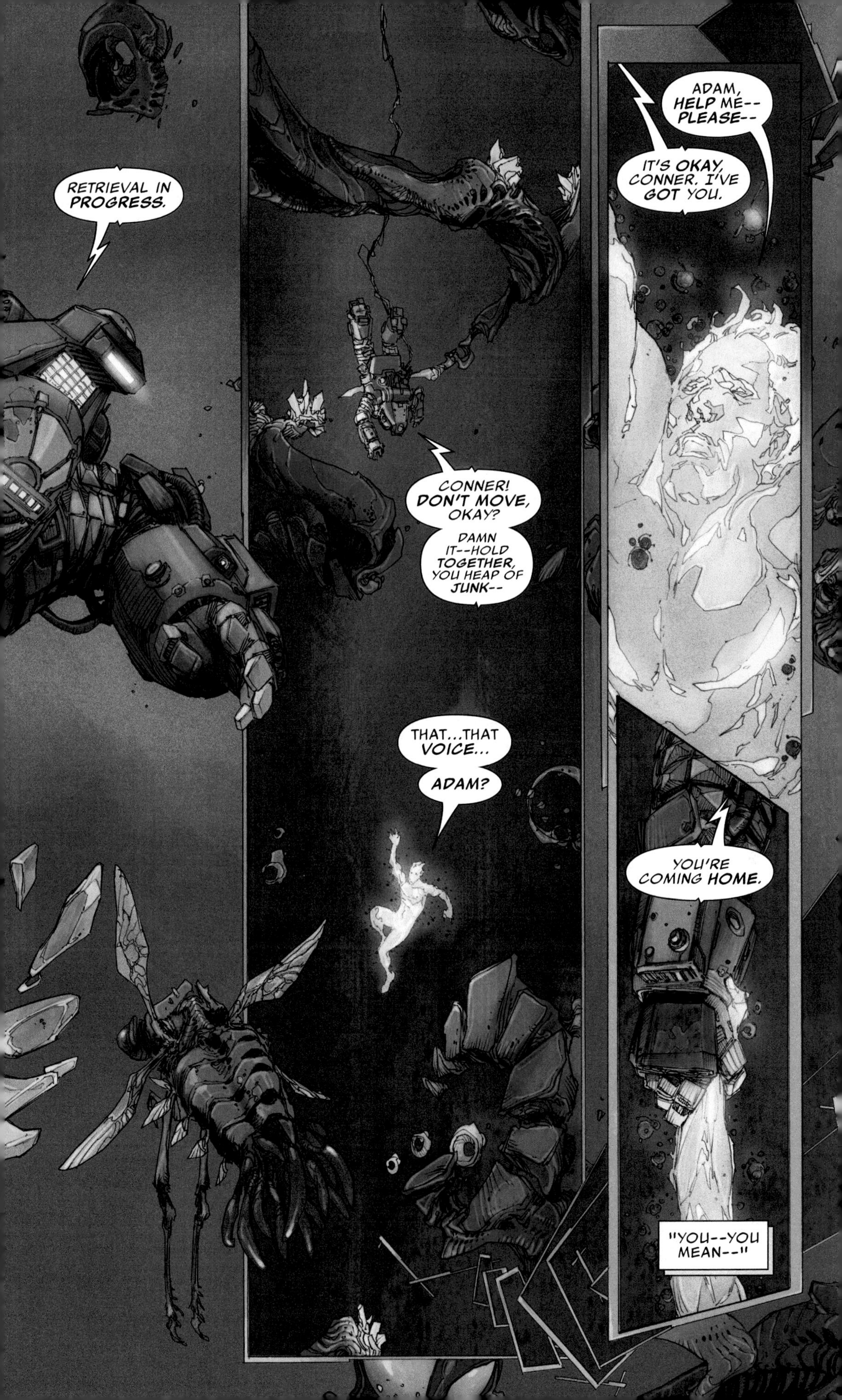

RETRIEVAL IN PROGRESS.
CONNER! DON'T MOVE, OKAY?
DAMN IT--HOLD TOGETHER, YOU HEAP OF JUNK--
THAT...THAT VOICE...
ADAM?
ADAM, HELP ME--PLEASE--
IT'S OKAY, CONNER. I'VE GOT YOU.
YOU'RE COMING HOME.
"YOU--YOU MEAN--"

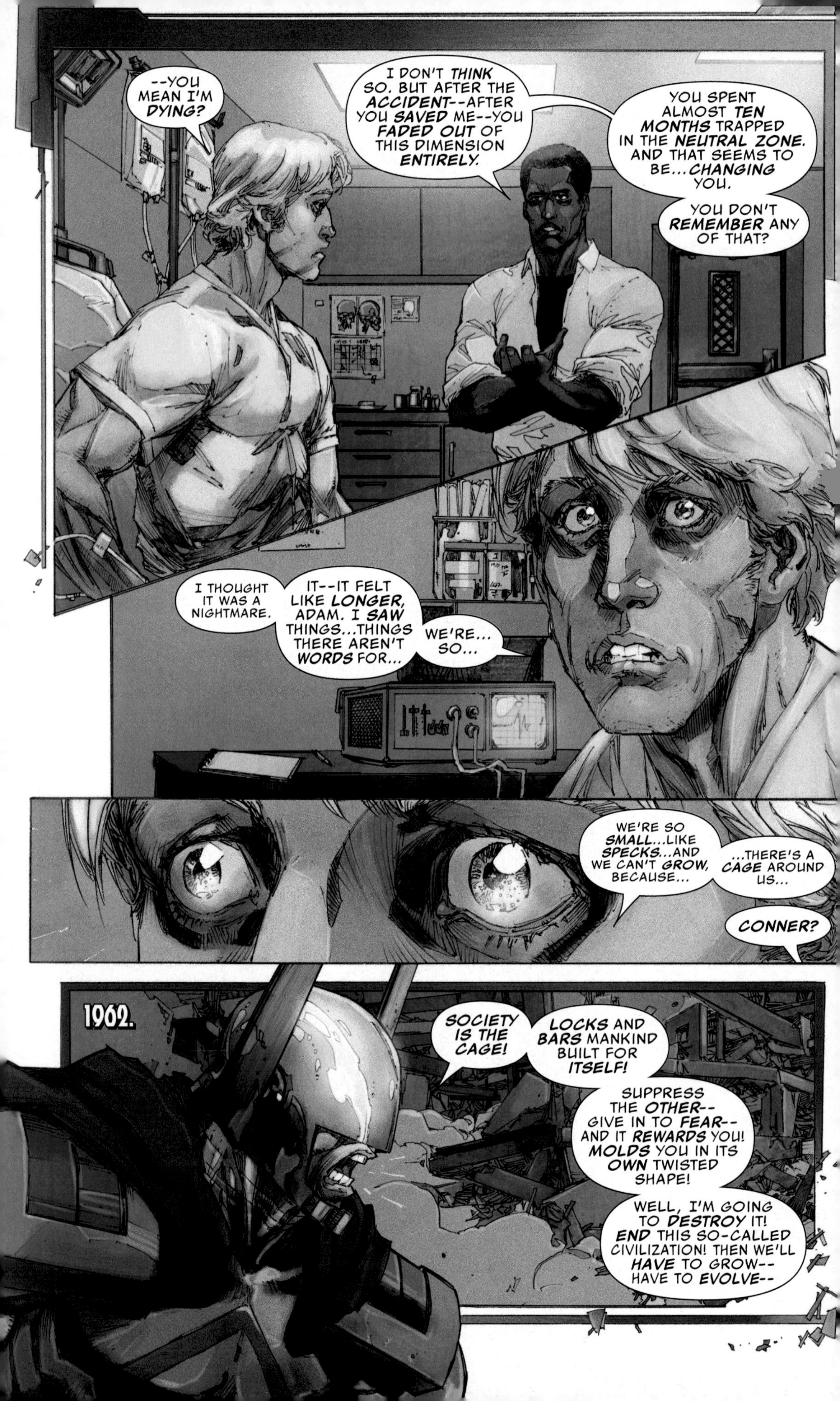
--YOU MEAN I'M DYING?
I DON'T THINK SO. BUT AFTER THE ACCIDENT--AFTER YOU SAVED ME--YOU FADED OUT OF THIS DIMENSION ENTIRELY.
YOU SPENT ALMOST TEN MONTHS TRAPPED IN THE NEUTRAL ZONE. AND THAT SEEMS TO BE...CHANGING YOU.
YOU DON'T REMEMBER ANY OF THAT?
I THOUGHT IT WAS A NIGHTMARE.
IT--IT FELT LIKE LONGER, ADAM. I SAW THINGS...THINGS THERE AREN'T WORDS FOR...
WE'RE... SO...
WE'RE SO SMALL...LIKE SPECKS...AND WE CAN'T GROW, BECAUSE...
...THERE'S A CAGE AROUND US...
CONNER?
1962.
SOCIETY IS THE CAGE!
LOCKS AND BARS MANKIND BUILT FOR ITSELF!
SUPPRESS THE OTHER--GIVE IN TO FEAR--AND IT REWARDS YOU! MOLDS YOU IN ITS OWN TWISTED SHAPE!
WELL, I'M GOING TO DESTROY IT! END THIS SO-CALLED CIVILIZATION! THEN WE'LL HAVE TO GROW--HAVE TO EVOLVE--

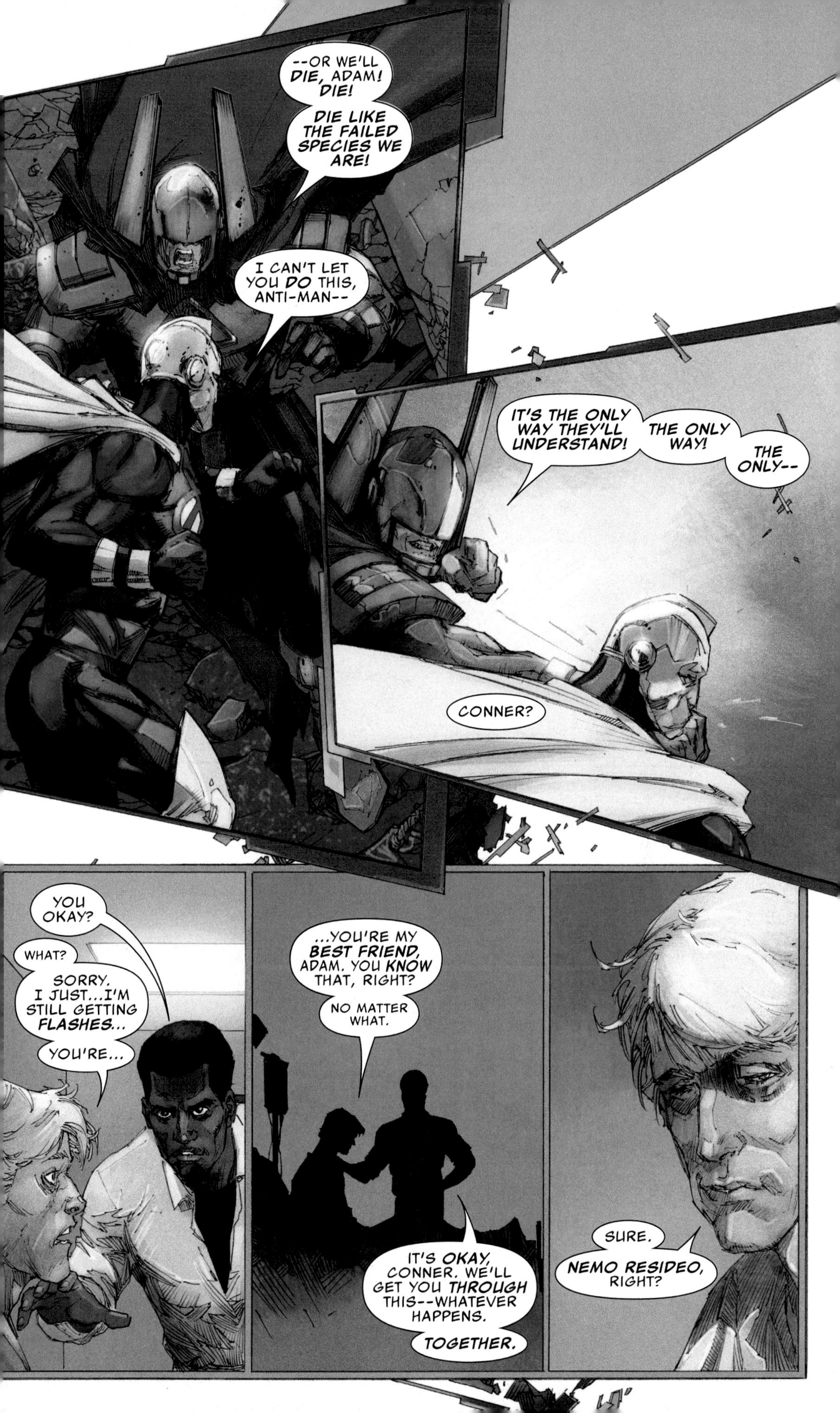
--OR WE'LL DIE, ADAM! DIE!
DIE LIKE THE FAILED SPECIES WE ARE!
I CAN'T LET YOU DO THIS, ANTI-MAN--
IT'S THE ONLY WAY THEY'LL UNDERSTAND!
THE ONLY WAY!
THE ONLY--
CONNER?
YOU OKAY?
WHAT?
SORRY. I JUST...I'M STILL GETTING FLASHES...
YOU'RE...
...YOU'RE MY BEST FRIEND, ADAM. YOU KNOW THAT, RIGHT?
NO MATTER WHAT.
IT'S OKAY, CONNER. WE'LL GET YOU THROUGH THIS--WHATEVER HAPPENS.
TOGETHER.
SURE.
NEMO RESIDEO, RIGHT?

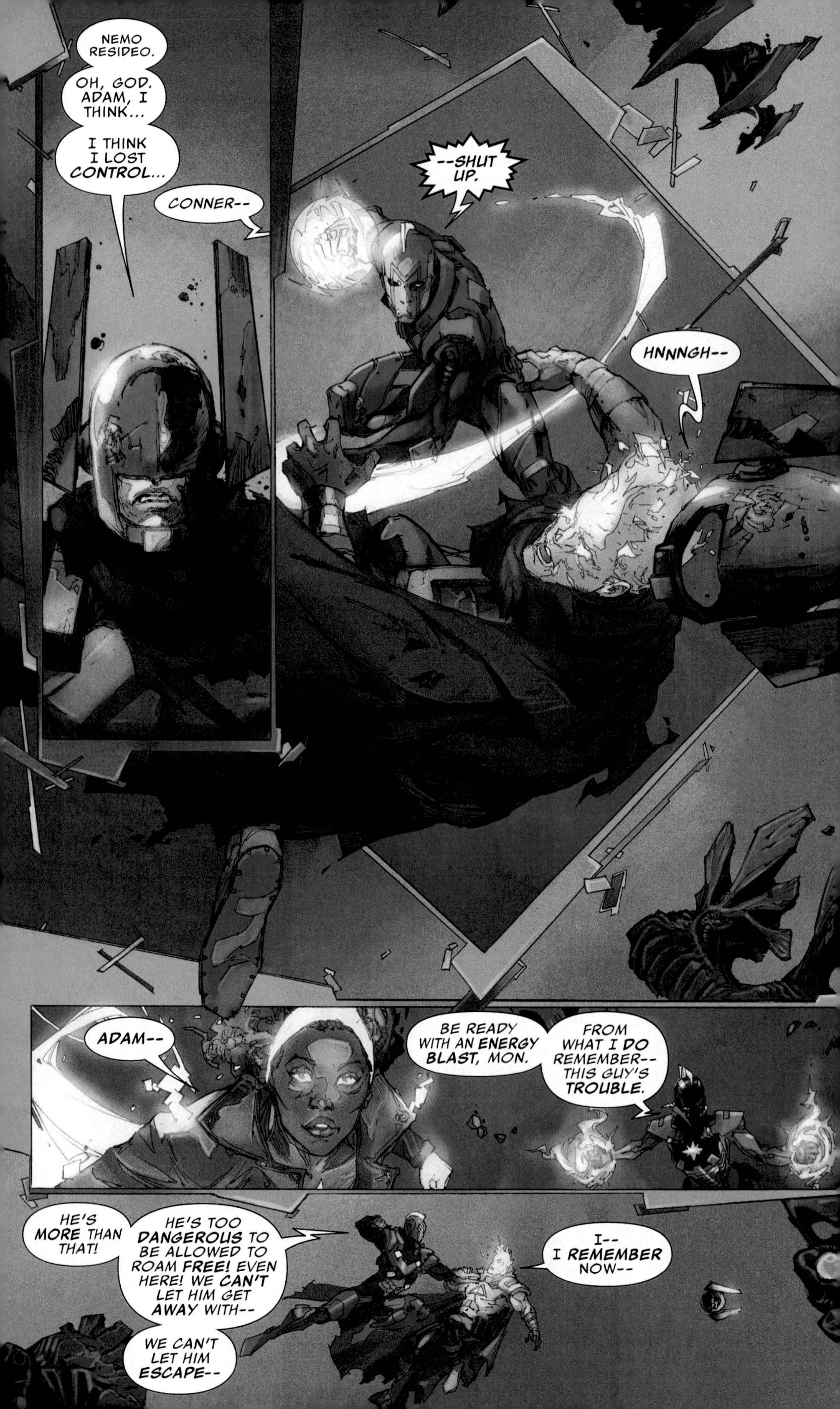
NEMO RESIDEO.
OH, GOD. ADAM, I THINK...
I THINK I LOST CONTROL...
CONNER--
--SHUT UP.
HNNNGH--
ADAM--
BE READY WITH AN ENERGY BLAST, MON.
FROM WHAT I DO REMEMBER-- THIS GUY'S TROUBLE.
HE'S MORE THAN THAT!
HE'S TOO DANGEROUS TO BE ALLOWED TO ROAM FREE! EVEN HERE! WE CAN'T LET HIM GET AWAY WITH--
WE CAN'T LET HIM ESCAPE--
I-- I REMEMBER NOW--

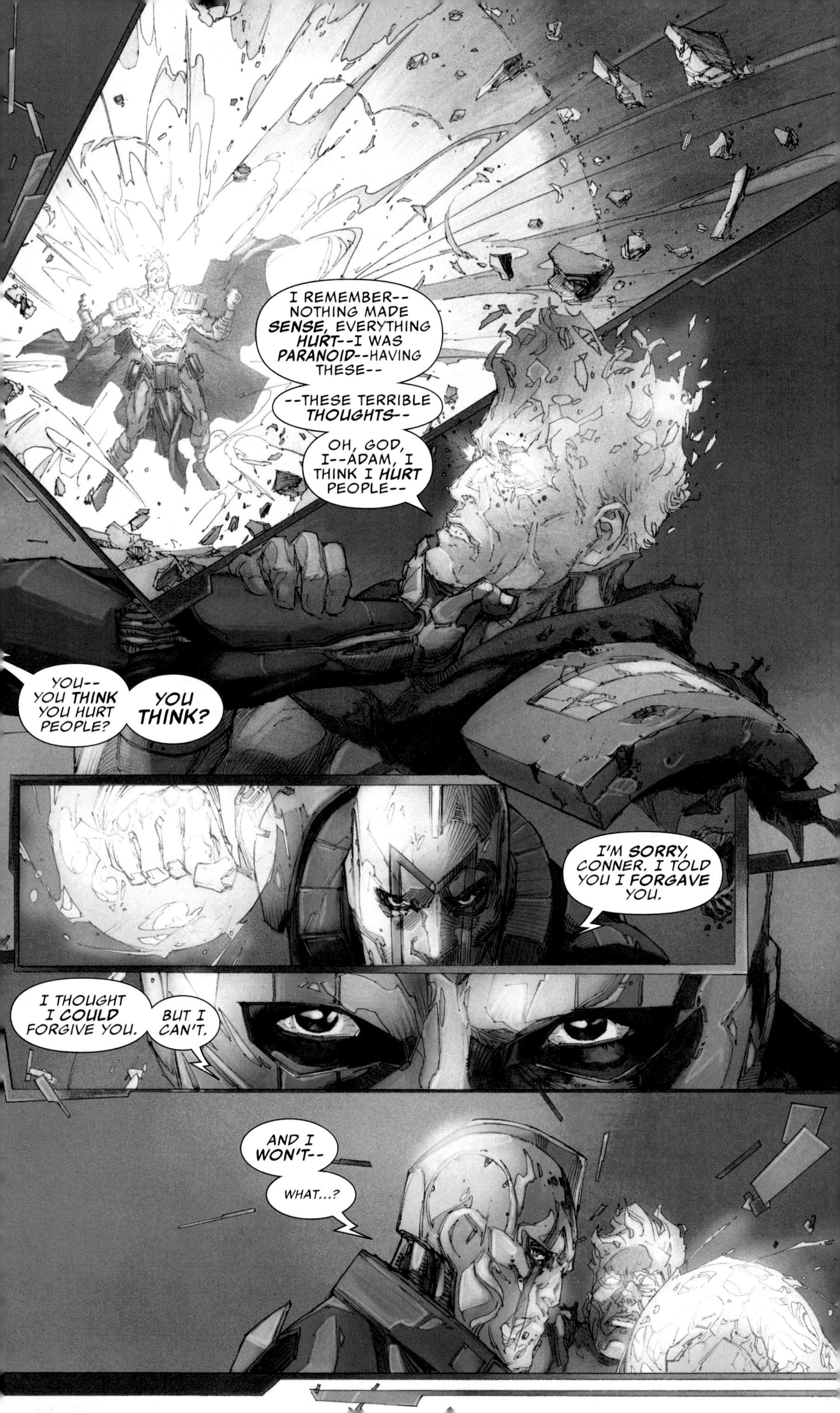
I REMEMBER--
NOTHING MADE
SENSE, EVERYTHING
HURT--I WAS
PARANOID--HAVING
THESE--
--THESE TERRIBLE
THOUGHTS--
OH, GOD,
I--ADAM, I
THINK I HURT
PEOPLE--
YOU--
YOU THINK
YOU HURT
PEOPLE?
YOU
THINK?
I'M SORRY,
CONNER. I TOLD
YOU I FORGAVE
YOU.
I THOUGHT
I COULD
FORGIVE YOU.
BUT I
CAN'T.
AND I
WON'T--
WHAT...?

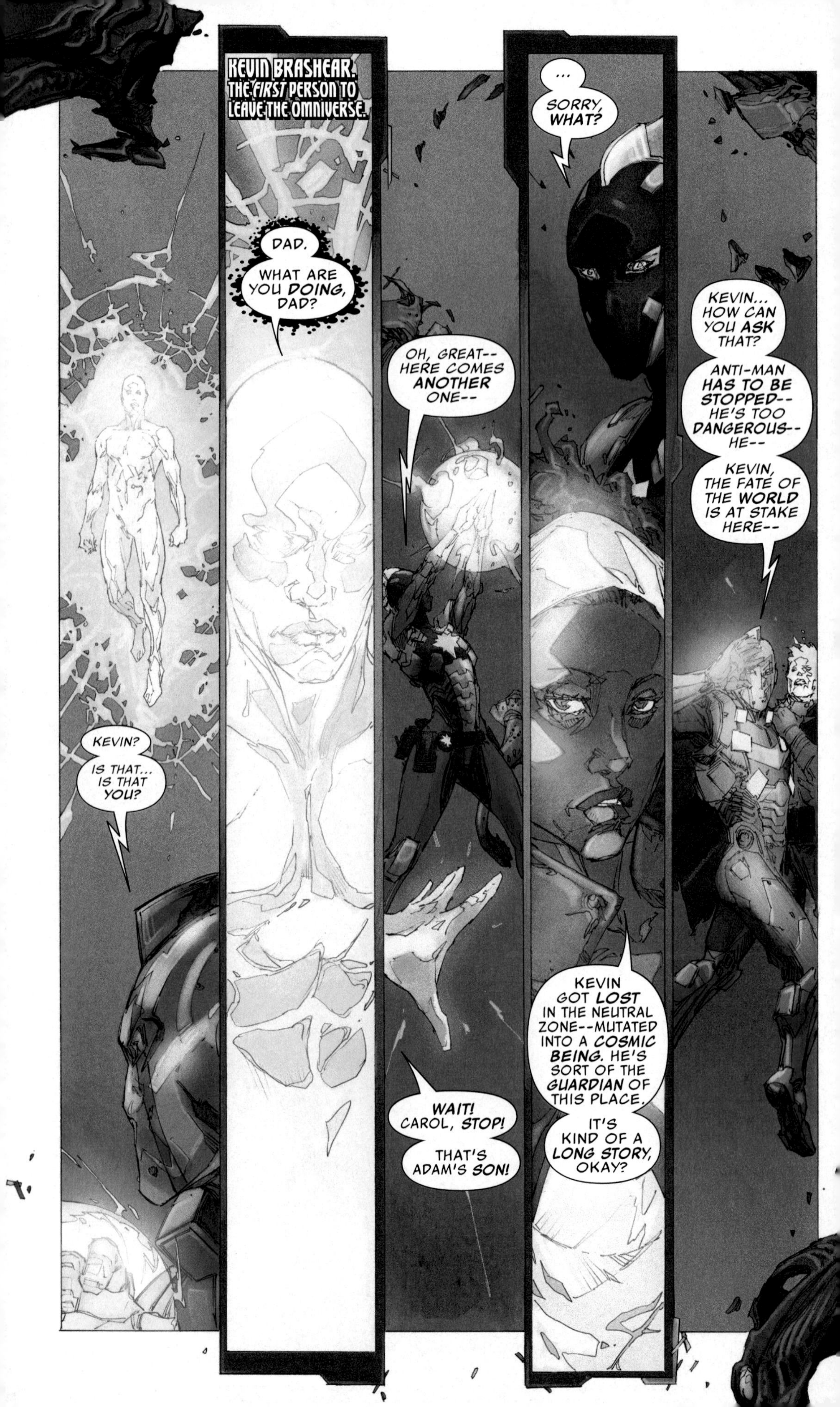

KEVIN BRASHEAR. THE FIRST PERSON TO LEAVE THE OMNIVERSE.
KEVIN?
IS THAT... IS THAT YOU?
DAD.
WHAT ARE YOU DOING, DAD?
OH, GREAT-- HERE COMES ANOTHER ONE--
WAIT! CAROL, STOP!
THAT'S ADAM'S SON!
...
SORRY, WHAT?
KEVIN GOT LOST IN THE NEUTRAL ZONE--MUTATED INTO A COSMIC BEING. HE'S SORT OF THE GUARDIAN OF THIS PLACE.
IT'S KIND OF A LONG STORY, OKAY?
KEVIN... HOW CAN YOU ASK THAT?
ANTI-MAN HAS TO BE STOPPED-- HE'S TOO DANGEROUS-- HE--
KEVIN, THE FATE OF THE WORLD IS AT STAKE HERE--

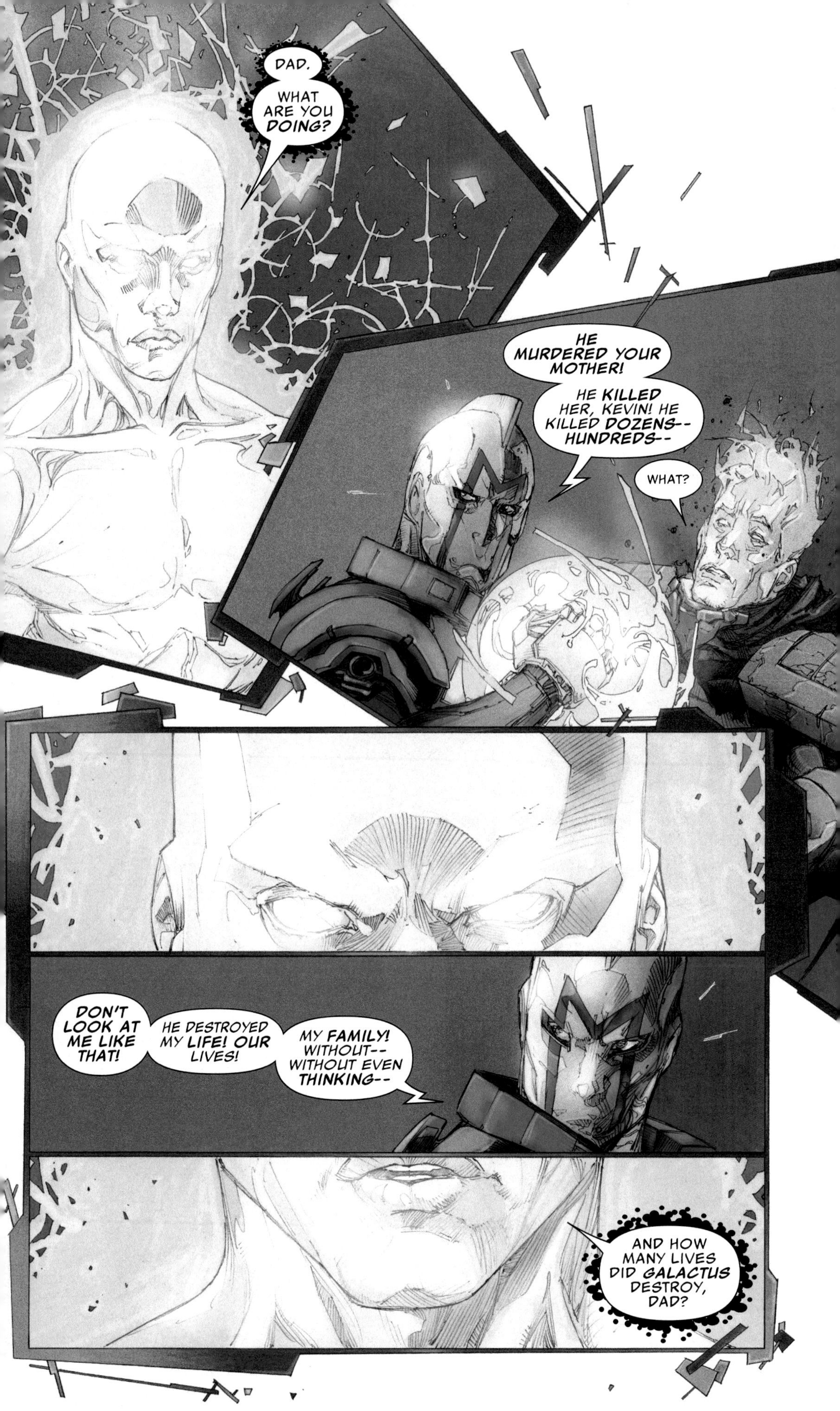
DAD.
WHAT ARE YOU DOING?
HE MURDERED YOUR MOTHER!
HE KILLED HER, KEVIN! HE KILLED DOZENS-- HUNDREDS--
WHAT?
DON'T LOOK AT ME LIKE THAT!
HE DESTROYED MY LIFE! OUR LIVES!
MY FAMILY! WITHOUT-- WITHOUT EVEN THINKING--
AND HOW MANY LIVES DID GALACTUS DESTROY, DAD?

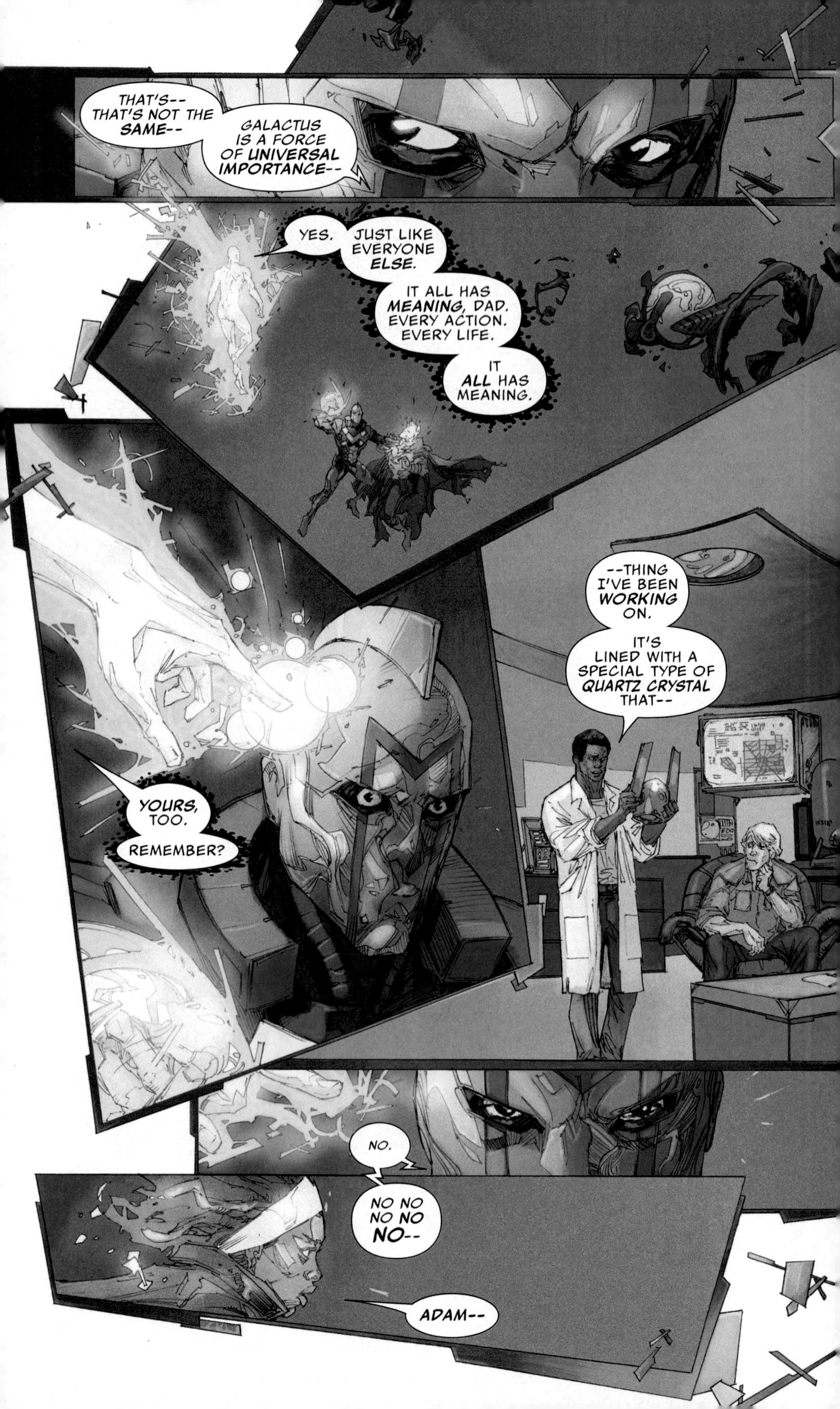
THAT'S--
THAT'S NOT THE SAME--
GALACTUS IS A FORCE OF UNIVERSAL IMPORTANCE--
YES.
JUST LIKE EVERYONE ELSE.
IT ALL HAS MEANING, DAD. EVERY ACTION. EVERY LIFE.
IT ALL HAS MEANING.
YOURS, TOO.
REMEMBER?
--THING I'VE BEEN WORKING ON.
IT'S LINED WITH A SPECIAL TYPE OF QUARTZ CRYSTAL THAT--
NO.
NO NO NO NO NO--
ADAM--

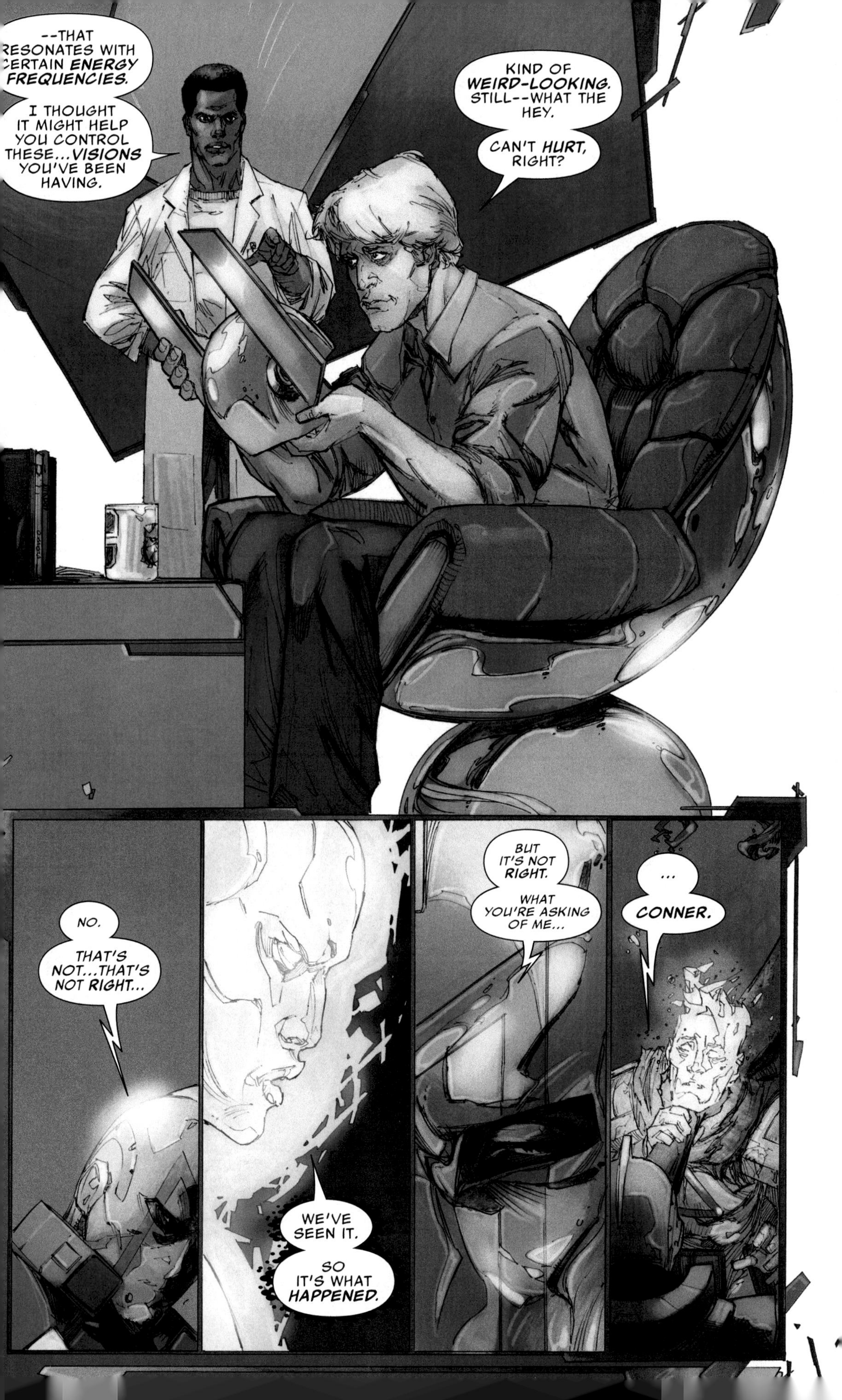
--THAT
RESONATES WITH
CERTAIN ENERGY
FREQUENCIES.
I THOUGHT
IT MIGHT HELP
YOU CONTROL
THESE...VISIONS
YOU'VE BEEN
HAVING.
KIND OF
WEIRD-LOOKING.
STILL--WHAT THE
HEY.
CAN'T HURT,
RIGHT?
NO.
THAT'S
NOT...THAT'S
NOT RIGHT...
WE'VE
SEEN IT.
SO
IT'S WHAT
HAPPENED.
BUT
IT'S NOT
RIGHT.
WHAT
YOU'RE ASKING
OF ME...
...
CONNER.

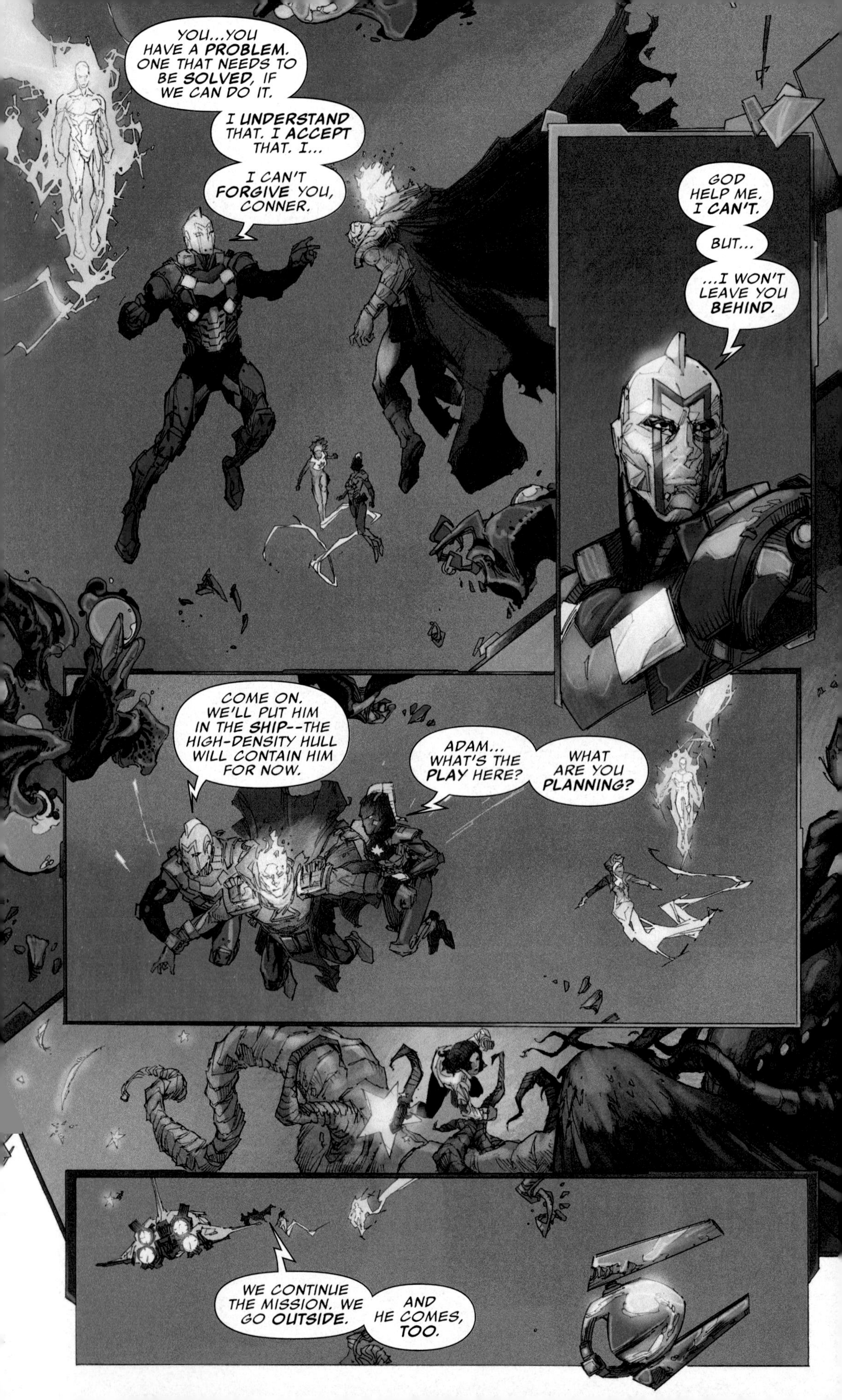
YOU...YOU HAVE A PROBLEM. ONE THAT NEEDS TO BE SOLVED, IF WE CAN DO IT.
I UNDERSTAND THAT. I ACCEPT THAT. I...
I CAN'T FORGIVE YOU, CONNER.
GOD HELP ME. I CAN'T.
BUT...
...I WON'T LEAVE YOU BEHIND.
COME ON. WE'LL PUT HIM IN THE SHIP--THE HIGH-DENSITY HULL WILL CONTAIN HIM FOR NOW.
ADAM... WHAT'S THE PLAY HERE?
WHAT ARE YOU PLANNING?
WE CONTINUE THE MISSION. WE GO OUTSIDE.
AND HE COMES, TOO.

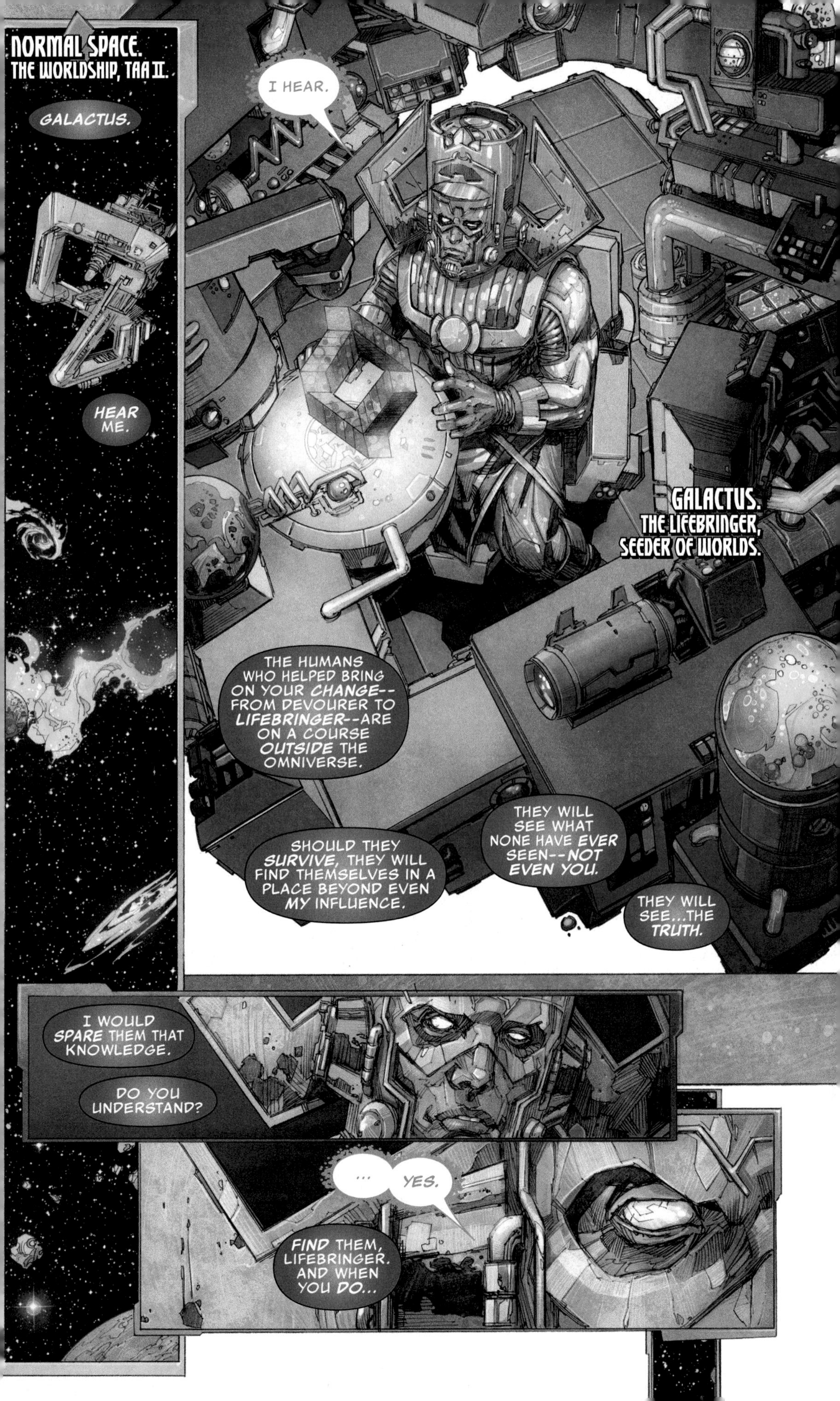
NORMAL SPACE.
THE WORLDSHIP, TAA II.
GALACTUS.
I HEAR.
HEAR ME.
GALACTUS.
THE LIFEBRINGER,
SEEDER OF WORLDS.
THE HUMANS WHO HELPED BRING ON YOUR CHANGE--FROM DEVOURER TO LIFEBRINGER--ARE ON A COURSE OUTSIDE THE OMNIVERSE.
SHOULD THEY SURVIVE, THEY WILL FIND THEMSELVES IN A PLACE BEYOND EVEN MY INFLUENCE.
THEY WILL SEE WHAT NONE HAVE EVER SEEN--NOT EVEN YOU.
THEY WILL SEE...THE TRUTH.
I WOULD SPARE THEM THAT KNOWLEDGE.
DO YOU UNDERSTAND?
...
YES.
FIND THEM, LIFEBRINGER. AND WHEN YOU DO...

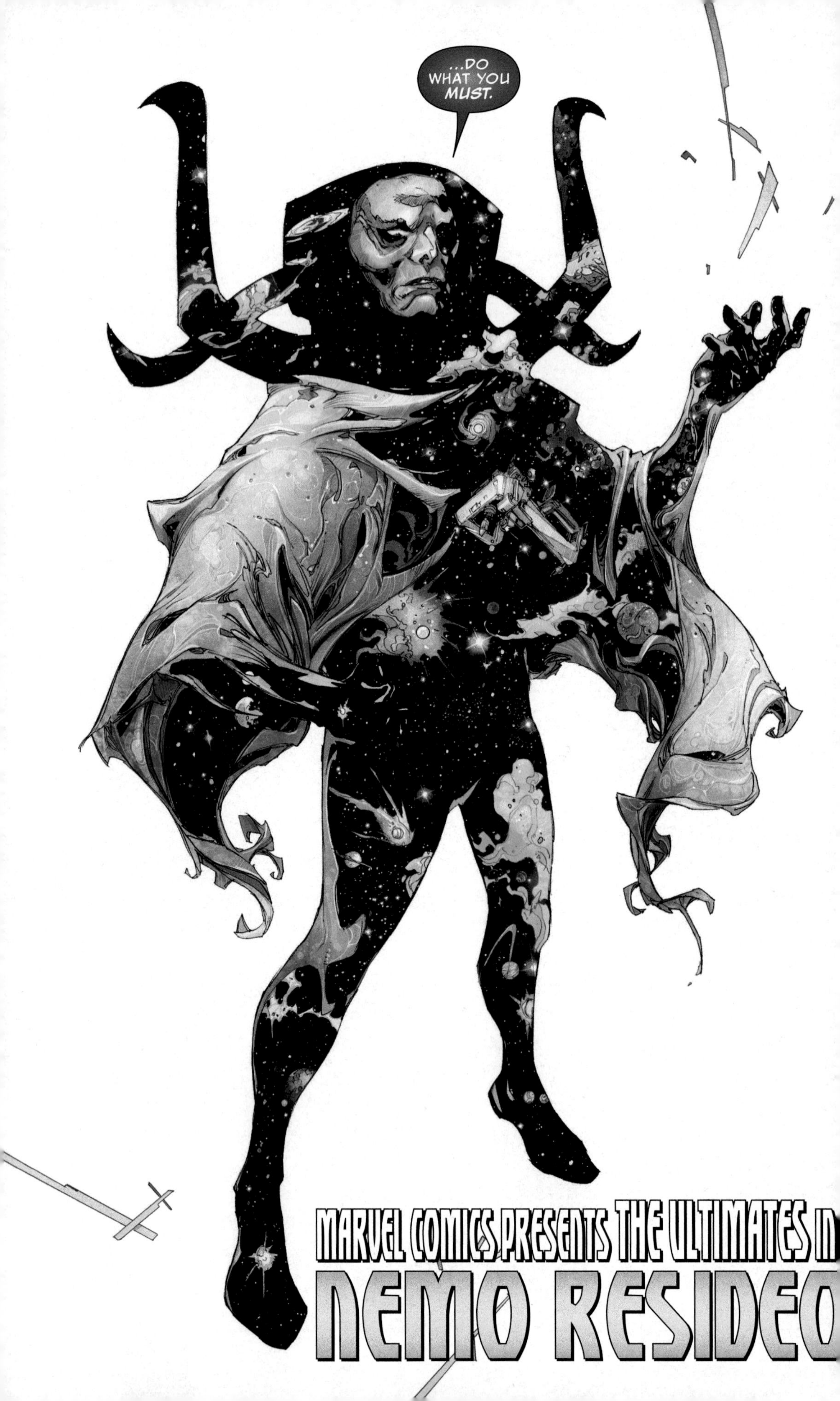
...DO WHAT YOU MUST.
MARVEL COMICS PRESENTS THE ULTIMATES IN
NEMO RESIDEO

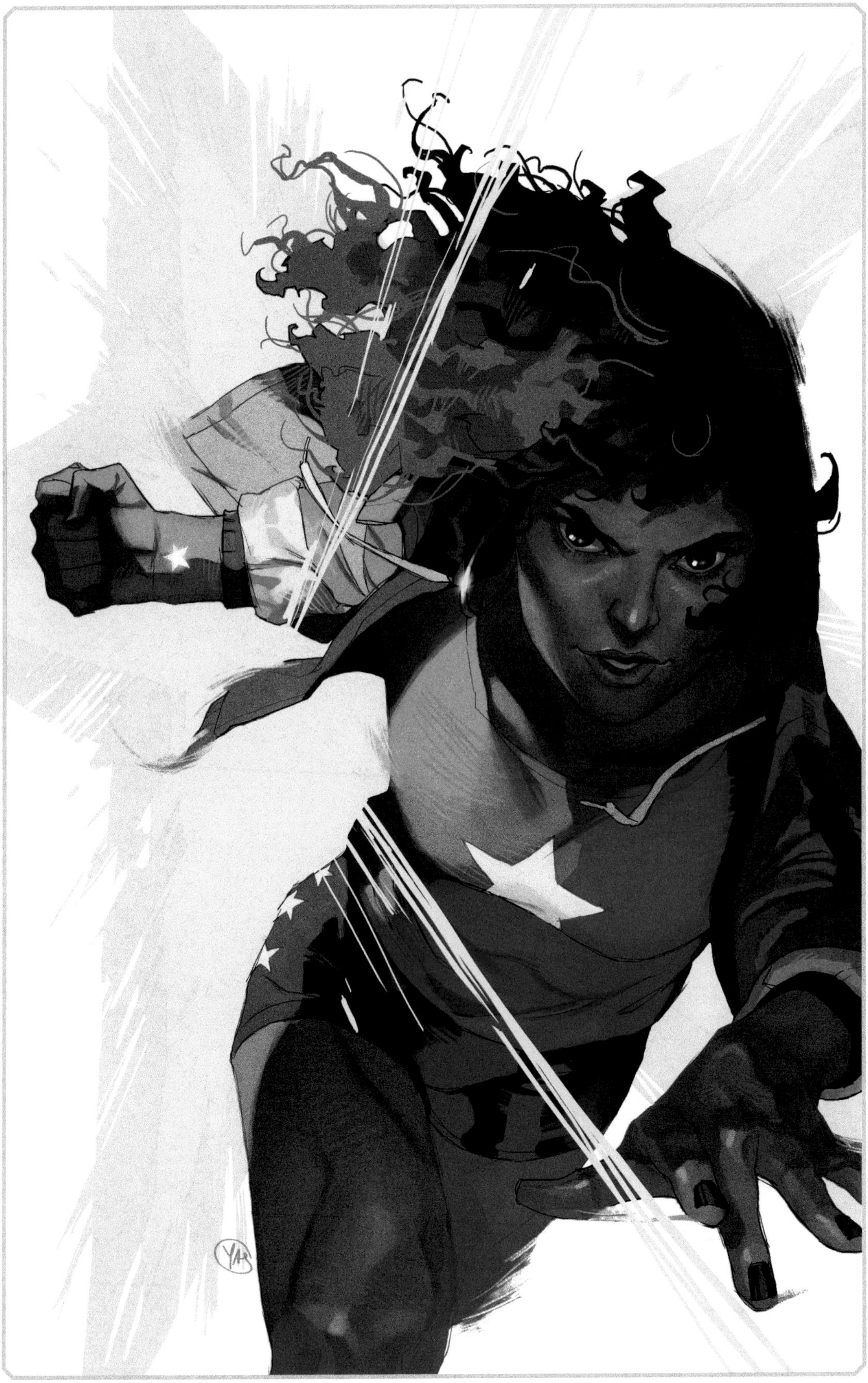
YAS

#5 WOMEN OF POWER VARIANT BY YASMINE PUTRI

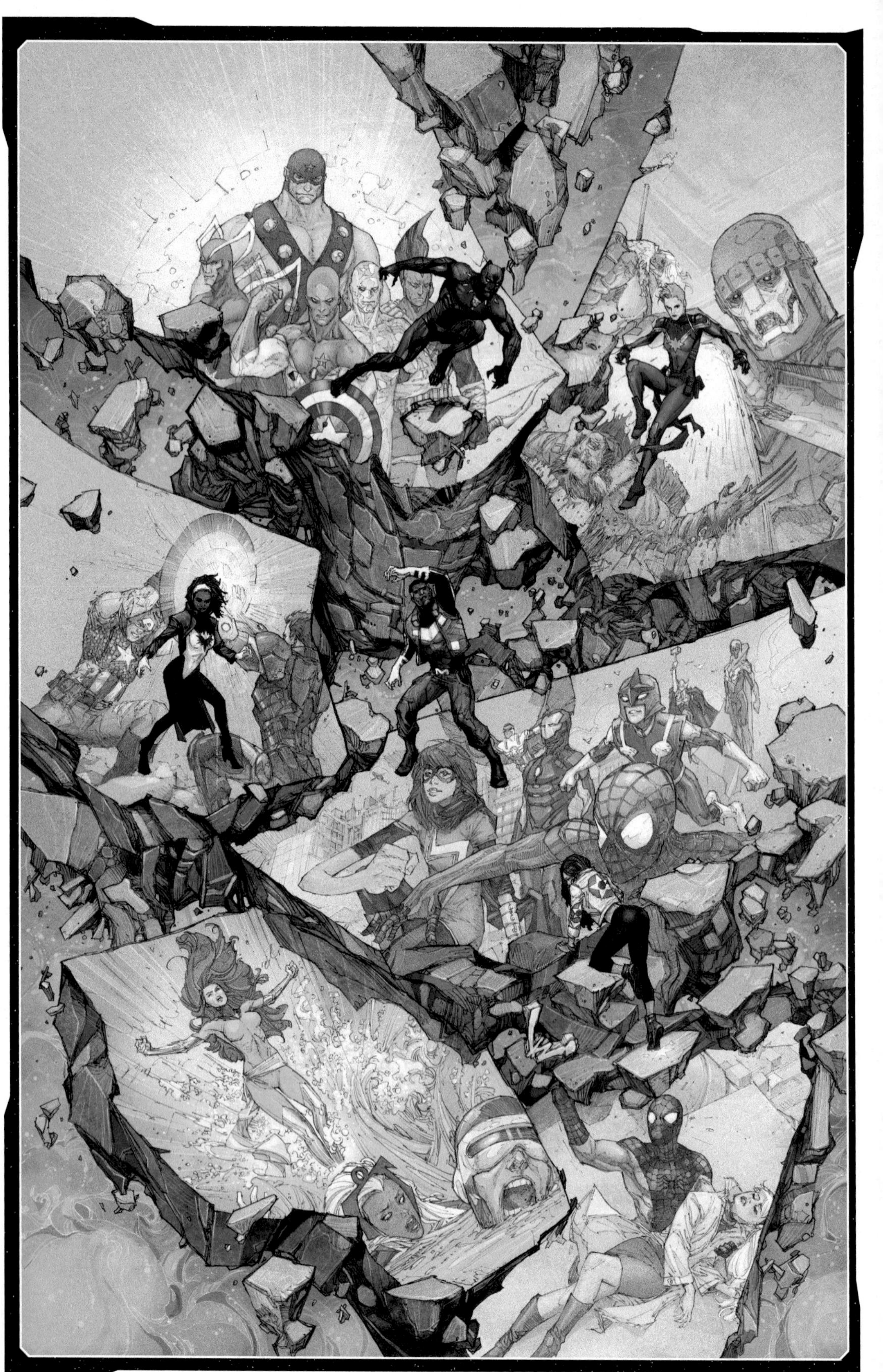

5

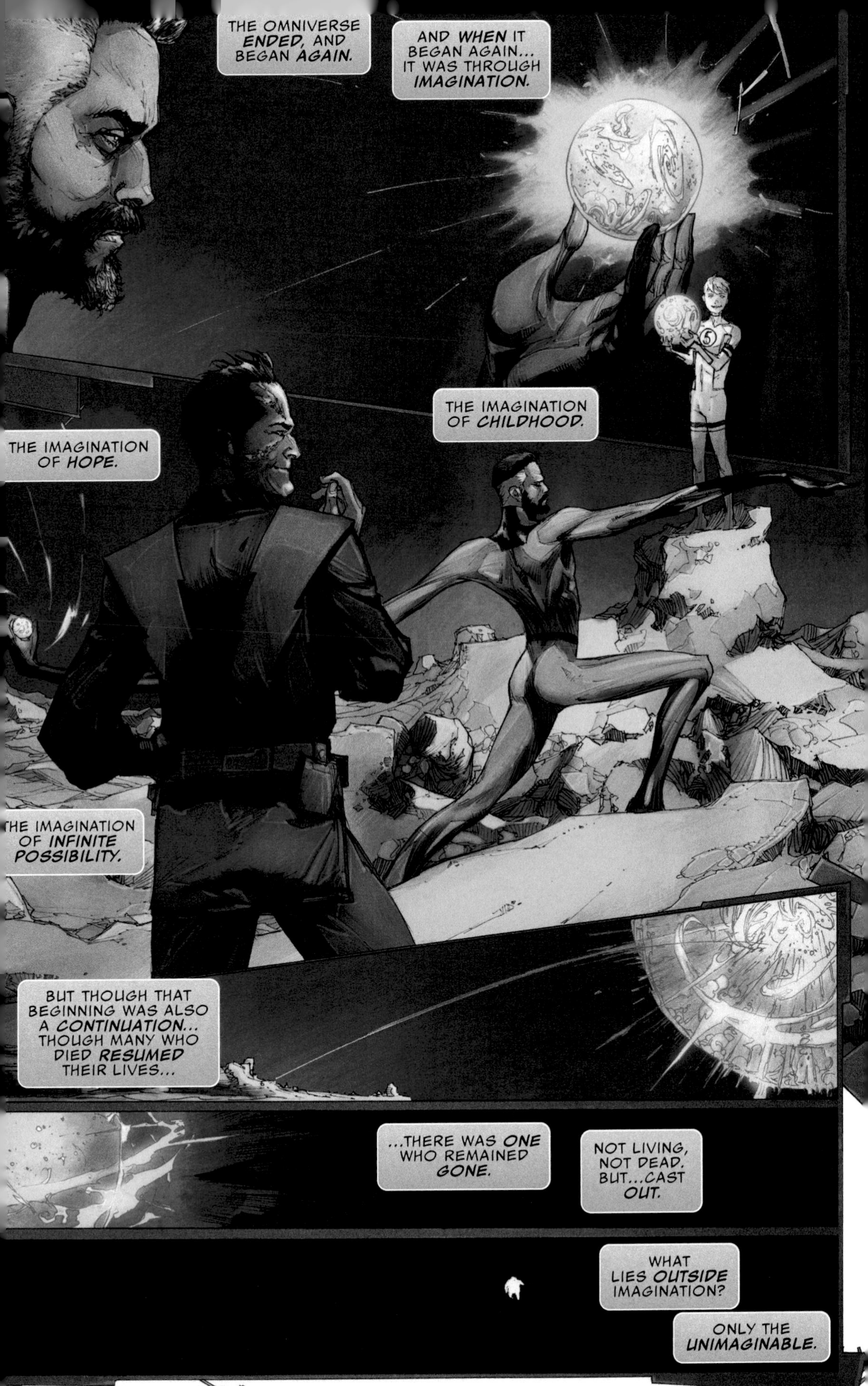
THE OMNIVERSE ENDED, AND BEGAN AGAIN.
AND WHEN IT BEGAN AGAIN... IT WAS THROUGH IMAGINATION.
THE IMAGINATION OF CHILDHOOD.
THE IMAGINATION OF HOPE.
THE IMAGINATION OF INFINITE POSSIBILITY.
BUT THOUGH THAT BEGINNING WAS ALSO A CONTINUATION... THOUGH MANY WHO DIED RESUMED THEIR LIVES...
...THERE WAS ONE WHO REMAINED GONE.
NOT LIVING, NOT DEAD. BUT...CAST OUT.
WHAT LIES OUTSIDE IMAGINATION?
ONLY THE UNIMAGINABLE.

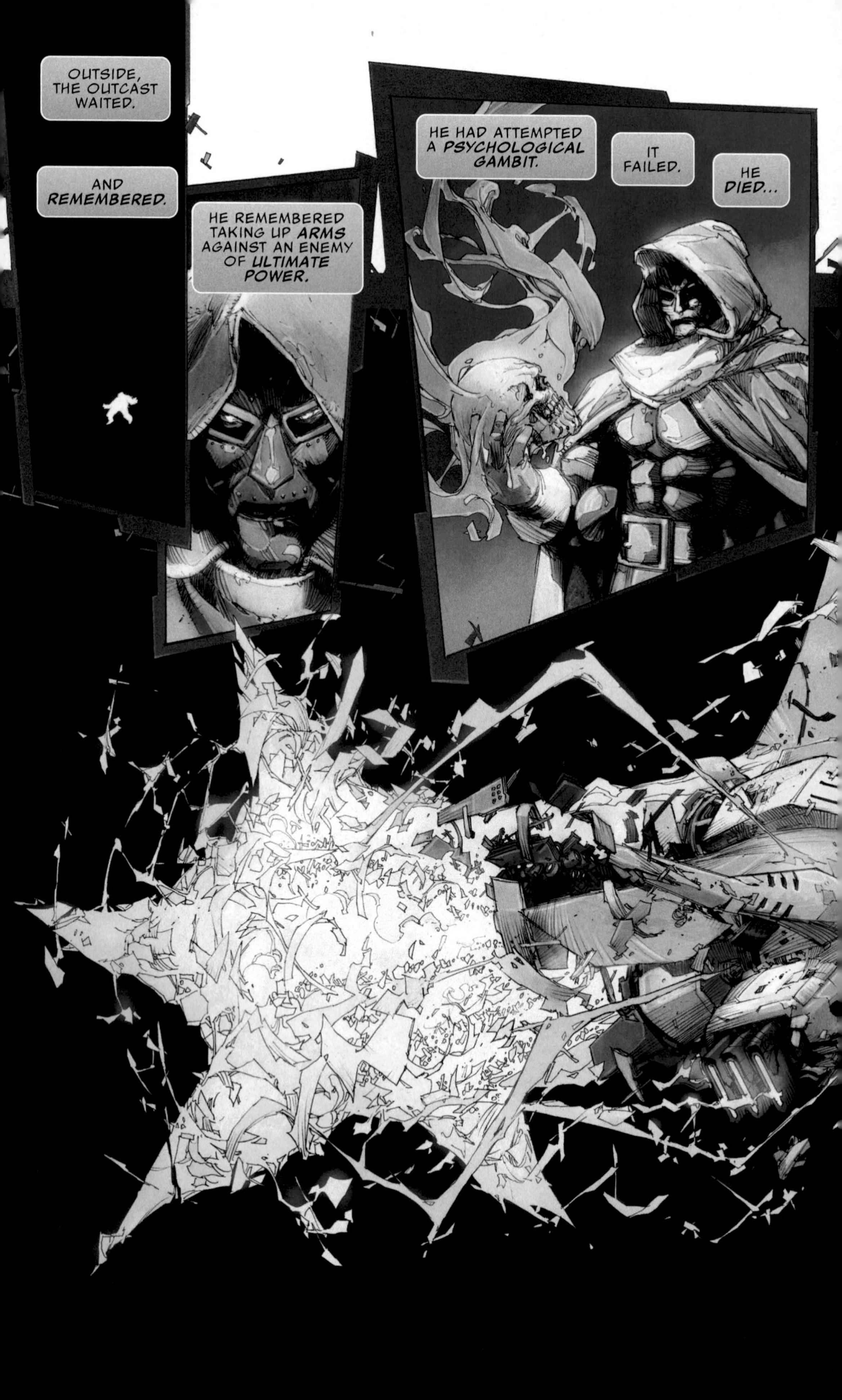

OUTSIDE, THE OUTCAST WAITED.
AND REMEMBERED.
HE REMEMBERED TAKING UP ARMS AGAINST AN ENEMY OF ULTIMATE POWER.
HE HAD ATTEMPTED A PSYCHOLOGICAL GAMBIT.
IT FAILED.
HE DIED...

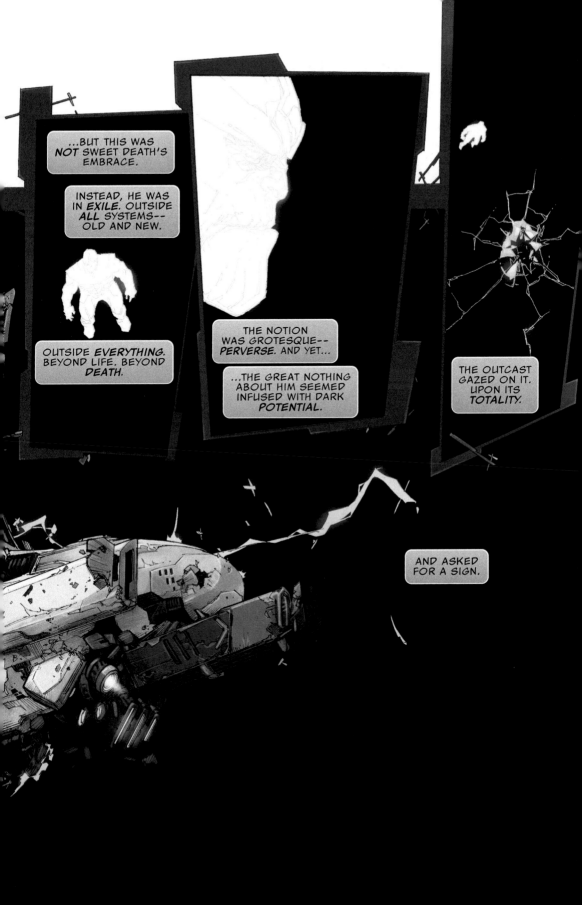

...BUT THIS WAS *NOT* SWEET DEATH'S EMBRACE.

INSTEAD, HE WAS IN *EXILE.* OUTSIDE *ALL* SYSTEMS-- OLD AND NEW.

OUTSIDE *EVERYTHING.* BEYOND LIFE. BEYOND *DEATH.*

THE NOTION WAS GROTESQUE-- *PERVERSE.* AND YET...

...THE GREAT NOTHING ABOUT HIM SEEMED INFUSED WITH DARK *POTENTIAL.*

THE OUTCAST GAZED ON IT. UPON ITS *TOTALITY.*

AND ASKED FOR A SIGN.

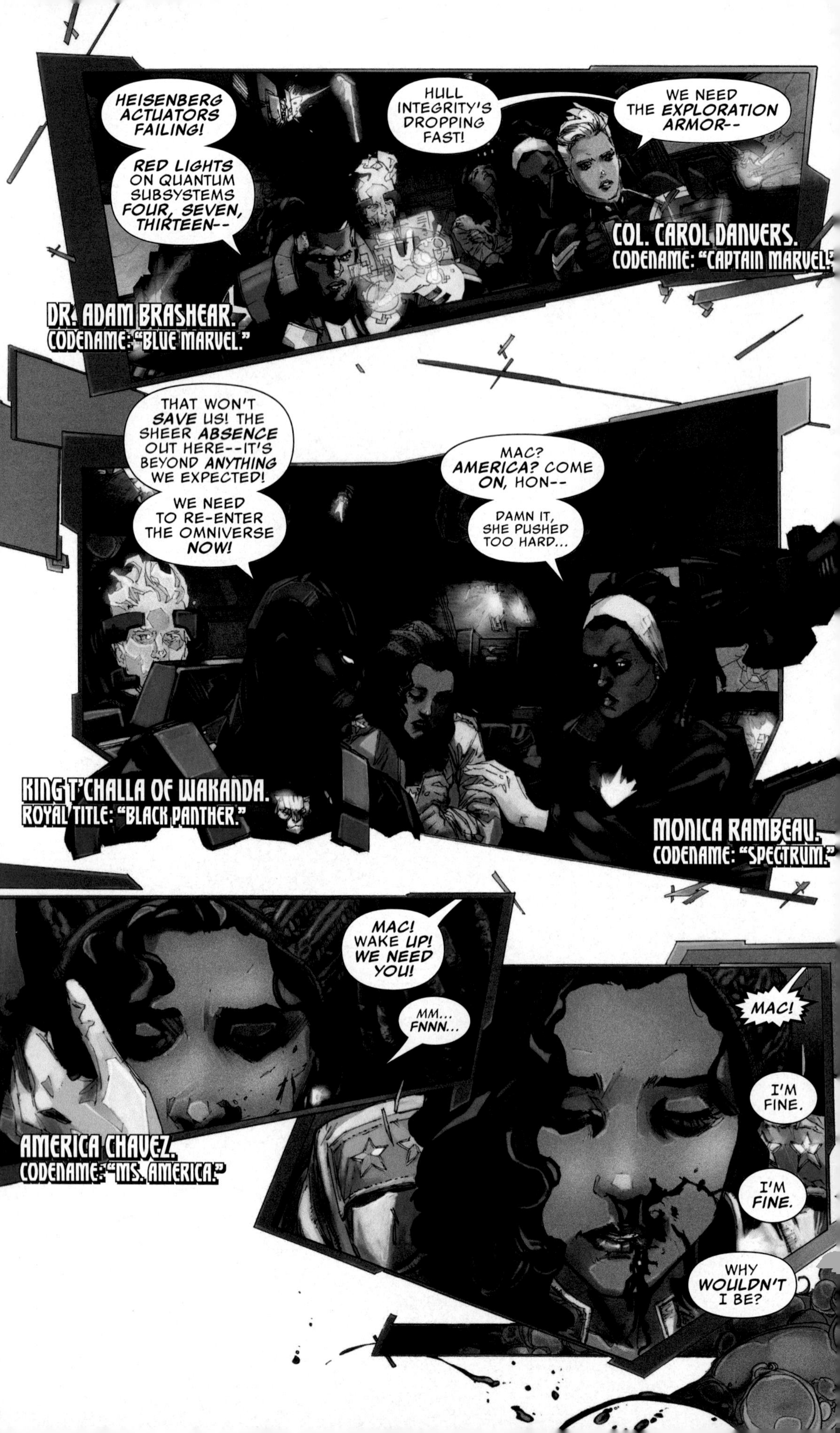
HEISENBERG ACTUATORS FAILING!
RED LIGHTS ON QUANTUM SUBSYSTEMS FOUR, SEVEN, THIRTEEN--
HULL INTEGRITY'S DROPPING FAST!
WE NEED THE EXPLORATION ARMOR--
COL. CAROL DANVERS.
CODENAME: "CAPTAIN MARVEL."
DR. ADAM BRASHEAR.
CODENAME: "BLUE MARVEL."
THAT WON'T SAVE US! THE SHEER ABSENCE OUT HERE--IT'S BEYOND ANYTHING WE EXPECTED!
WE NEED TO RE-ENTER THE OMNIVERSE NOW!
MAC? AMERICA? COME ON, HON--
DAMN IT, SHE PUSHED TOO HARD...
KING T'CHALLA OF WAKANDA.
ROYAL TITLE: "BLACK PANTHER."
MONICA RAMBEAU.
CODENAME: "SPECTRUM."
MAC! WAKE UP! WE NEED YOU!
MM... FNNN...
AMERICA CHAVEZ.
CODENAME: "MS. AMERICA."
MAC!
I'M FINE.
I'M FINE.
WHY WOULDN'T I BE?

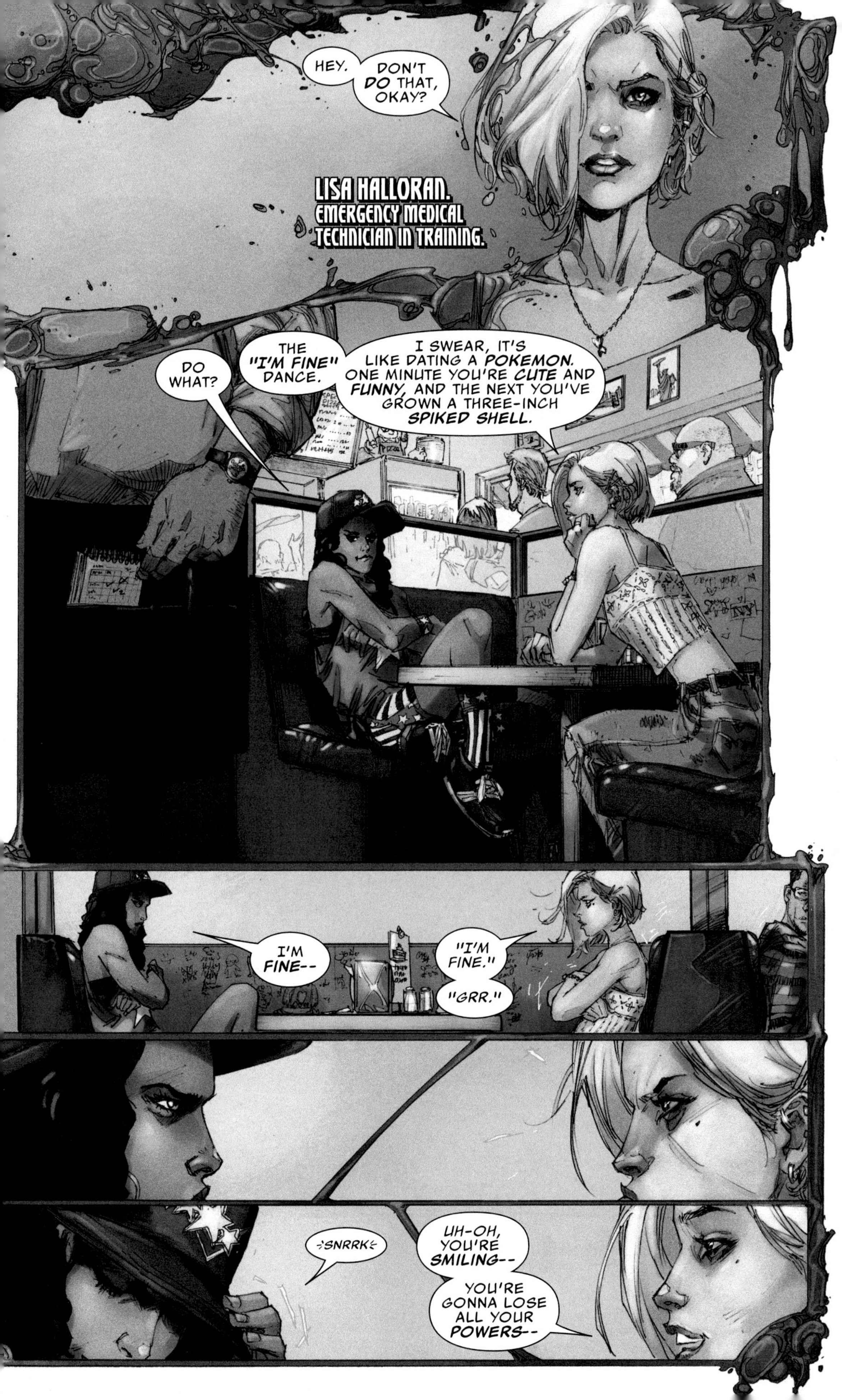
HEY.
DON'T DO THAT, OKAY?
LISA HALLORAN. EMERGENCY MEDICAL TECHNICIAN IN TRAINING.
DO WHAT?
THE "I'M FINE" DANCE.
I SWEAR, IT'S LIKE DATING A POKEMON. ONE MINUTE YOU'RE CUTE AND FUNNY, AND THE NEXT YOU'VE GROWN A THREE-INCH SPIKED SHELL.
I'M FINE--
"I'M FINE."
"GRR."
SNRRK
UH-OH, YOU'RE SMILING--
YOU'RE GONNA LOSE ALL YOUR POWERS--

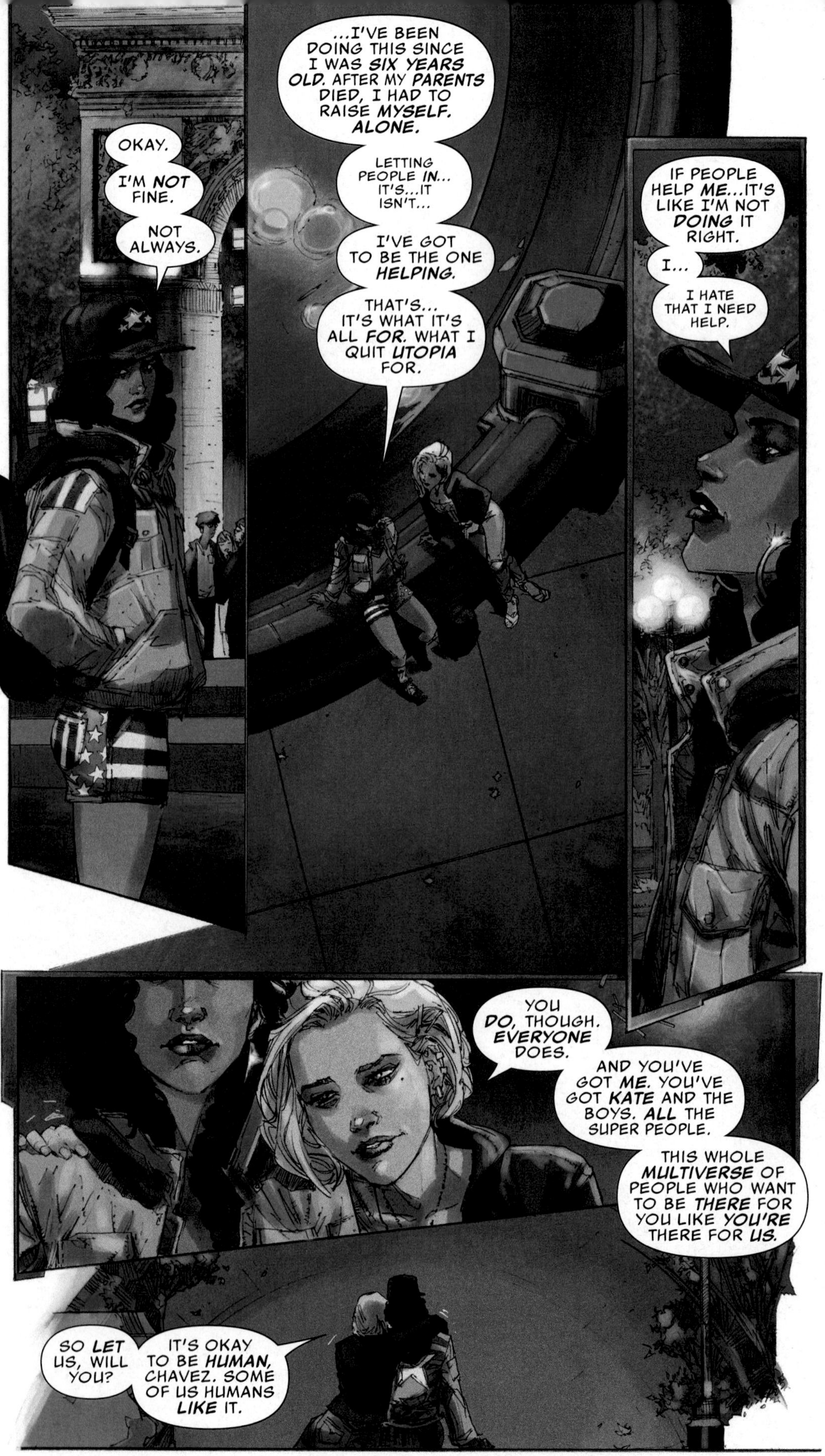
OKAY.
I'M NOT FINE.
NOT ALWAYS.
...I'VE BEEN DOING THIS SINCE I WAS SIX YEARS OLD. AFTER MY PARENTS DIED, I HAD TO RAISE MYSELF. ALONE.
LETTING PEOPLE IN... IT'S...IT ISN'T...
I'VE GOT TO BE THE ONE HELPING.
THAT'S... IT'S WHAT IT'S ALL FOR. WHAT I QUIT UTOPIA FOR.
IF PEOPLE HELP ME...IT'S LIKE I'M NOT DOING IT RIGHT.
I...
I HATE THAT I NEED HELP.
YOU DO, THOUGH. EVERYONE DOES.
AND YOU'VE GOT ME. YOU'VE GOT KATE AND THE BOYS. ALL THE SUPER PEOPLE.
THIS WHOLE MULTIVERSE OF PEOPLE WHO WANT TO BE THERE FOR YOU LIKE YOU'RE THERE FOR US.
IT'S OKAY TO BE HUMAN, CHAVEZ. SOME OF US HUMANS LIKE IT.
SO LET US, WILL YOU?

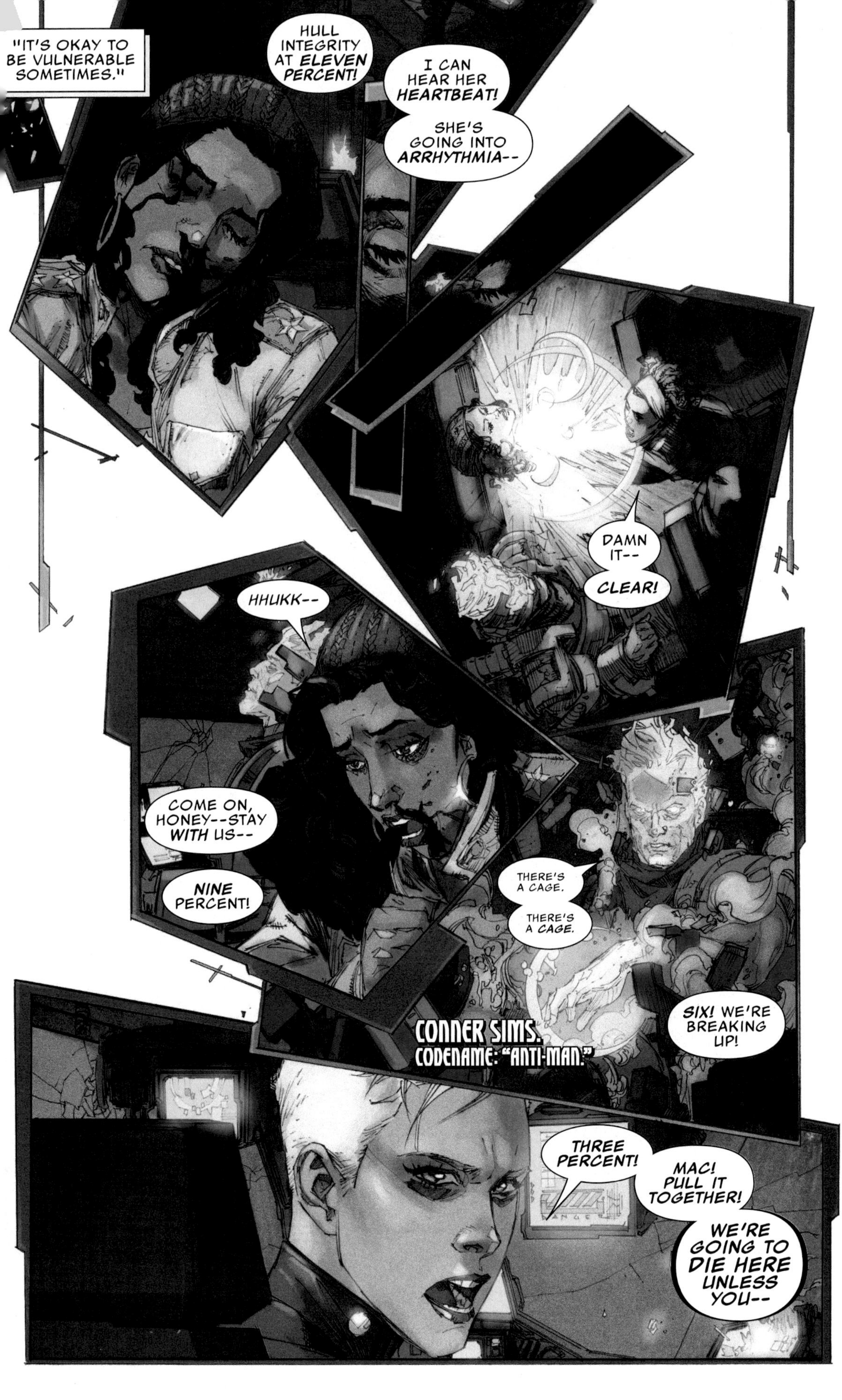
"IT'S OKAY TO BE VULNERABLE SOMETIMES."
HULL INTEGRITY AT ELEVEN PERCENT!
I CAN HEAR HER HEARTBEAT!
SHE'S GOING INTO ARRHYTHMIA--
DAMN IT--
CLEAR!
HHUKK--
COME ON, HONEY--STAY WITH US--
NINE PERCENT!
THERE'S A CAGE.
THERE'S A CAGE.
SIX! WE'RE BREAKING UP!
CONNER SIMS.
CODENAME: "ANTI-MAN."
THREE PERCENT!
MAC! PULL IT TOGETHER!
WE'RE GOING TO DIE HERE UNLESS YOU--

ZERO PERCENT.
NO.

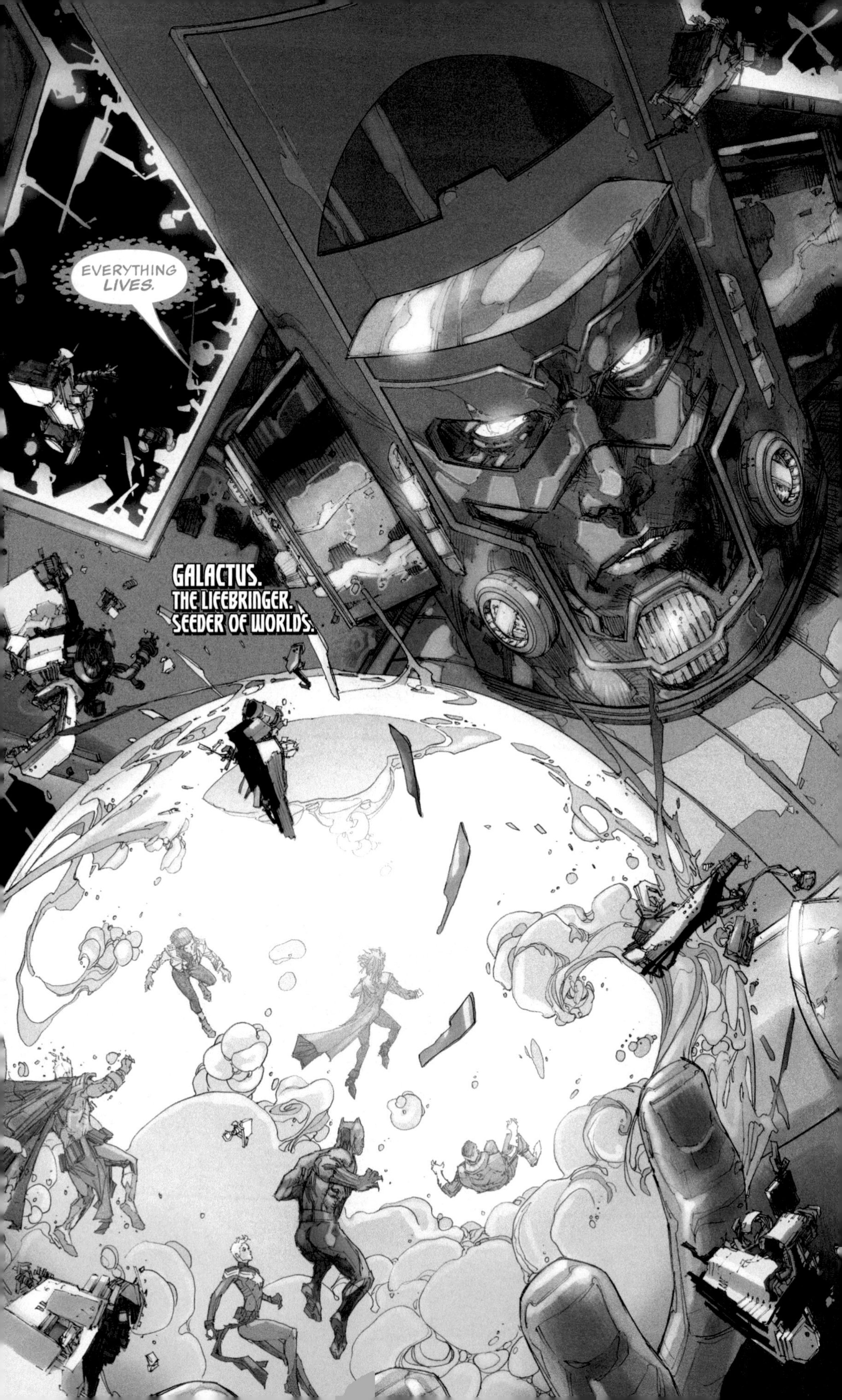
EVERYTHING LIVES.
GALACTUS.
THE LIFEBRINGER.
SEEDER OF WORLDS.

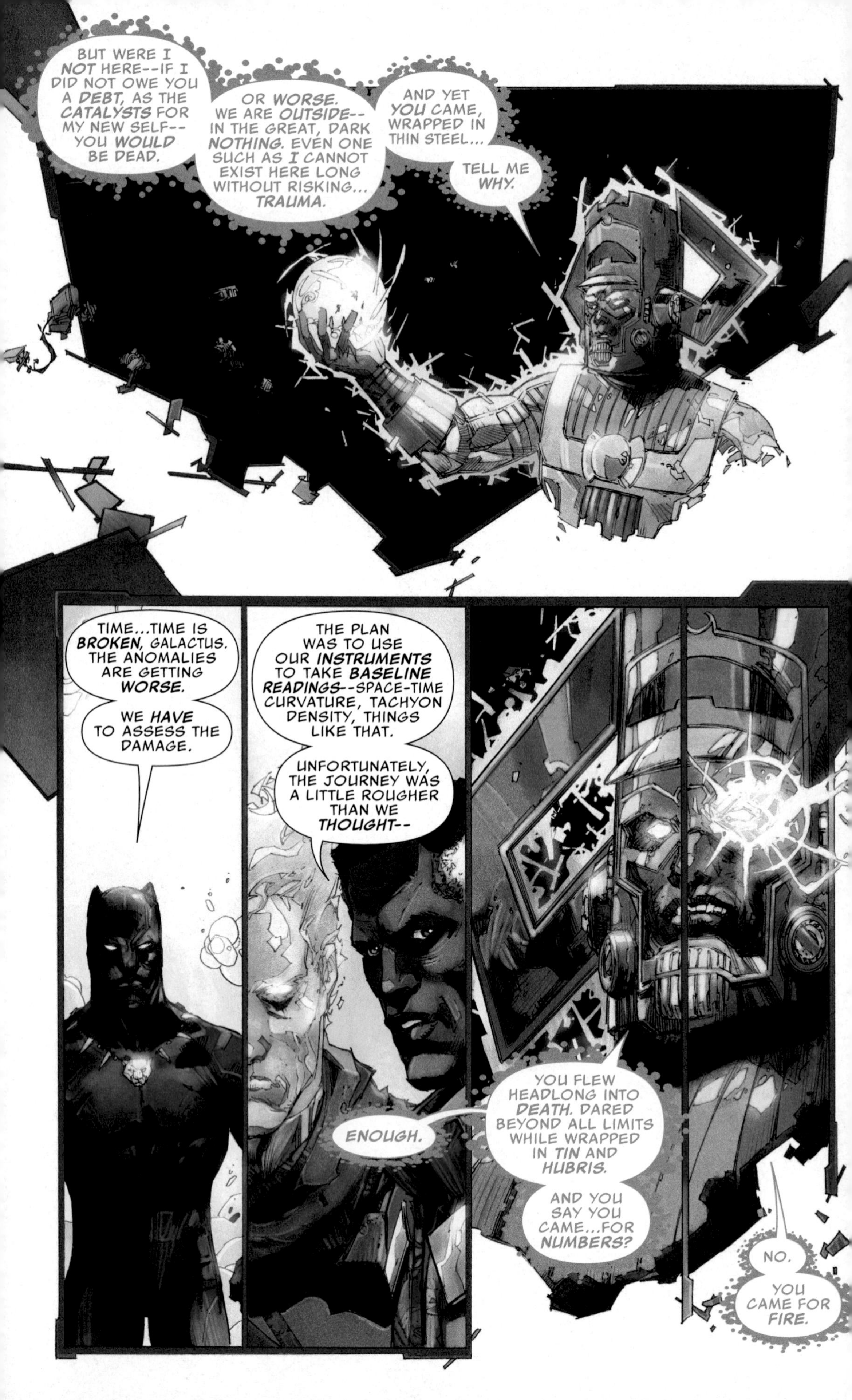

BUT WERE I NOT HERE--IF I DID NOT OWE YOU A DEBT, AS THE CATALYSTS FOR MY NEW SELF--YOU WOULD BE DEAD.
OR WORSE. WE ARE OUTSIDE--IN THE GREAT, DARK NOTHING. EVEN ONE SUCH AS I CANNOT EXIST HERE LONG WITHOUT RISKING... TRAUMA.
AND YET YOU CAME, WRAPPED IN THIN STEEL...
TELL ME WHY.
TIME...TIME IS BROKEN, GALACTUS. THE ANOMALIES ARE GETTING WORSE.
WE HAVE TO ASSESS THE DAMAGE.
THE PLAN WAS TO USE OUR INSTRUMENTS TO TAKE BASELINE READINGS--SPACE-TIME CURVATURE, TACHYON DENSITY, THINGS LIKE THAT.
UNFORTUNATELY, THE JOURNEY WAS A LITTLE ROUGHER THAN WE THOUGHT--
ENOUGH.
YOU FLEW HEADLONG INTO DEATH. DARED BEYOND ALL LIMITS WHILE WRAPPED IN TIN AND HUBRIS.
AND YOU SAY YOU CAME...FOR NUMBERS?
NO.
YOU CAME FOR FIRE.

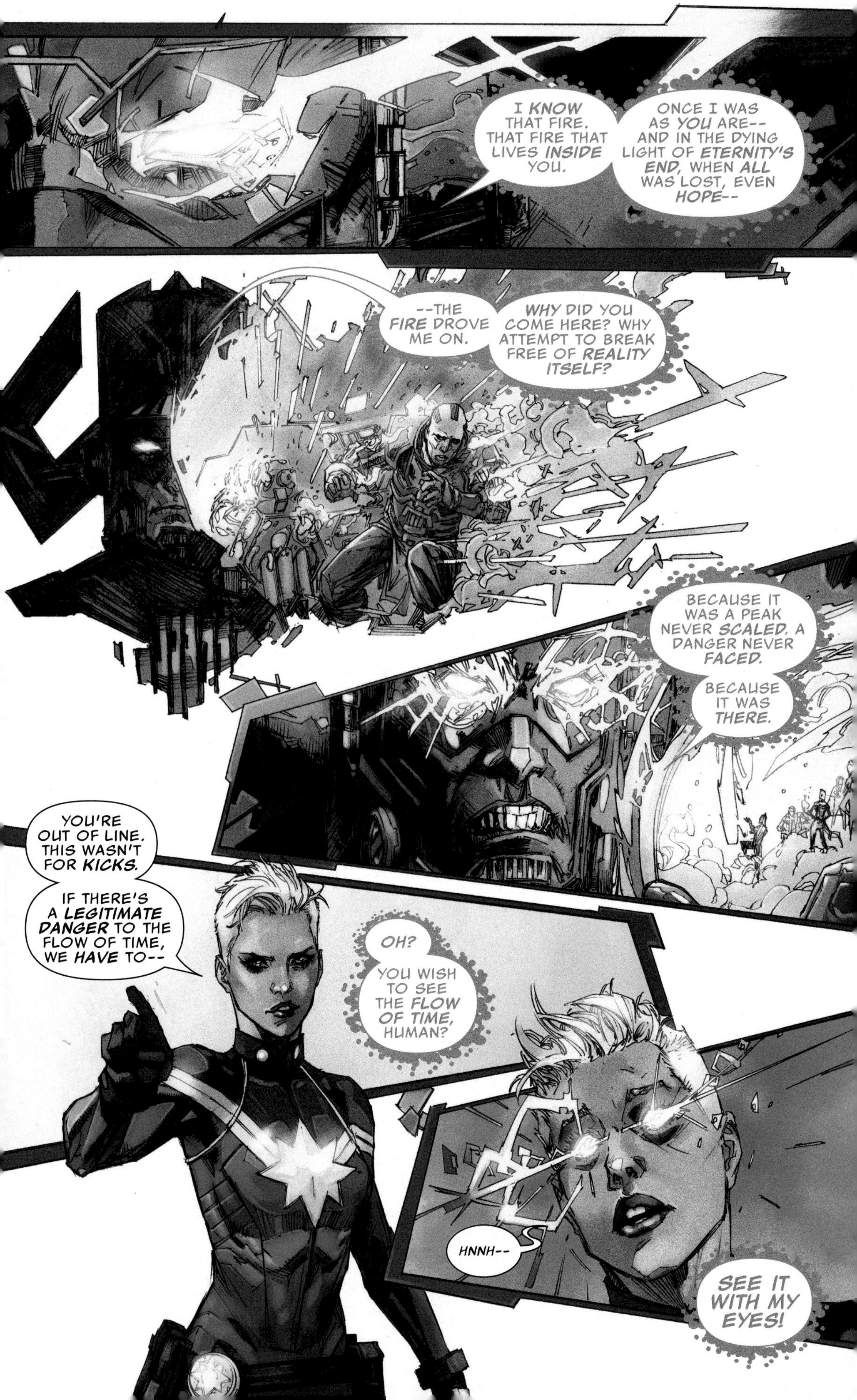

I KNOW THAT FIRE. THAT FIRE THAT LIVES INSIDE YOU.
ONCE I WAS AS YOU ARE-- AND IN THE DYING LIGHT OF ETERNITY'S END, WHEN ALL WAS LOST, EVEN HOPE--
--THE FIRE DROVE ME ON.
WHY DID YOU COME HERE? WHY ATTEMPT TO BREAK FREE OF REALITY ITSELF?
BECAUSE IT WAS A PEAK NEVER SCALED. A DANGER NEVER FACED.
BECAUSE IT WAS THERE.
YOU'RE OUT OF LINE. THIS WASN'T FOR KICKS.
IF THERE'S A LEGITIMATE DANGER TO THE FLOW OF TIME, WE HAVE TO--
OH?
YOU WISH TO SEE THE FLOW OF TIME, HUMAN?
HNNH--
SEE IT WITH MY EYES!

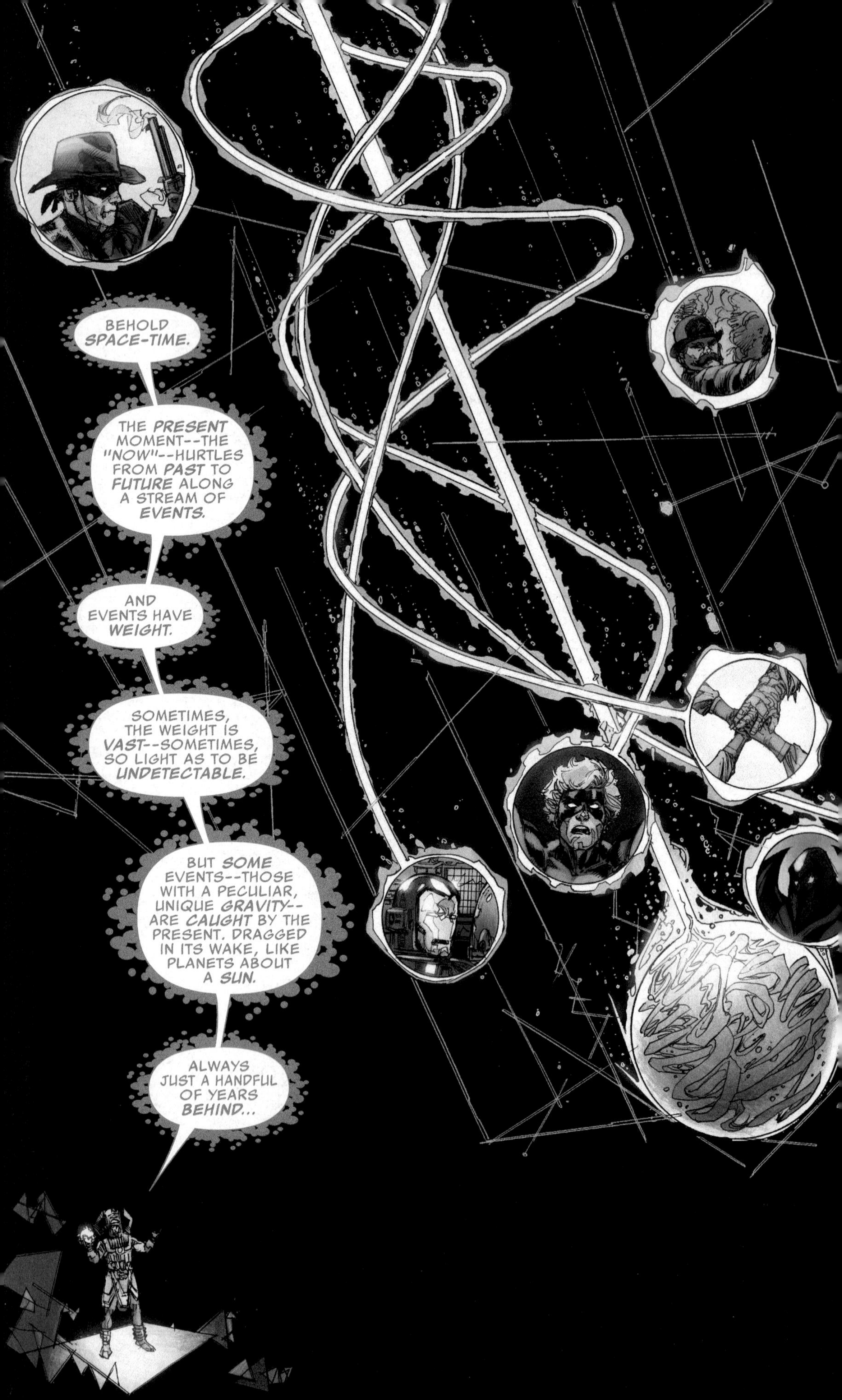
BEHOLD SPACE-TIME.
THE PRESENT MOMENT--THE "NOW"--HURTLES FROM PAST TO FUTURE ALONG A STREAM OF EVENTS.
AND EVENTS HAVE WEIGHT.
SOMETIMES, THE WEIGHT IS VAST--SOMETIMES, SO LIGHT AS TO BE UNDETECTABLE.
BUT SOME EVENTS--THOSE WITH A PECULIAR, UNIQUE GRAVITY--ARE CAUGHT BY THE PRESENT. DRAGGED IN ITS WAKE, LIKE PLANETS ABOUT A SUN.
ALWAYS JUST A HANDFUL OF YEARS BEHIND...

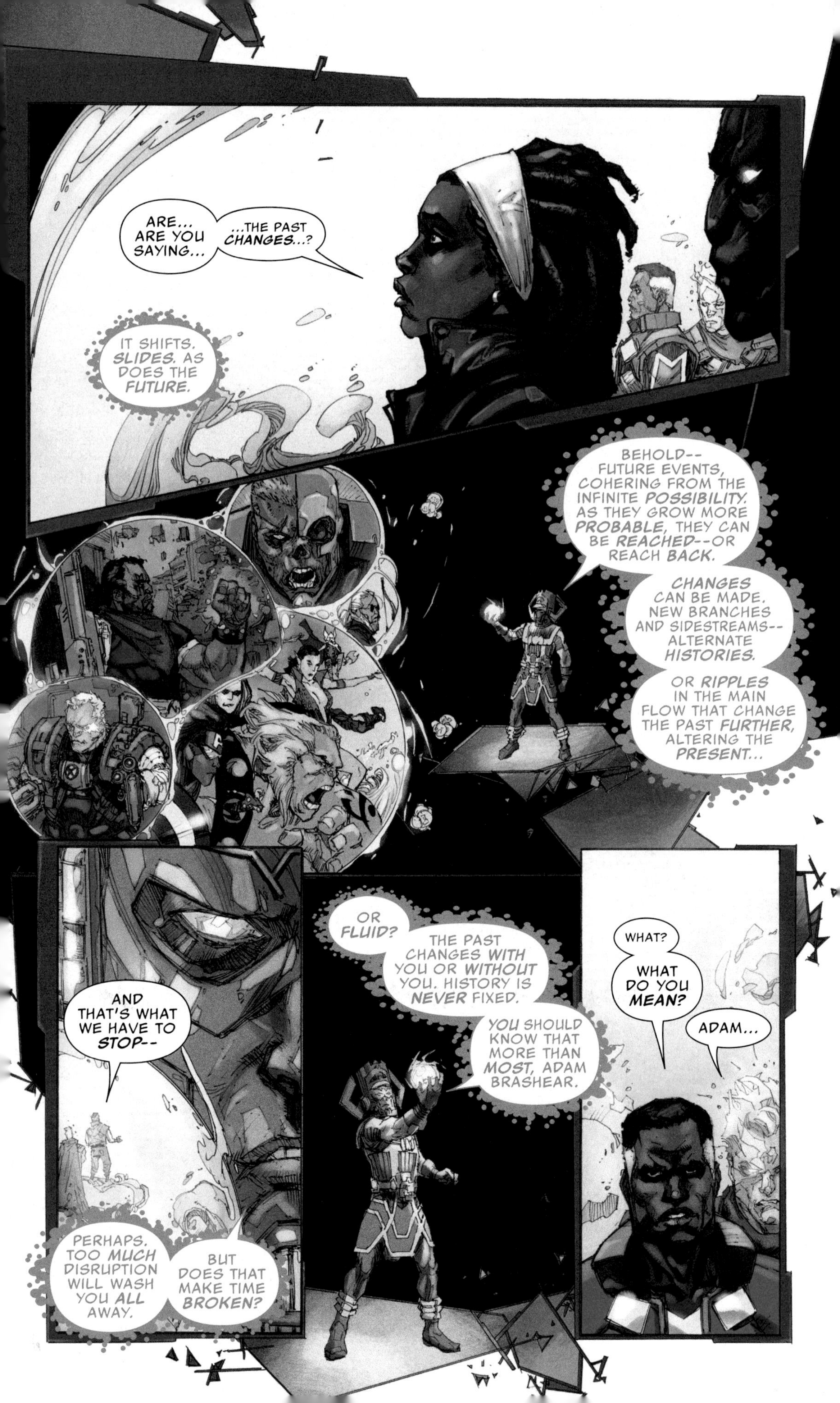
ARE... ARE YOU SAYING...
...THE PAST CHANGES...?
IT SHIFTS. SLIDES. AS DOES THE FUTURE.
BEHOLD-- FUTURE EVENTS, COHERING FROM THE INFINITE POSSIBILITY. AS THEY GROW MORE PROBABLE, THEY CAN BE REACHED--OR REACH BACK.
CHANGES CAN BE MADE. NEW BRANCHES AND SIDESTREAMS-- ALTERNATE HISTORIES.
OR RIPPLES IN THE MAIN FLOW THAT CHANGE THE PAST FURTHER, ALTERING THE PRESENT...
AND THAT'S WHAT WE HAVE TO STOP--
PERHAPS. TOO MUCH DISRUPTION WILL WASH YOU ALL AWAY.
BUT DOES THAT MAKE TIME BROKEN?
OR FLUID?
THE PAST CHANGES WITH YOU OR WITHOUT YOU. HISTORY IS NEVER FIXED.
YOU SHOULD KNOW THAT MORE THAN MOST, ADAM BRASHEAR.
WHAT?
WHAT DO YOU MEAN?
ADAM...

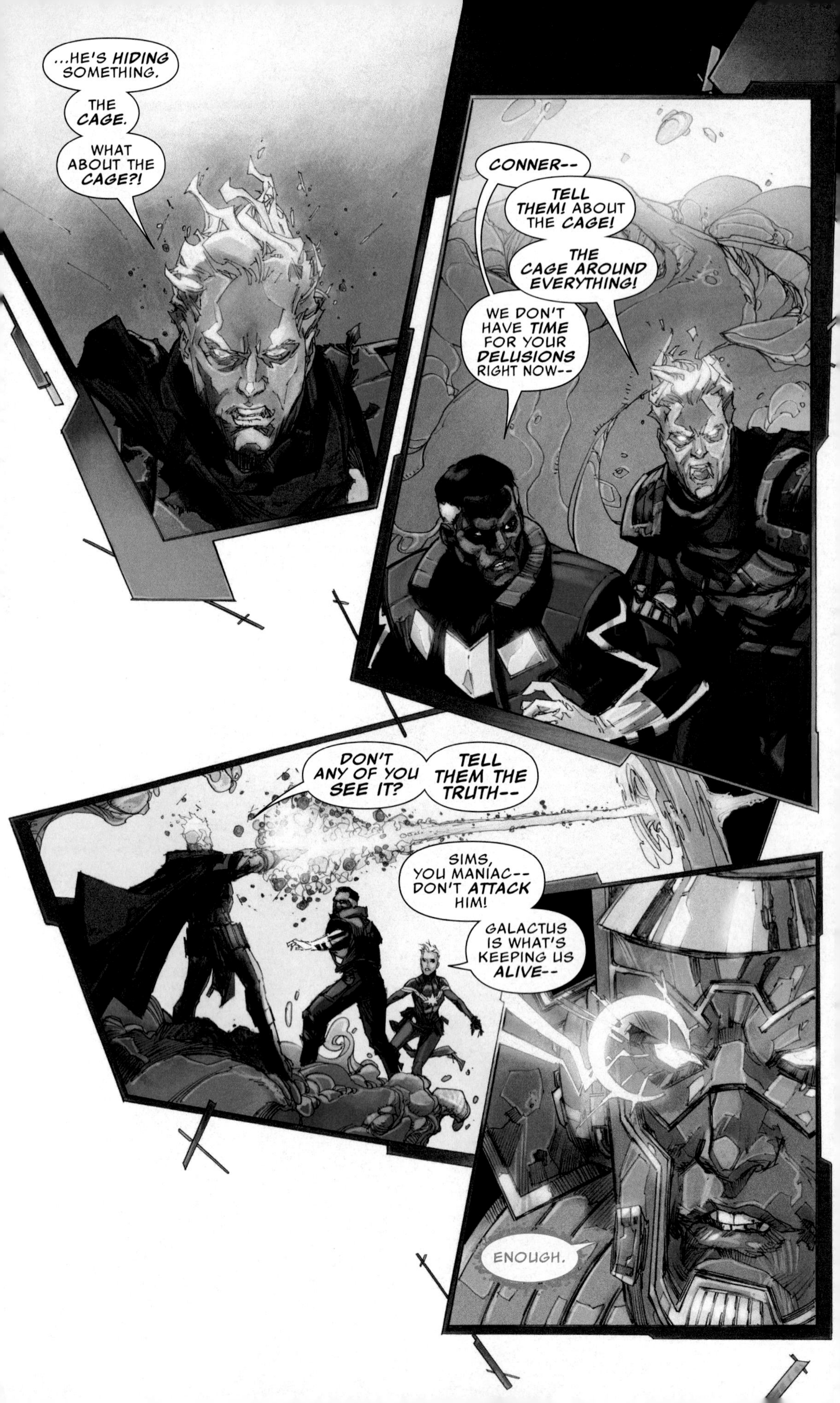

...HE'S HIDING SOMETHING.
THE CAGE.
WHAT ABOUT THE CAGE?!
CONNER--
TELL THEM! ABOUT THE CAGE!
THE CAGE AROUND EVERYTHING!
WE DON'T HAVE TIME FOR YOUR DELUSIONS RIGHT NOW--
DON'T ANY OF YOU SEE IT?
TELL THEM THE TRUTH--
SIMS, YOU MANIAC-- DON'T ATTACK HIM!
GALACTUS IS WHAT'S KEEPING US ALIVE--
ENOUGH.

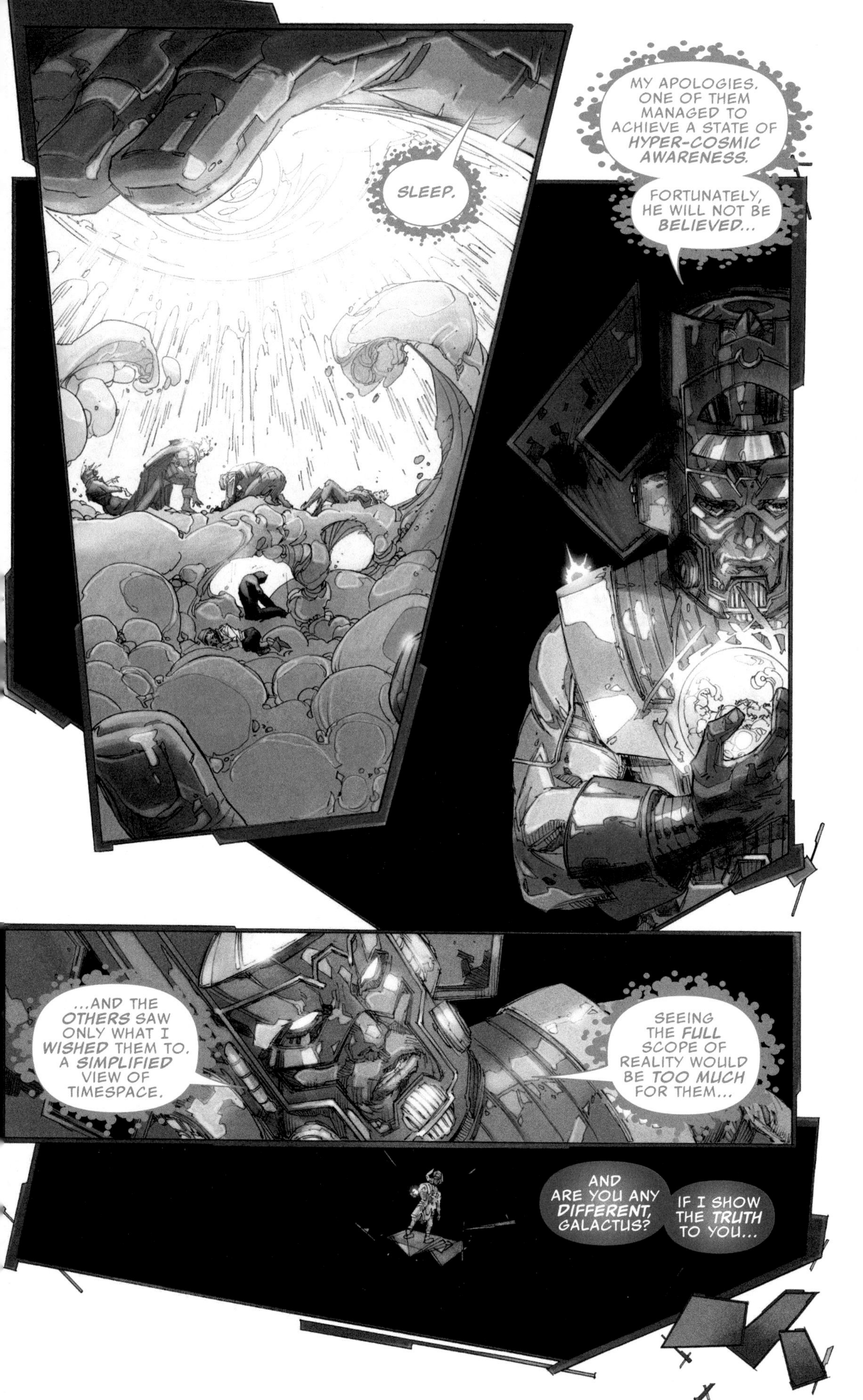
SLEEP.
MY APOLOGIES. ONE OF THEM MANAGED TO ACHIEVE A STATE OF HYPER-COSMIC AWARENESS.
FORTUNATELY, HE WILL NOT BE BELIEVED...
...AND THE OTHERS SAW ONLY WHAT I WISHED THEM TO. A SIMPLIFIED VIEW OF TIMESPACE.
SEEING THE FULL SCOPE OF REALITY WOULD BE TOO MUCH FOR THEM...
AND ARE YOU ANY DIFFERENT, GALACTUS?
IF I SHOW THE TRUTH TO YOU...

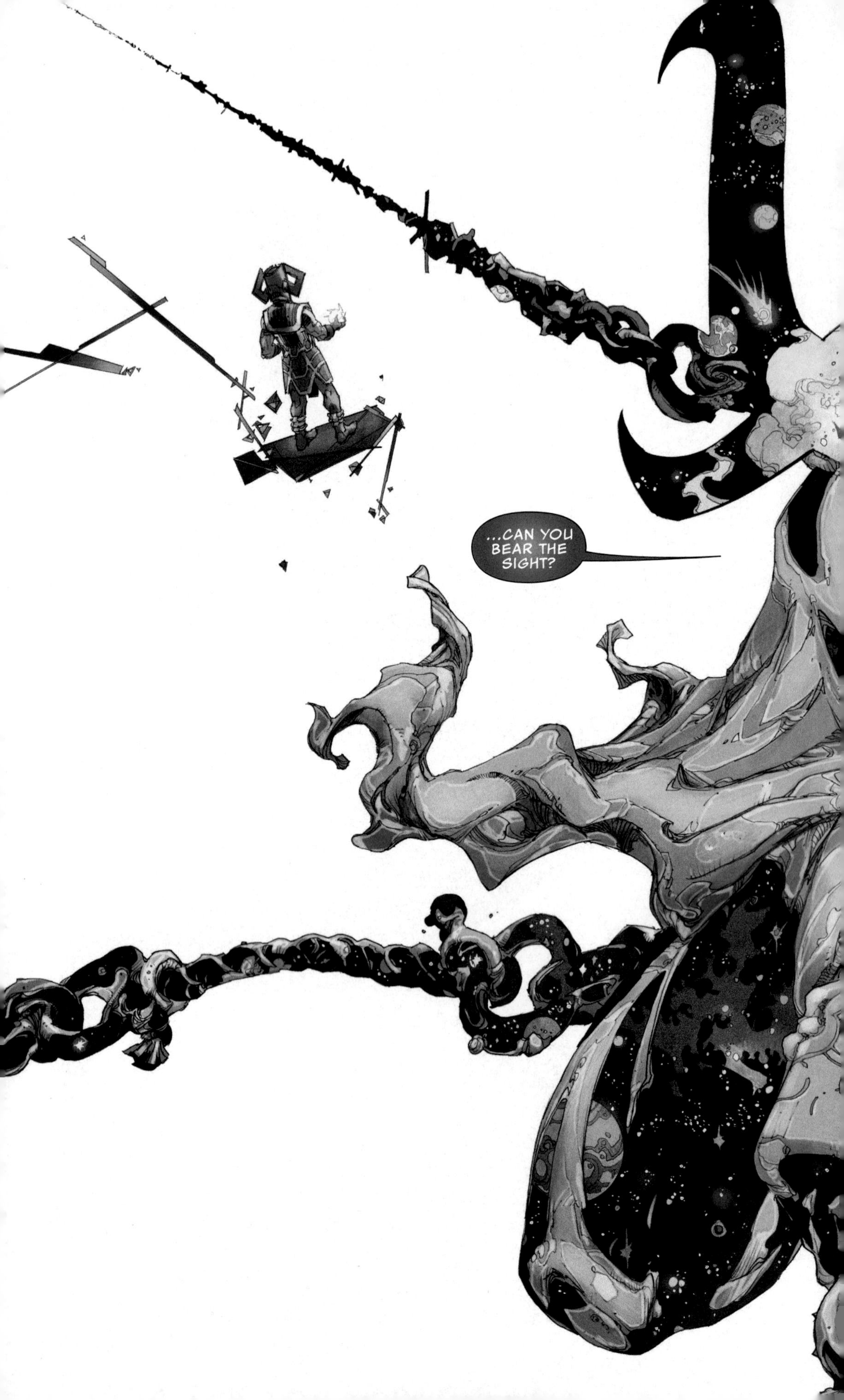
...CAN YOU BEAR THE SIGHT?

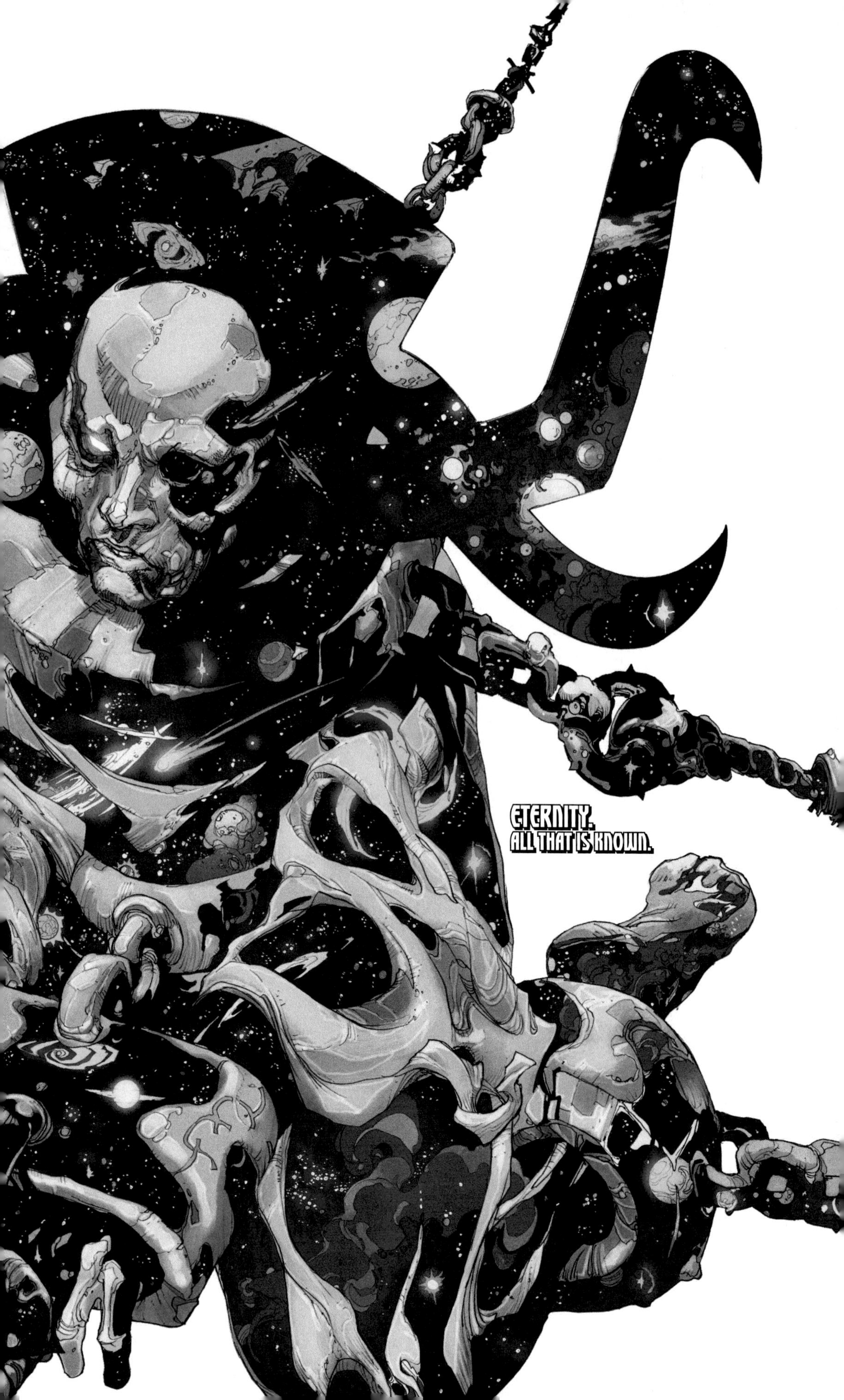
ETERNITY.
ALL THAT IS KNOWN.

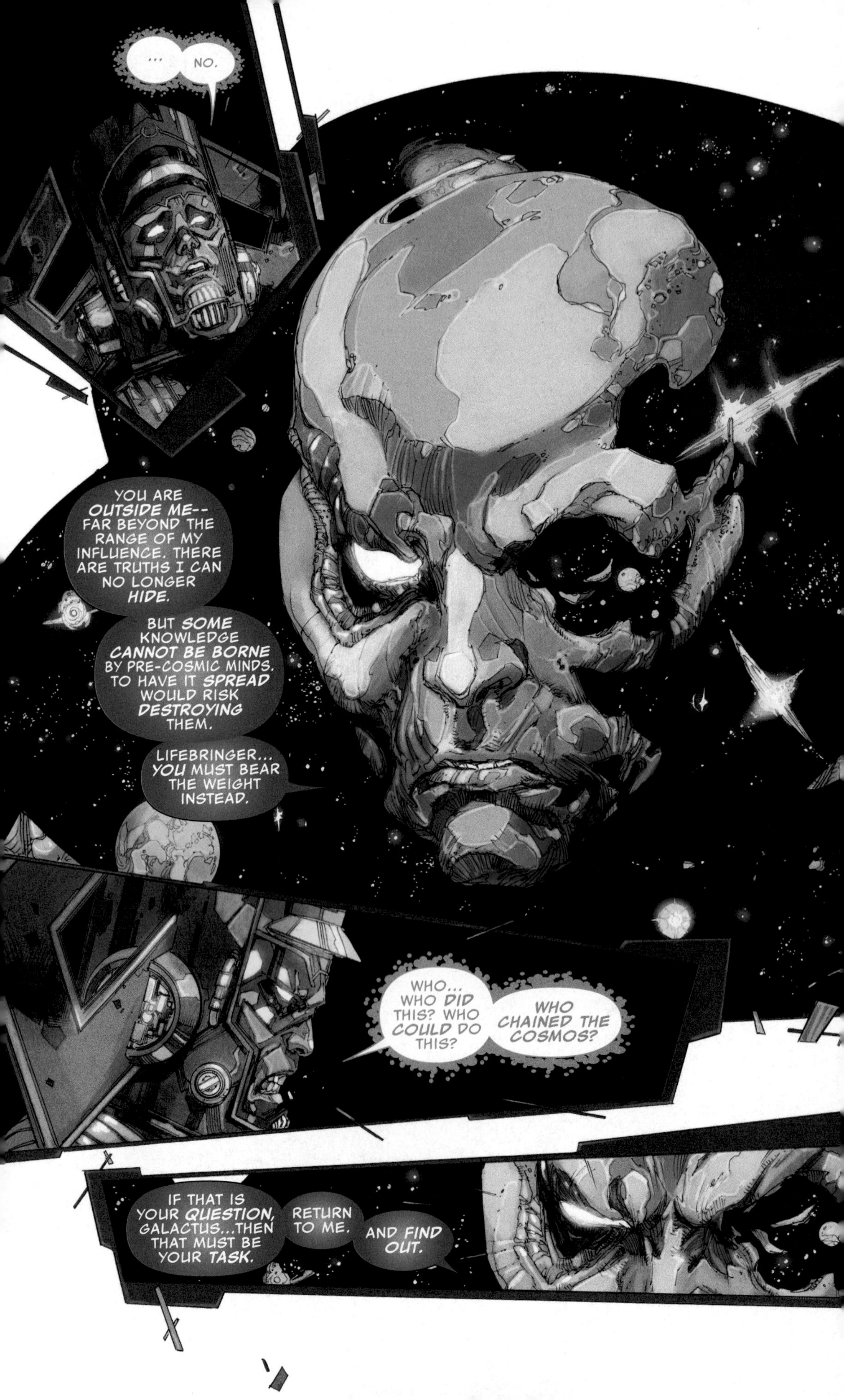
...
NO.
YOU ARE OUTSIDE ME-- FAR BEYOND THE RANGE OF MY INFLUENCE. THERE ARE TRUTHS I CAN NO LONGER HIDE.
BUT SOME KNOWLEDGE CANNOT BE BORNE BY PRE-COSMIC MINDS. TO HAVE IT SPREAD WOULD RISK DESTROYING THEM.
LIFEBRINGER... YOU MUST BEAR THE WEIGHT INSTEAD.
WHO... WHO DID THIS? WHO COULD DO THIS?
WHO CHAINED THE COSMOS?
IF THAT IS YOUR QUESTION, GALACTUS...THEN THAT MUST BE YOUR TASK.
RETURN TO ME.
AND FIND OUT.

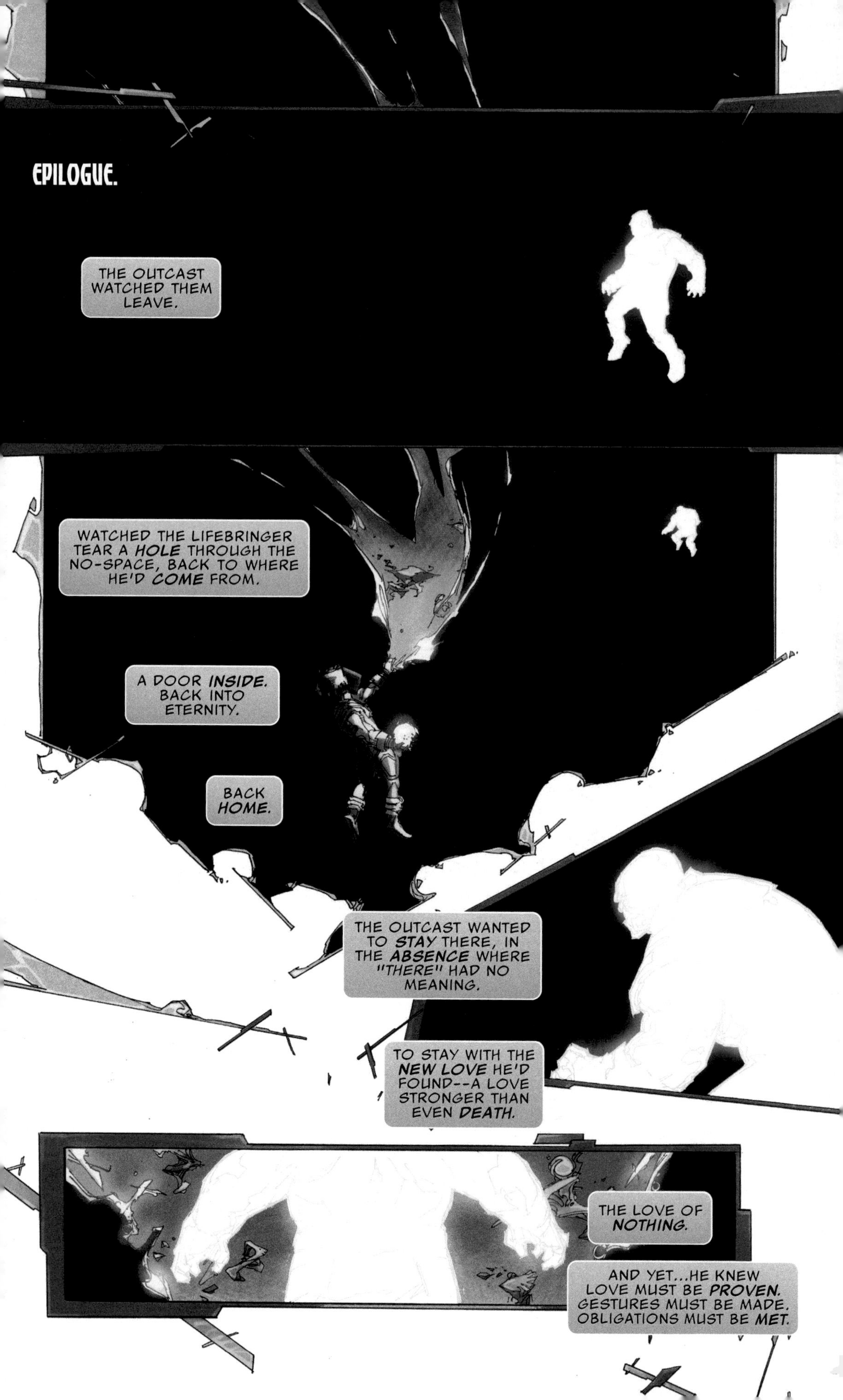

EPILOGUE.
THE OUTCAST WATCHED THEM LEAVE.
WATCHED THE LIFEBRINGER TEAR A HOLE THROUGH THE NO-SPACE, BACK TO WHERE HE'D COME FROM.
A DOOR INSIDE. BACK INTO ETERNITY.
BACK HOME.
THE OUTCAST WANTED TO STAY THERE, IN THE ABSENCE WHERE "THERE" HAD NO MEANING.
TO STAY WITH THE NEW LOVE HE'D FOUND--A LOVE STRONGER THAN EVEN DEATH.
THE LOVE OF NOTHING.
AND YET...HE KNEW LOVE MUST BE PROVEN. GESTURES MUST BE MADE. OBLIGATIONS MUST BE MET.

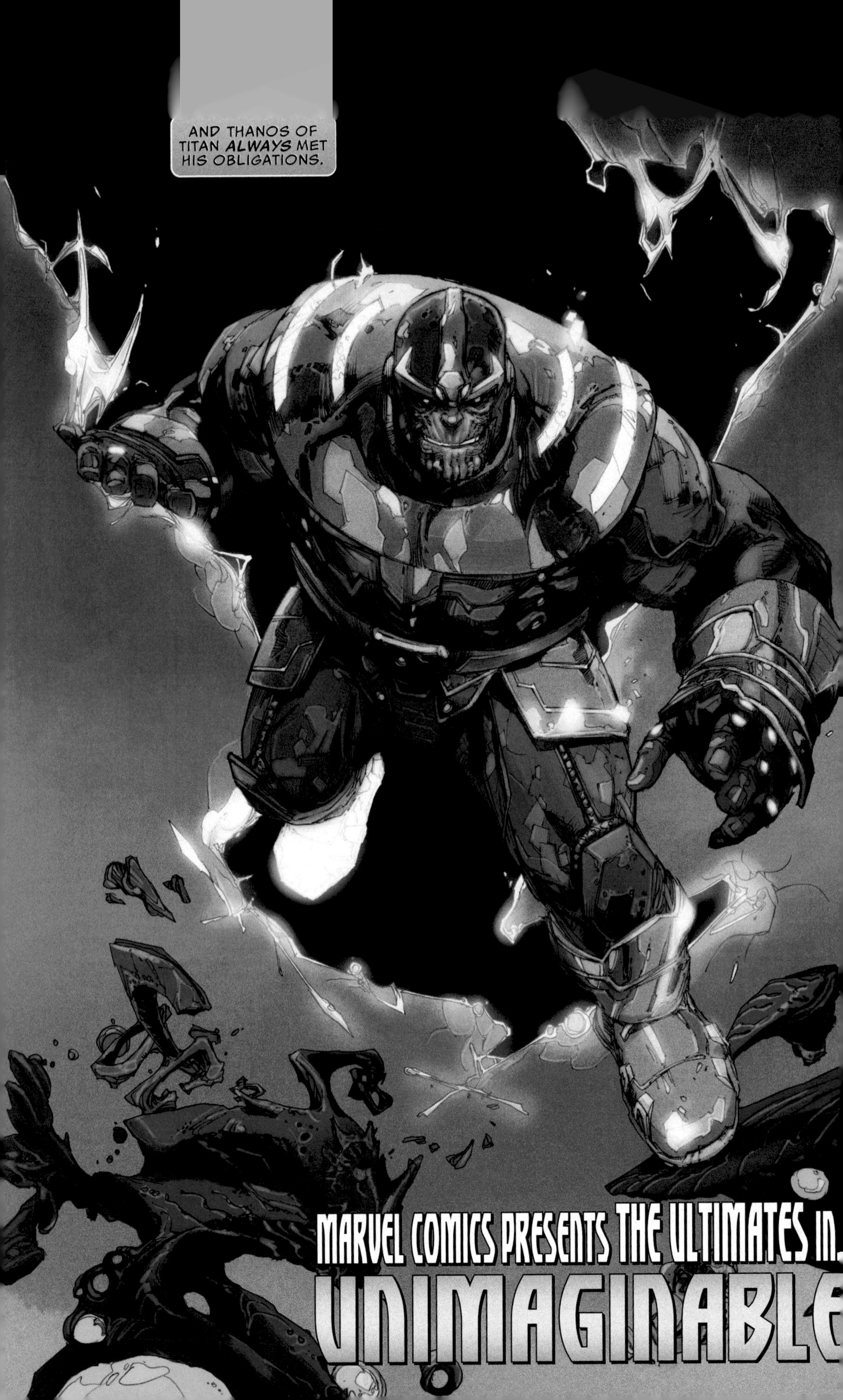
AND THANOS OF TITAN *ALWAYS* MET HIS OBLIGATIONS.
MARVEL COMICS PRESENTS THE ULTIMATES IN...
UNIMAGINABLE

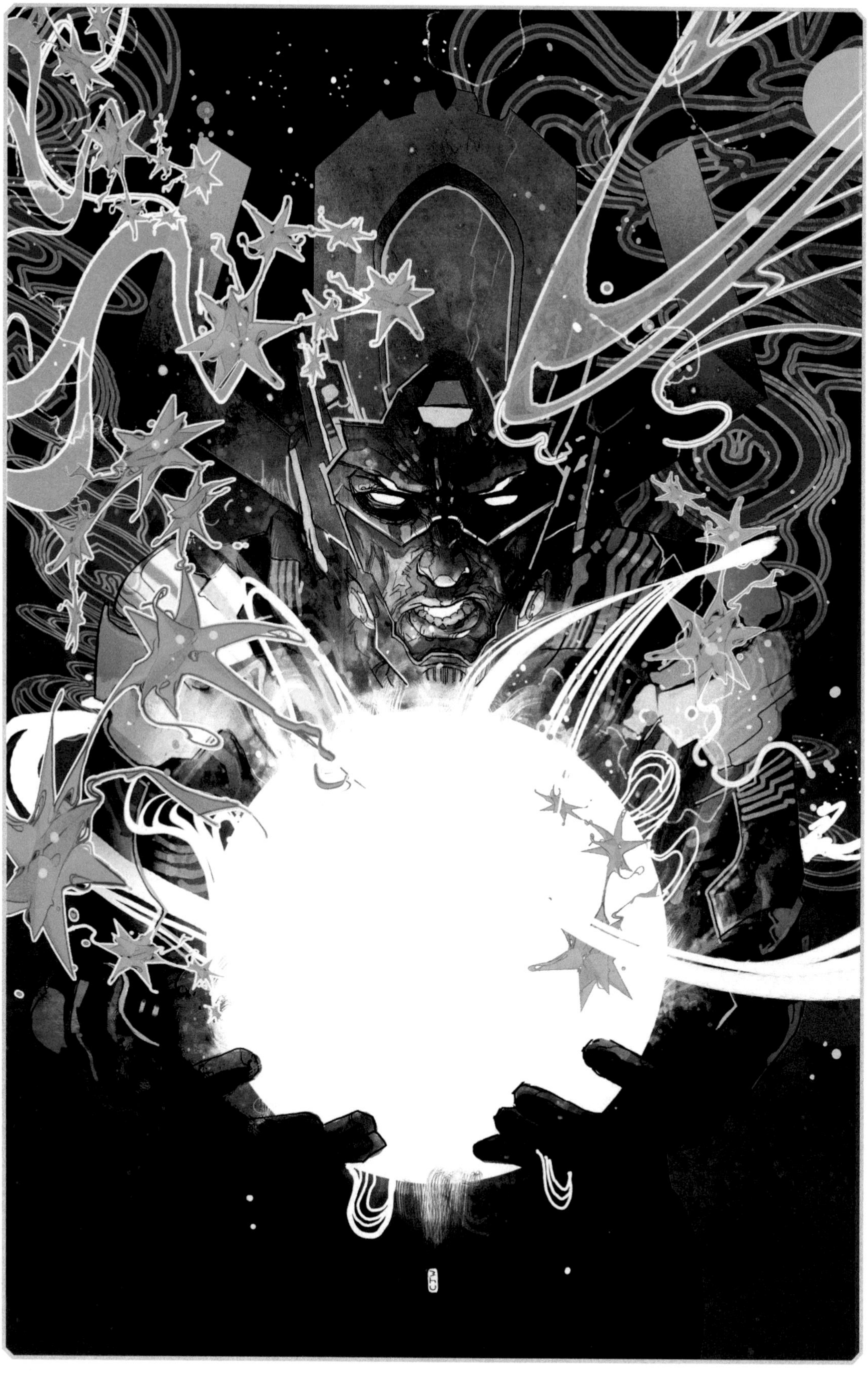
CTW

#6 VARIANT BY CHRISTIAN WARD

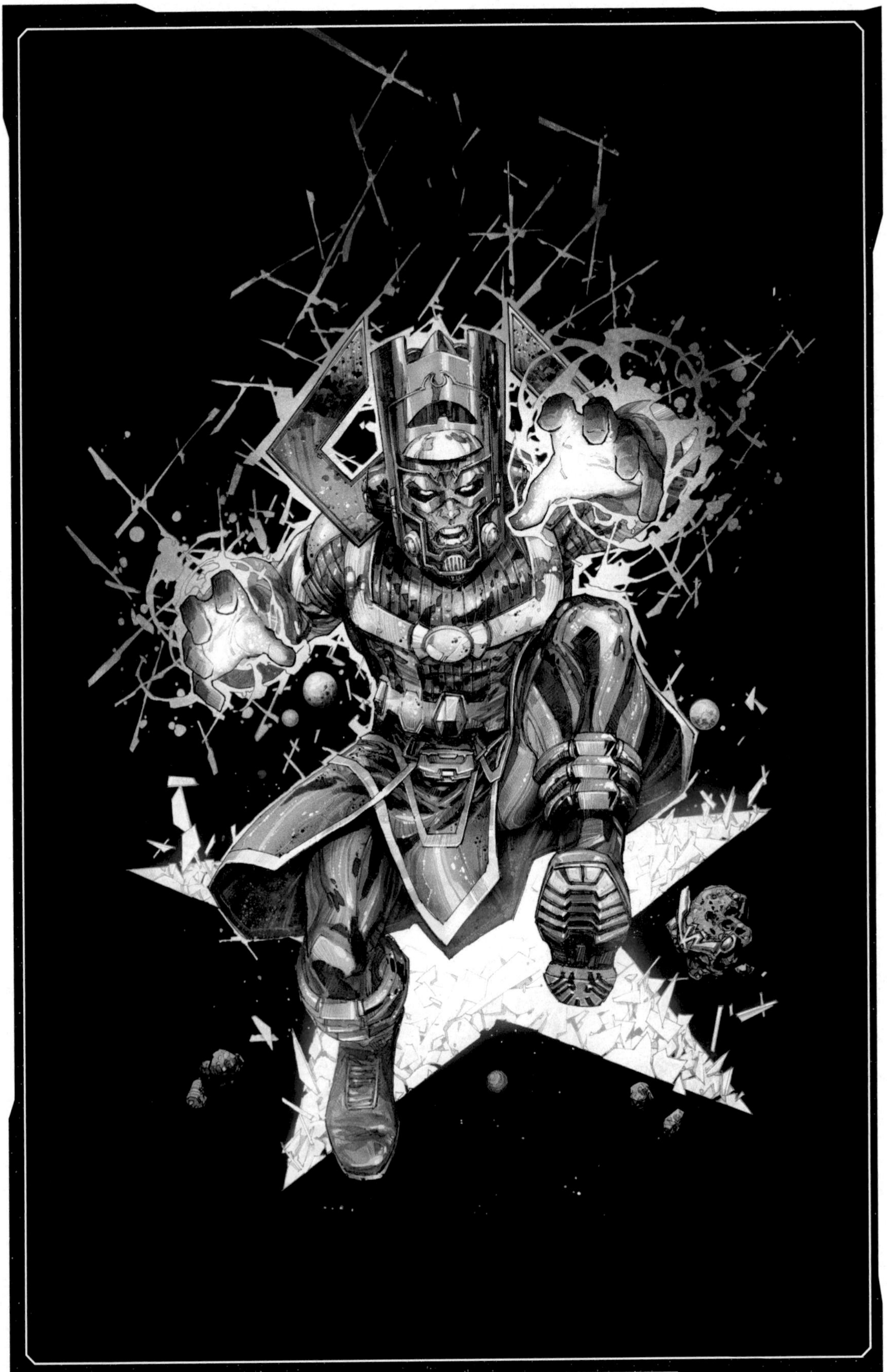

6

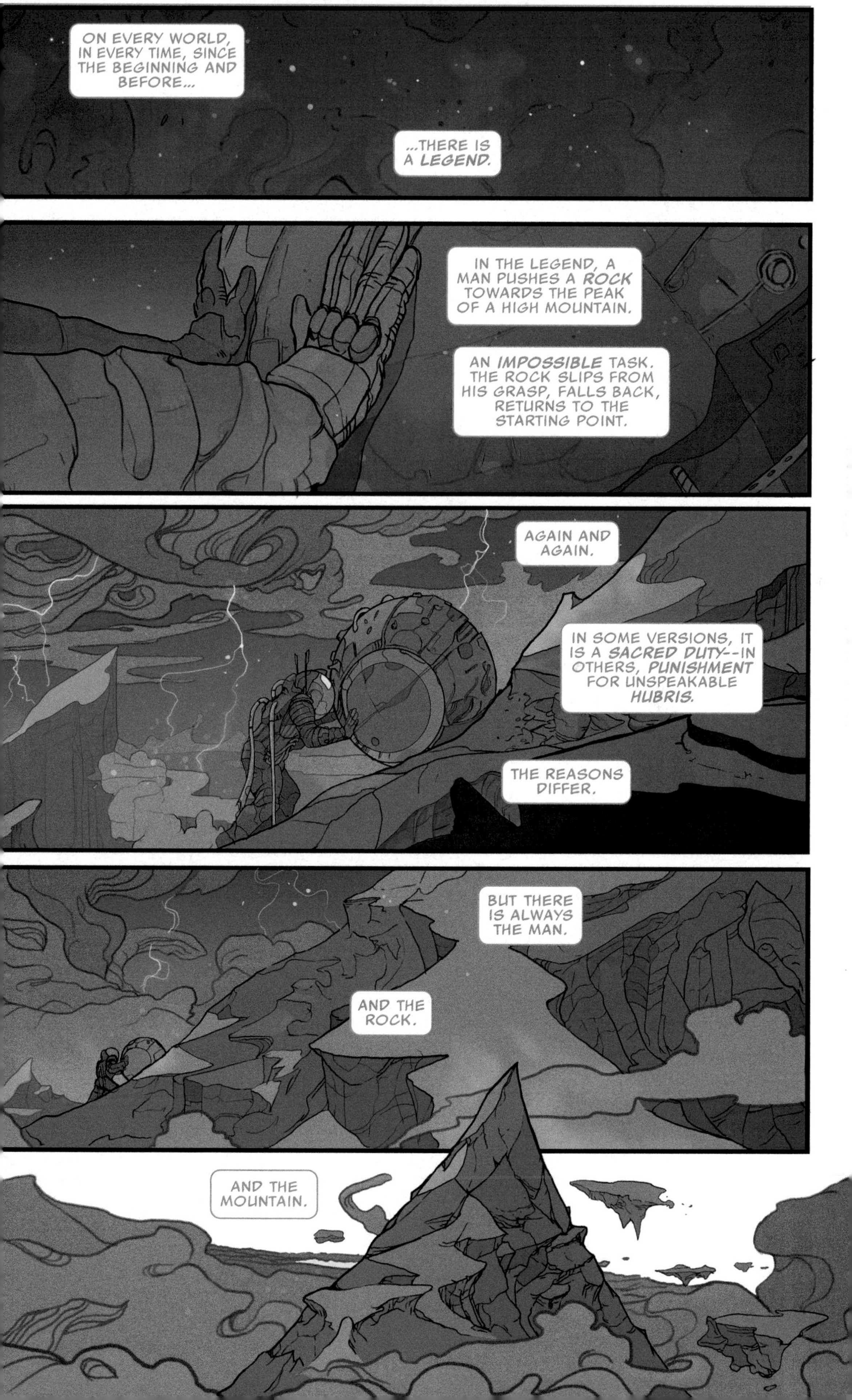
ON EVERY WORLD, IN EVERY TIME, SINCE THE BEGINNING AND BEFORE...
...THERE IS A LEGEND.
IN THE LEGEND, A MAN PUSHES A ROCK TOWARDS THE PEAK OF A HIGH MOUNTAIN.
AN IMPOSSIBLE TASK. THE ROCK SLIPS FROM HIS GRASP, FALLS BACK, RETURNS TO THE STARTING POINT.
AGAIN AND AGAIN.
IN SOME VERSIONS, IT IS A SACRED DUTY--IN OTHERS, PUNISHMENT FOR UNSPEAKABLE HUBRIS.
THE REASONS DIFFER.
BUT THERE IS ALWAYS THE MAN.
AND THE ROCK.
AND THE MOUNTAIN.

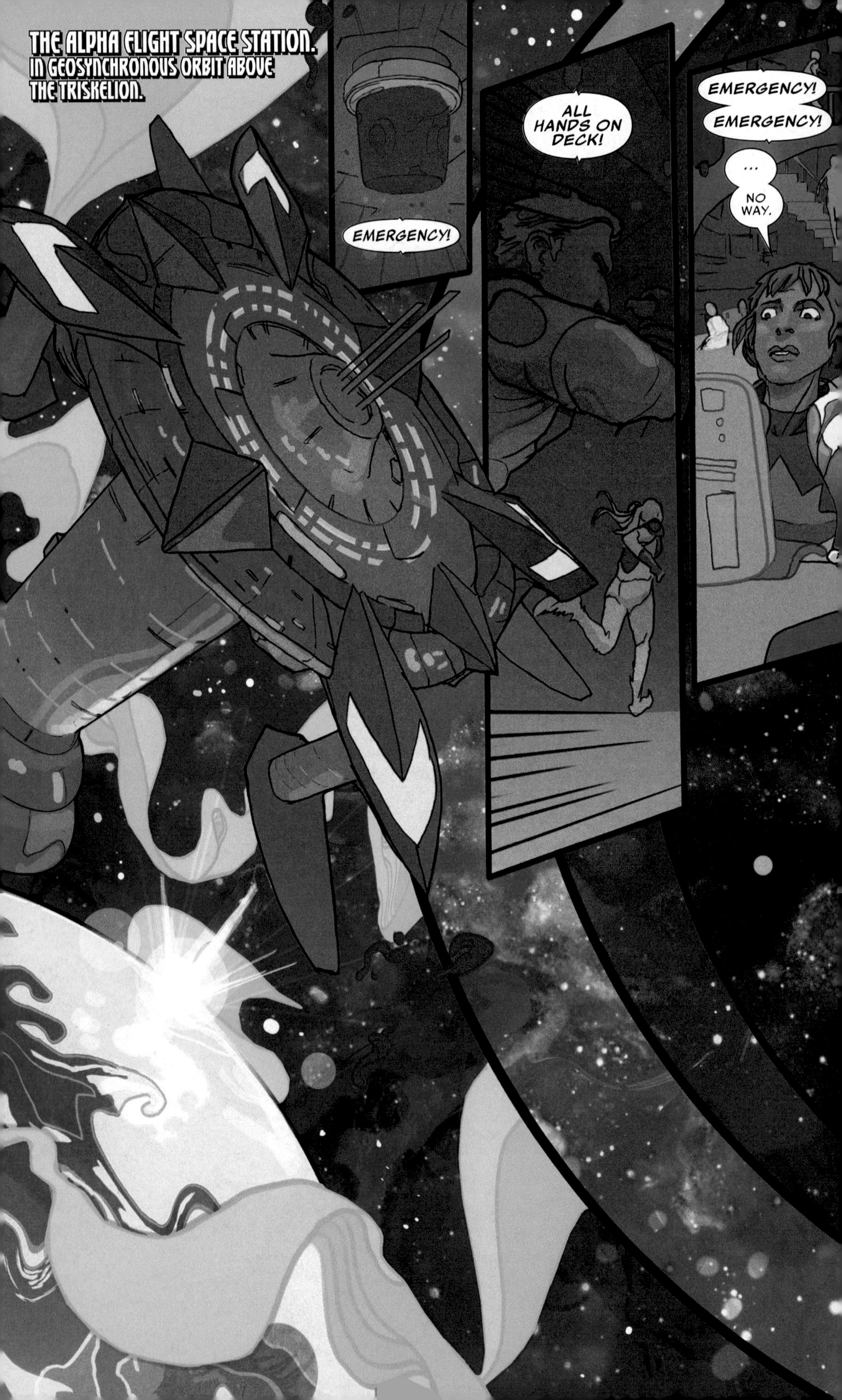
THE ALPHA FLIGHT SPACE STATION.
IN GEOSYNCHRONOUS ORBIT ABOVE THE TRISKELION.
EMERGENCY!
ALL HANDS ON DECK!
EMERGENCY!
EMERGENCY!
...
NO WAY.

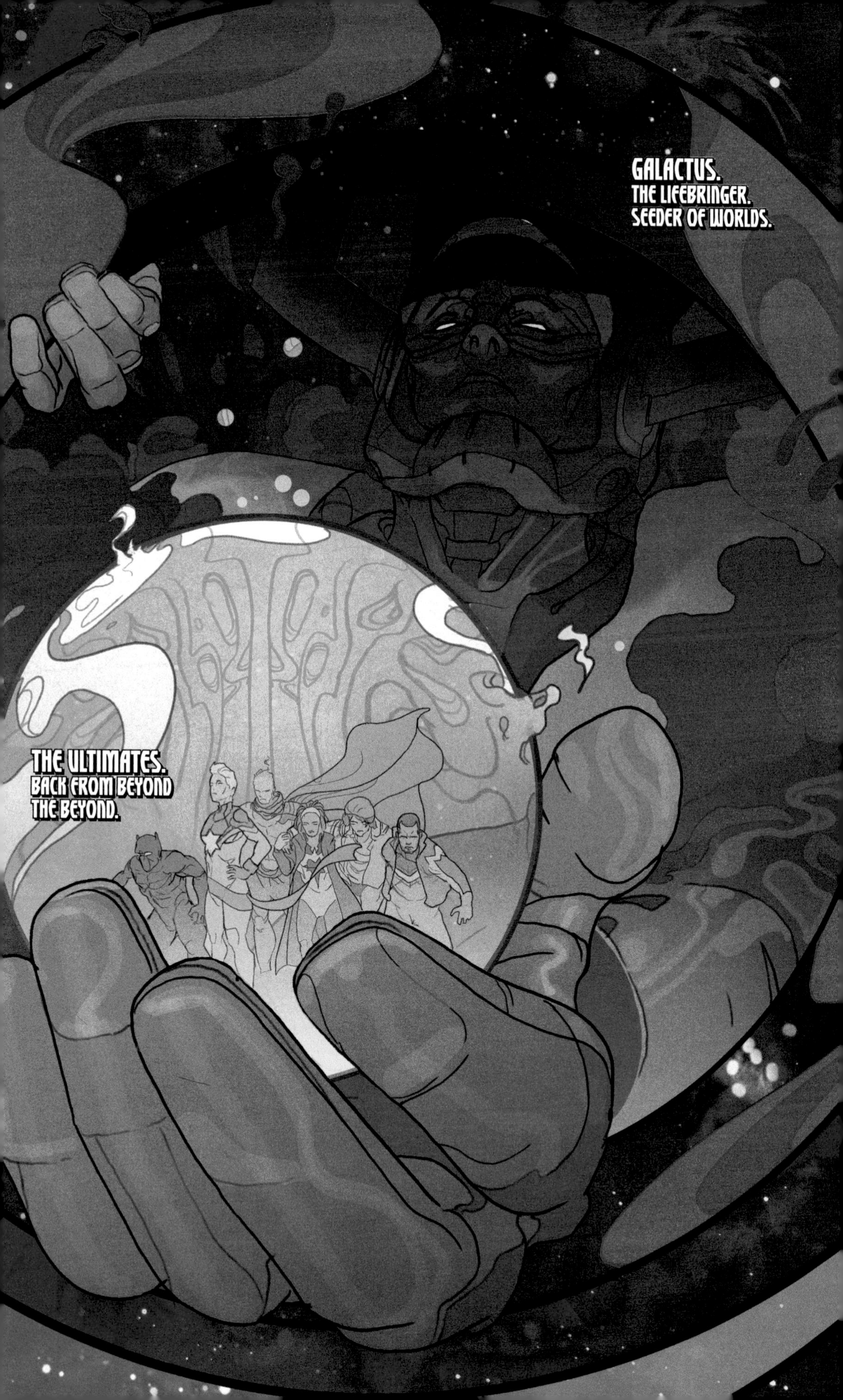
GALACTUS.
THE LIFEBRINGER.
SEEDER OF WORLDS.
THE ULTIMATES.
BACK FROM BEYOND
THE BEYOND.

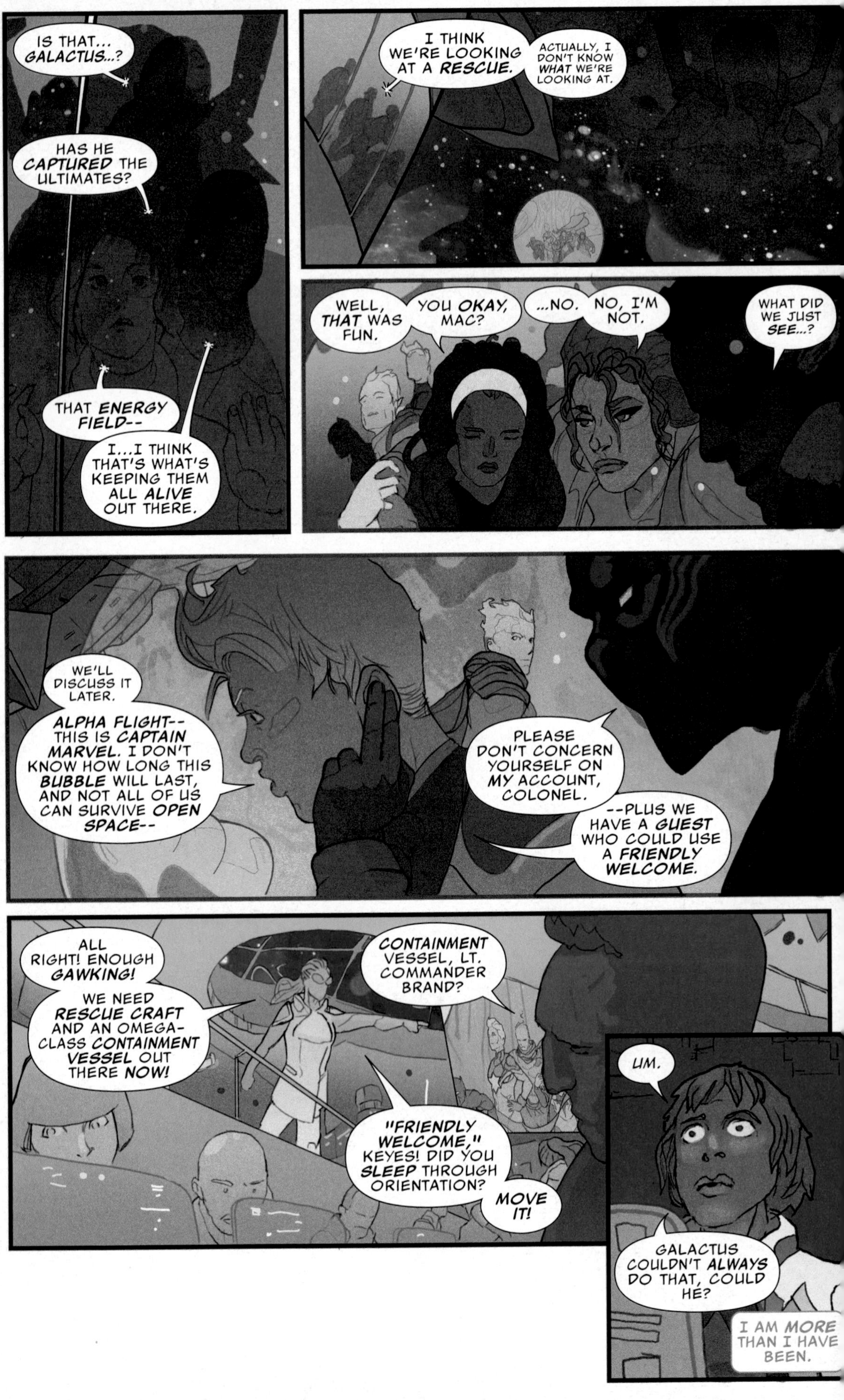

IS THAT... GALACTUS...?
HAS HE CAPTURED THE ULTIMATES?
THAT ENERGY FIELD--
I...I THINK THAT'S WHAT'S KEEPING THEM ALL ALIVE OUT THERE.
I THINK WE'RE LOOKING AT A RESCUE.
ACTUALLY, I DON'T KNOW WHAT WE'RE LOOKING AT.
WELL, THAT WAS FUN.
YOU OKAY, MAC?
...NO.
NO, I'M NOT.
WHAT DID WE JUST SEE...?
WE'LL DISCUSS IT LATER.
ALPHA FLIGHT--THIS IS CAPTAIN MARVEL. I DON'T KNOW HOW LONG THIS BUBBLE WILL LAST, AND NOT ALL OF US CAN SURVIVE OPEN SPACE--
PLEASE DON'T CONCERN YOURSELF ON MY ACCOUNT, COLONEL.
--PLUS WE HAVE A GUEST WHO COULD USE A FRIENDLY WELCOME.
ALL RIGHT! ENOUGH GAWKING!
WE NEED RESCUE CRAFT AND AN OMEGA-CLASS CONTAINMENT VESSEL OUT THERE NOW!
CONTAINMENT VESSEL, LT. COMMANDER BRAND?
"FRIENDLY WELCOME," KEYES! DID YOU SLEEP THROUGH ORIENTATION?
MOVE IT!
UM.
GALACTUS COULDN'T ALWAYS DO THAT, COULD HE?
I AM MORE THAN I HAVE BEEN.

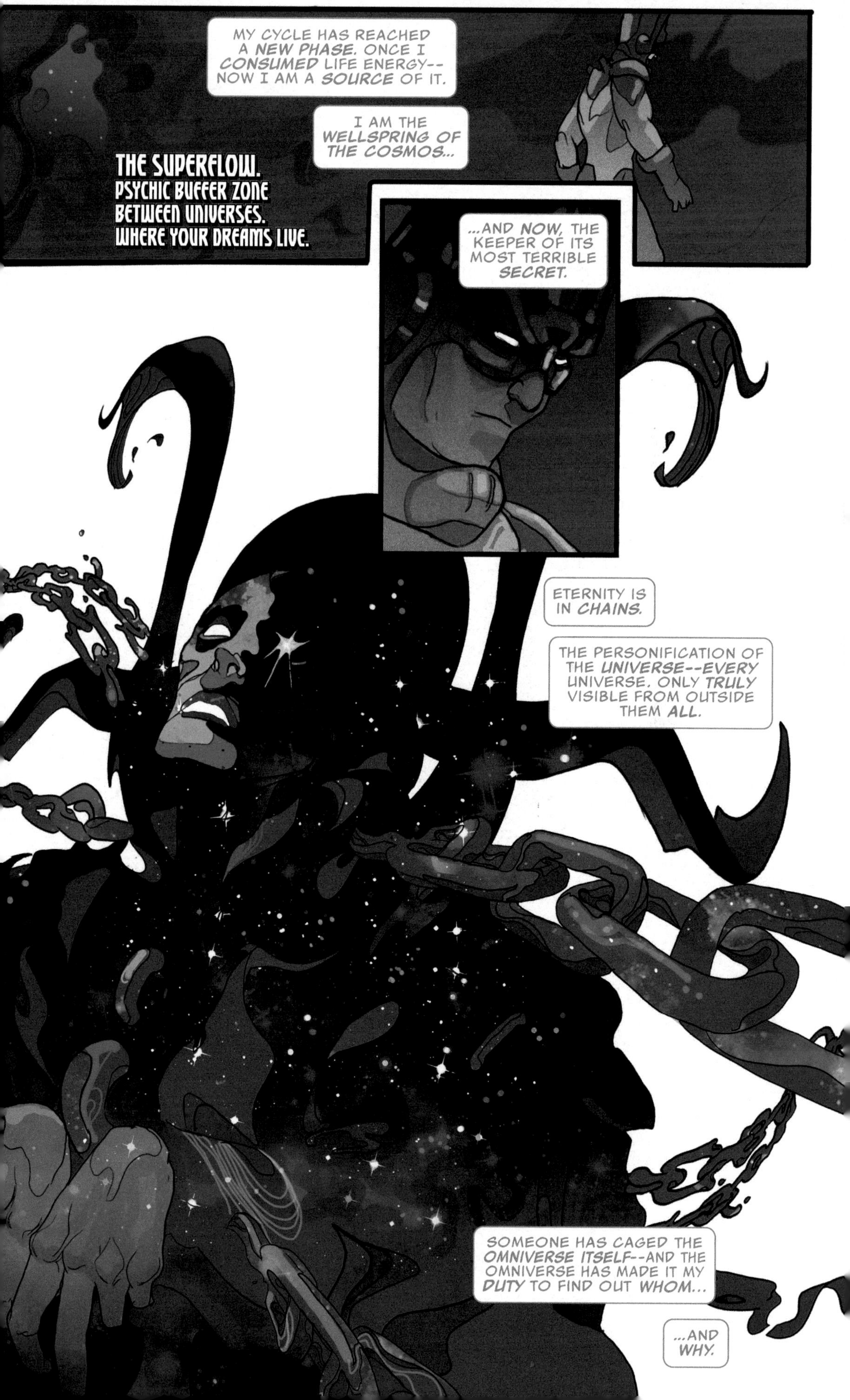

MY CYCLE HAS REACHED A NEW PHASE. ONCE I CONSUMED LIFE ENERGY--NOW I AM A SOURCE OF IT.
I AM THE WELLSPRING OF THE COSMOS...
THE SUPERFLOW. PSYCHIC BUFFER ZONE BETWEEN UNIVERSES. WHERE YOUR DREAMS LIVE.
...AND NOW, THE KEEPER OF ITS MOST TERRIBLE SECRET.
ETERNITY IS IN CHAINS.
THE PERSONIFICATION OF THE UNIVERSE--EVERY UNIVERSE. ONLY TRULY VISIBLE FROM OUTSIDE THEM ALL.
SOMEONE HAS CAGED THE OMNIVERSE ITSELF--AND THE OMNIVERSE HAS MADE IT MY DUTY TO FIND OUT WHOM...
...AND WHY.

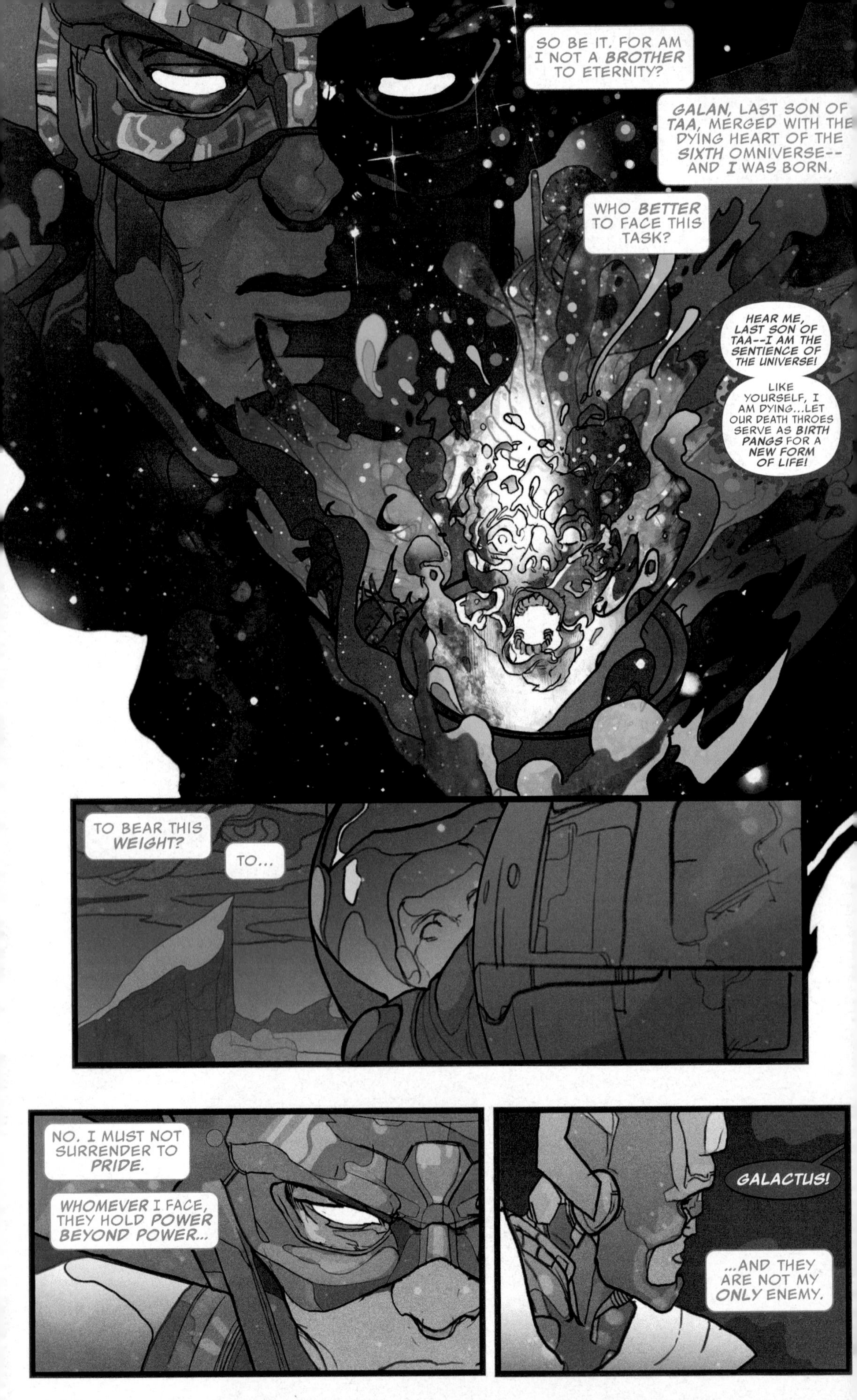
SO BE IT. FOR AM I NOT A BROTHER TO ETERNITY?
GALAN, LAST SON OF TAA, MERGED WITH THE DYING HEART OF THE SIXTH OMNIVERSE-- AND I WAS BORN.
WHO BETTER TO FACE THIS TASK?
HEAR ME, LAST SON OF TAA--I AM THE SENTIENCE OF THE UNIVERSE!
LIKE YOURSELF, I AM DYING...LET OUR DEATH THROES SERVE AS BIRTH PANGS FOR A NEW FORM OF LIFE!
TO BEAR THIS WEIGHT?
TO...
NO. I MUST NOT SURRENDER TO PRIDE.
WHOMEVER I FACE, THEY HOLD POWER BEYOND POWER...
GALACTUS!
...AND THEY ARE NOT MY ONLY ENEMY.

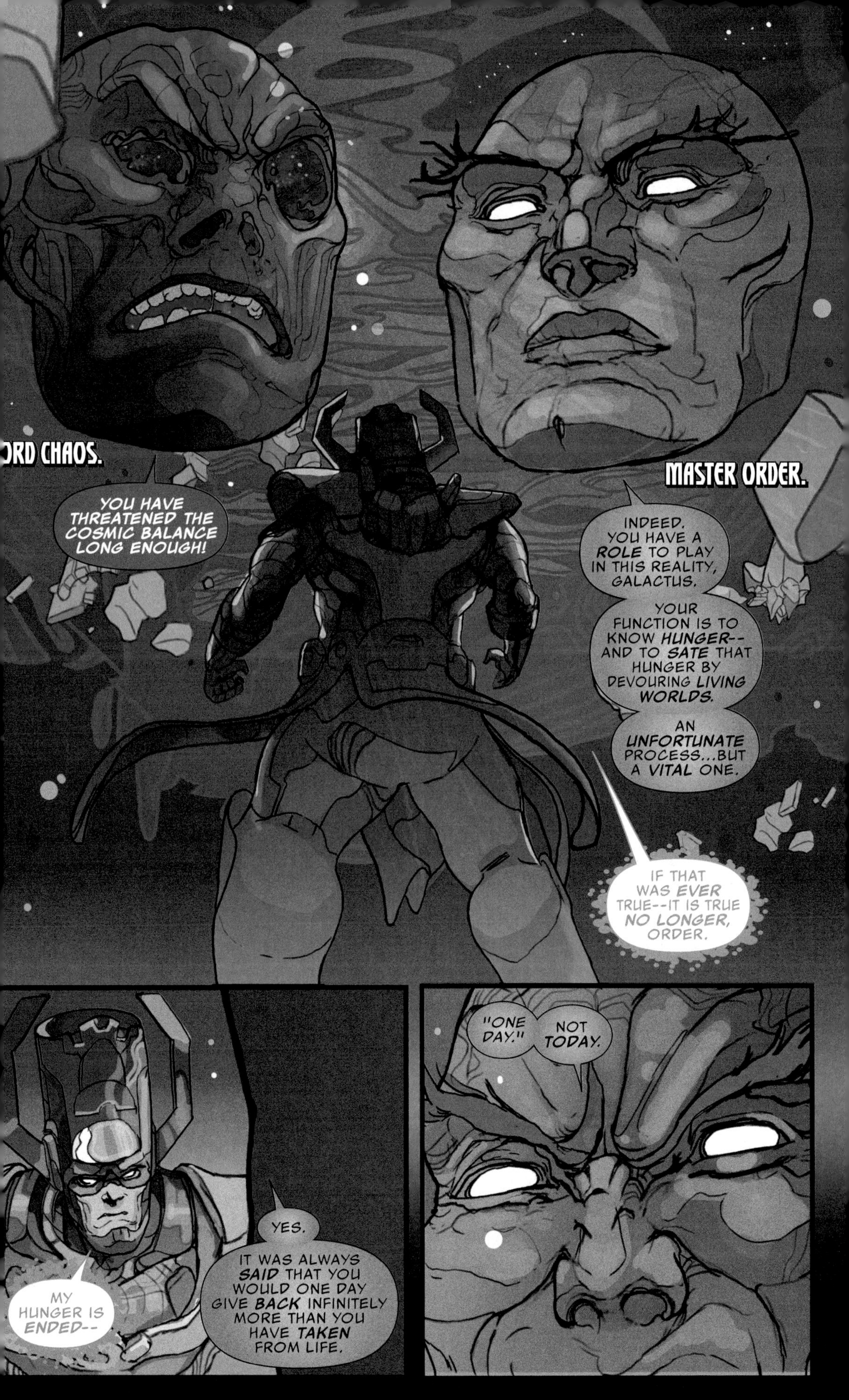
ORD CHAOS.
YOU HAVE THREATENED THE COSMIC BALANCE LONG ENOUGH!
MASTER ORDER.
INDEED. YOU HAVE A ROLE TO PLAY IN THIS REALITY, GALACTUS.
YOUR FUNCTION IS TO KNOW HUNGER-- AND TO SATE THAT HUNGER BY DEVOURING LIVING WORLDS.
AN UNFORTUNATE PROCESS...BUT A VITAL ONE.
IF THAT WAS EVER TRUE--IT IS TRUE NO LONGER, ORDER.
MY HUNGER IS ENDED--
YES.
IT WAS ALWAYS SAID THAT YOU WOULD ONE DAY GIVE BACK INFINITELY MORE THAN YOU HAVE TAKEN FROM LIFE.
"ONE DAY."
NOT TODAY.

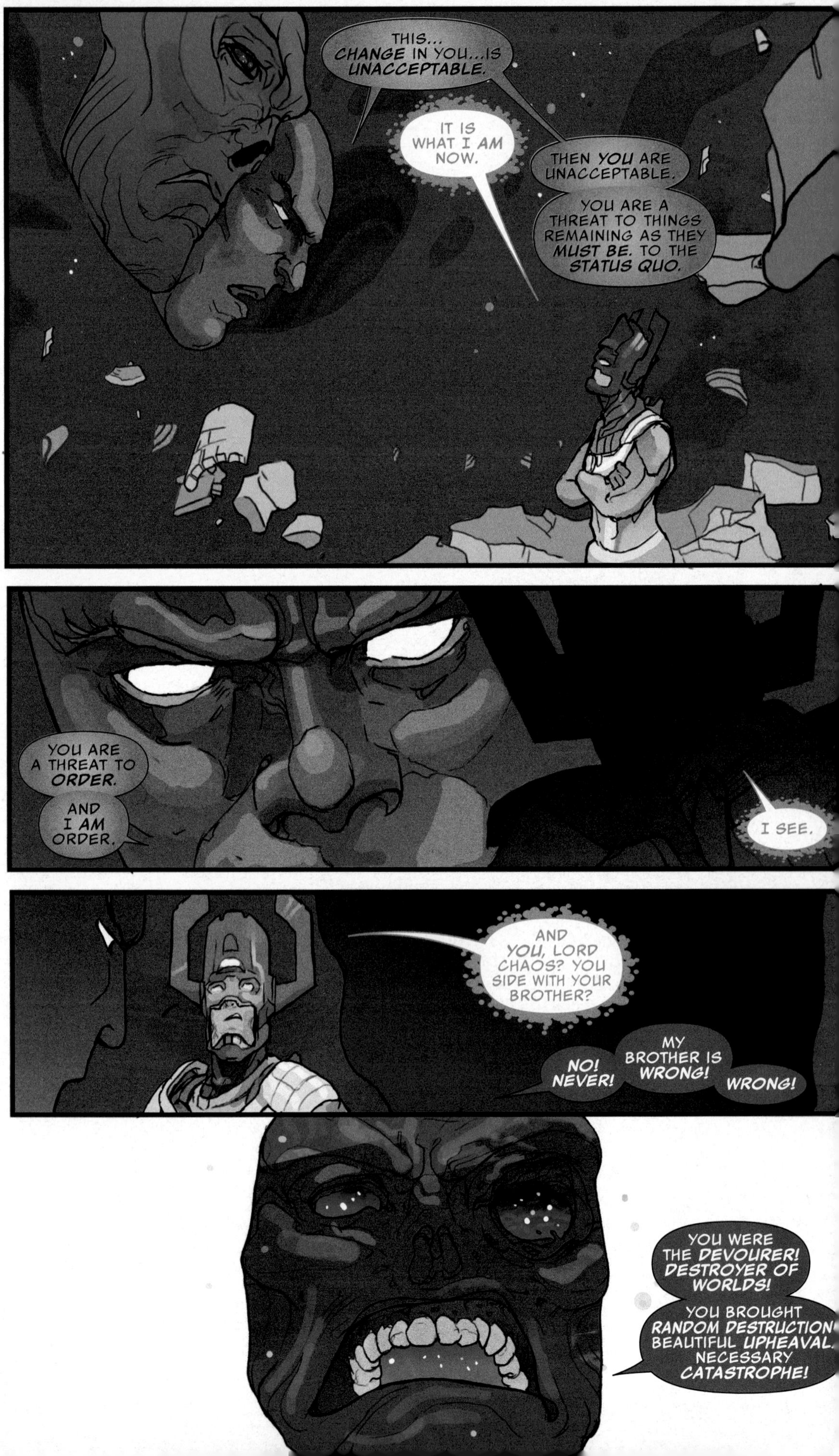
THIS... CHANGE IN YOU...IS UNACCEPTABLE.
IT IS WHAT I AM NOW.
THEN YOU ARE UNACCEPTABLE.
YOU ARE A THREAT TO THINGS REMAINING AS THEY MUST BE. TO THE STATUS QUO.
YOU ARE A THREAT TO ORDER.
AND I AM ORDER.
I SEE.
AND YOU, LORD CHAOS? YOU SIDE WITH YOUR BROTHER?
NO! NEVER!
MY BROTHER IS WRONG!
WRONG!
YOU WERE THE DEVOURER! DESTROYER OF WORLDS!
YOU BROUGHT RANDOM DESTRUCTION BEAUTIFUL UPHEAVAL NECESSARY CATASTROPHE!

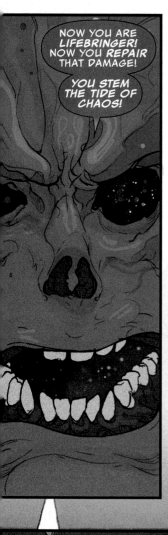

NOW YOU ARE *LIFEBRINGER!* NOW YOU *REPAIR* THAT DAMAGE!

YOU STEM THE TIDE OF CHAOS!

AND I AM--

ENOUGH.

YOUR REASONS ARE DIFFERENT, BUT THE GOAL IS THE SAME.

YOU ASK ME TO *UNDO* MY PROGRESS. TO BE AS I *WAS.*

THE ANSWER IS *NO.*

THEN WE WILL BRING YOU TO HEEL!

IN THIS DREAMSPACE-- THIS *SUPERFLOW*-- WE CAN UTILIZE OUR FULL POWER WITHOUT *DAMAGING* NORMAL SPACE. WE CAN *FORCE* YOU TO RESUME YOUR ROLE.

WE WERE ALWAYS YOUR *SUPERIORS* IN THE COSMIC HIERARCHY, AFTER ALL--

YES. YOU *WERE.*

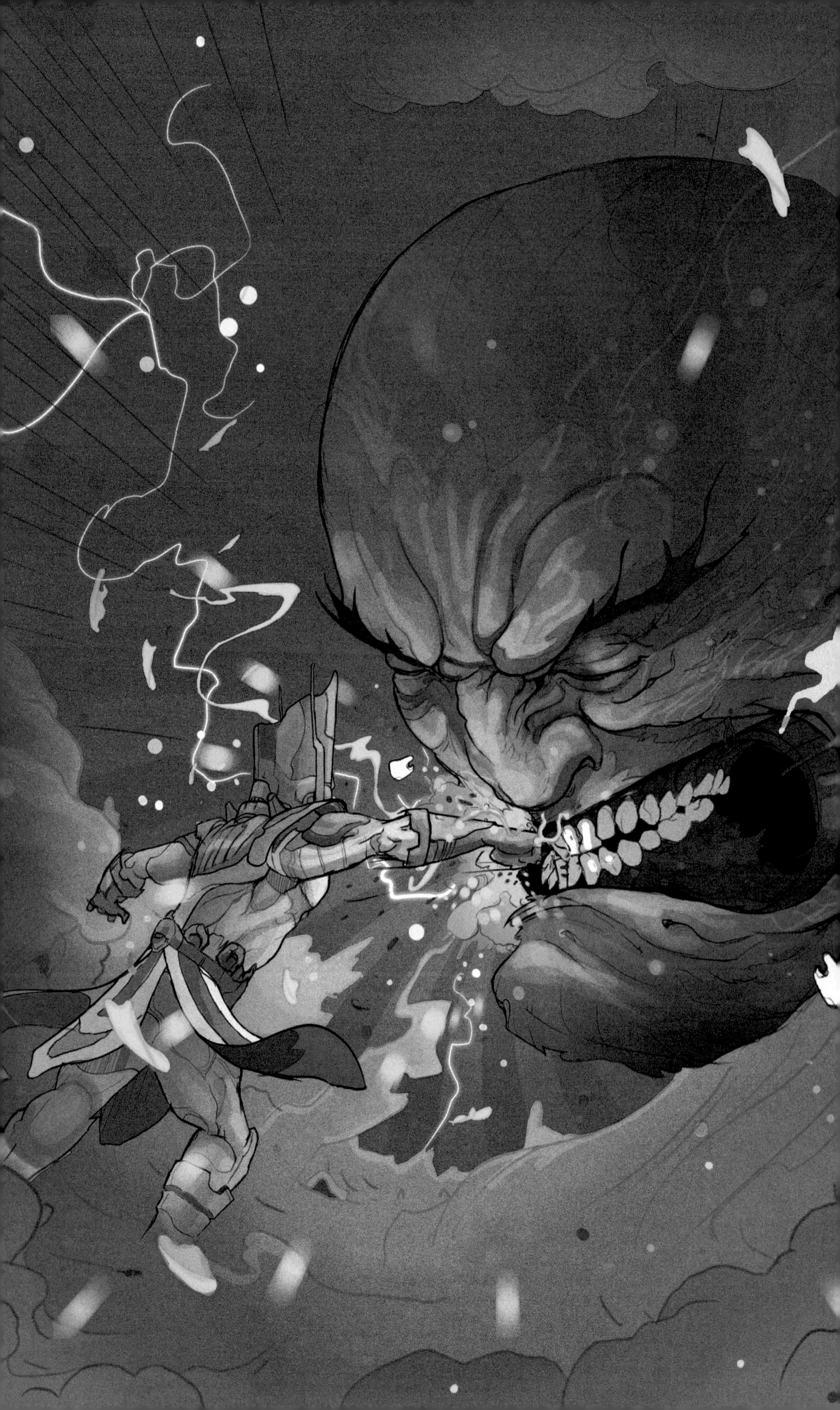

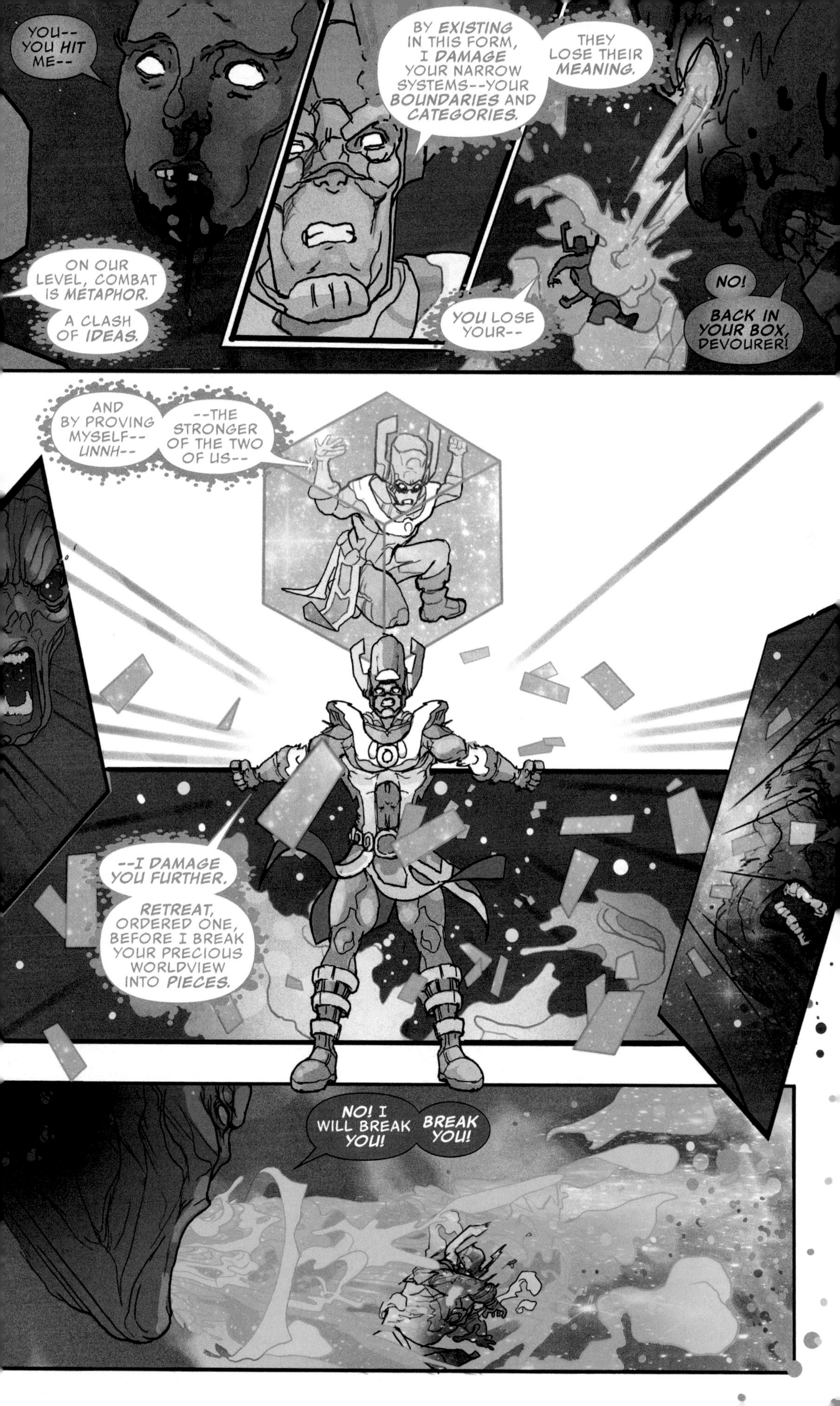
YOU--
YOU HIT ME--
BY EXISTING IN THIS FORM, I DAMAGE YOUR NARROW SYSTEMS--YOUR BOUNDARIES AND CATEGORIES.
THEY LOSE THEIR MEANING.
ON OUR LEVEL, COMBAT IS METAPHOR.
A CLASH OF IDEAS.
YOU LOSE YOUR--
NO!
BACK IN YOUR BOX, DEVOURER!
AND BY PROVING MYSELF--
UNNH--
--THE STRONGER OF THE TWO OF US--
--I DAMAGE YOU FURTHER.
RETREAT, ORDERED ONE, BEFORE I BREAK YOUR PRECIOUS WORLDVIEW INTO PIECES.
NO! I WILL BREAK YOU!
BREAK YOU!

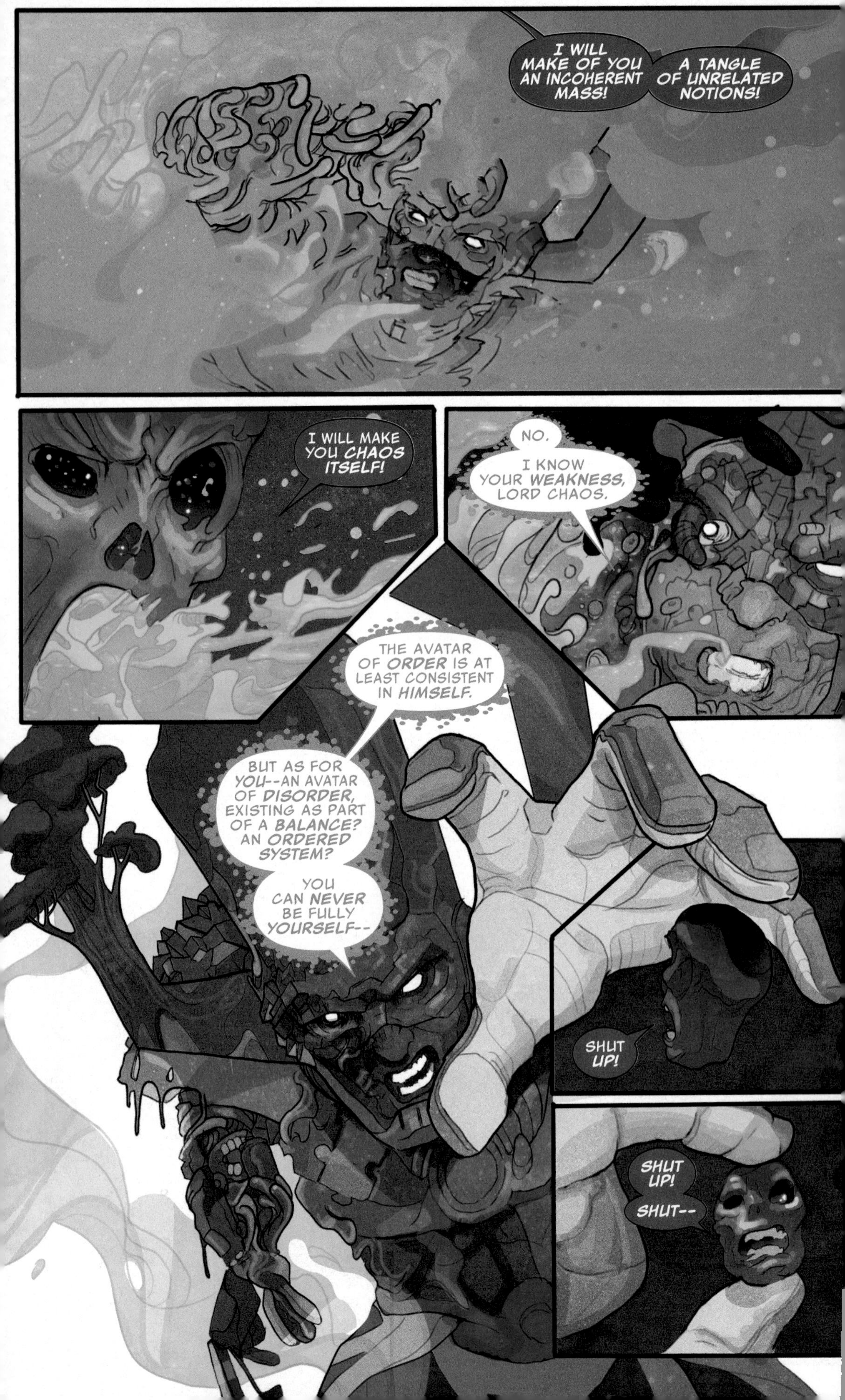
I WILL MAKE OF YOU AN INCOHERENT MASS!
A TANGLE OF UNRELATED NOTIONS!
I WILL MAKE YOU CHAOS ITSELF!
NO.
I KNOW YOUR WEAKNESS, LORD CHAOS.
THE AVATAR OF ORDER IS AT LEAST CONSISTENT IN HIMSELF.
BUT AS FOR YOU--AN AVATAR OF DISORDER, EXISTING AS PART OF A BALANCE? AN ORDERED SYSTEM?
YOU CAN NEVER BE FULLY YOURSELF--
SHUT UP!
SHUT UP!
SHUT--

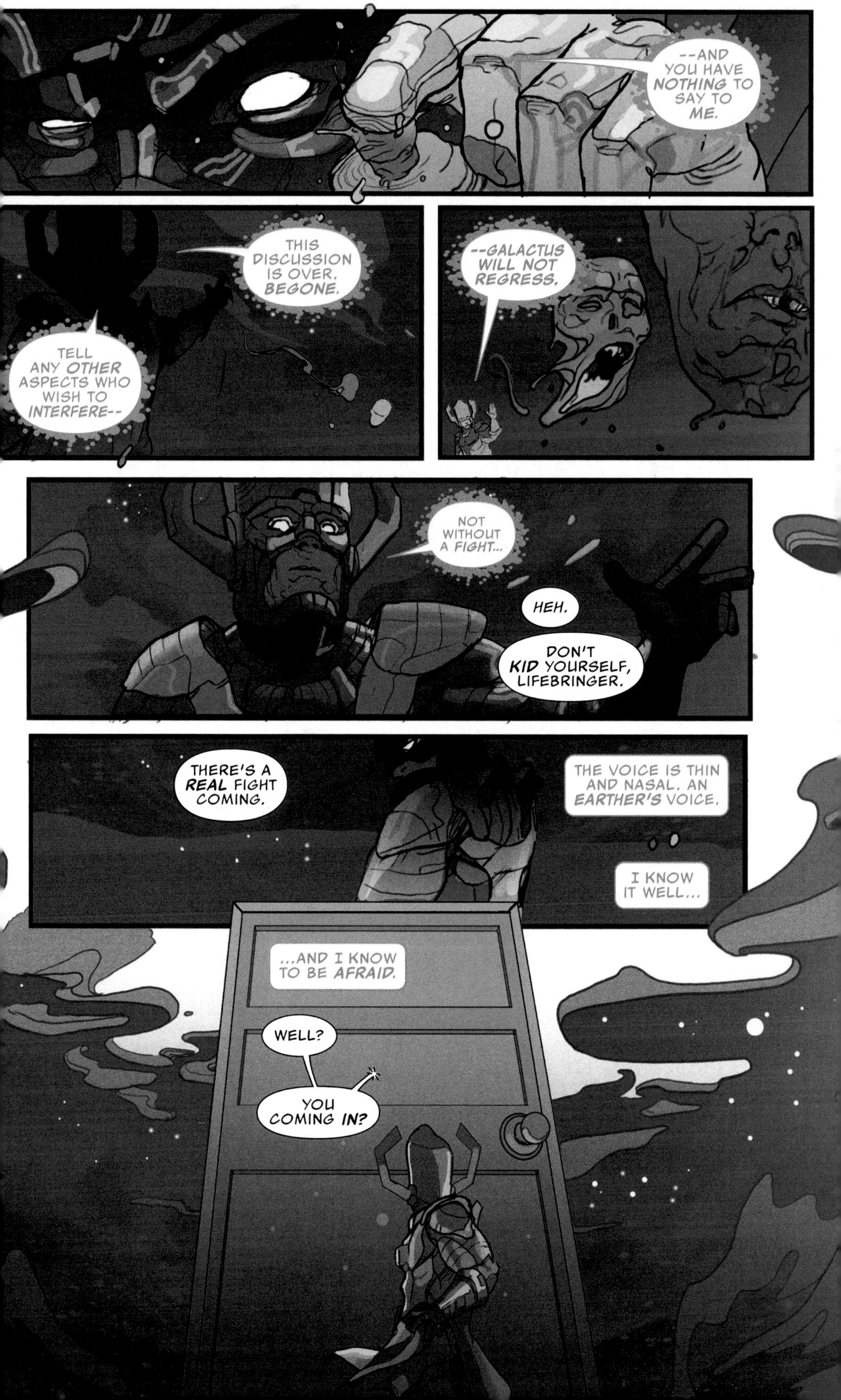

--AND YOU HAVE NOTHING TO SAY TO ME.
THIS DISCUSSION IS OVER. BEGONE.
TELL ANY OTHER ASPECTS WHO WISH TO INTERFERE--
--GALACTUS WILL NOT REGRESS.
NOT WITHOUT A FIGHT...
HEH.
DON'T KID YOURSELF, LIFEBRINGER.
THERE'S A REAL FIGHT COMING.
THE VOICE IS THIN AND NASAL. AN EARTHER'S VOICE.
I KNOW IT WELL...
...AND I KNOW TO BE AFRAID.
WELL?
YOU COMING IN?

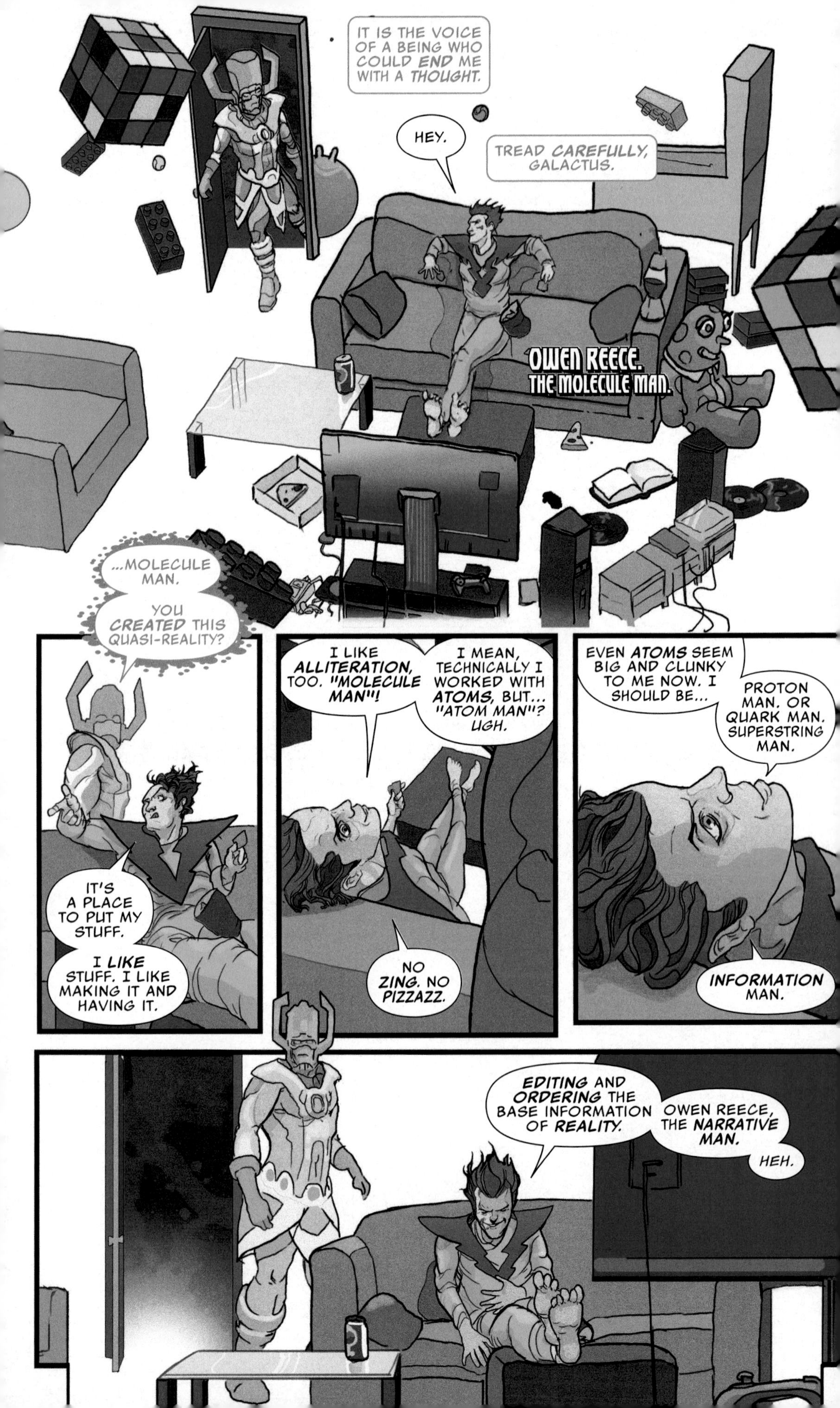
IT IS THE VOICE OF A BEING WHO COULD END ME WITH A THOUGHT.
HEY.
TREAD CAREFULLY, GALACTUS.
OWEN REECE. THE MOLECULE MAN.
...MOLECULE MAN.
YOU CREATED THIS QUASI-REALITY?
IT'S A PLACE TO PUT MY STUFF.
I LIKE STUFF. I LIKE MAKING IT AND HAVING IT.
I LIKE ALLITERATION, TOO. "MOLECULE MAN"!
I MEAN, TECHNICALLY I WORKED WITH ATOMS, BUT... "ATOM MAN"? UGH.
NO ZING. NO PIZZAZZ.
EVEN ATOMS SEEM BIG AND CLUNKY TO ME NOW. I SHOULD BE...
PROTON MAN. OR QUARK MAN. SUPERSTRING MAN.
INFORMATION MAN.
EDITING AND ORDERING THE BASE INFORMATION OF REALITY.
OWEN REECE, THE NARRATIVE MAN.
HEH.

ANYWAY. YOU SHOULD SIT DOWN.

THANK YOU, BUT I WOULD RATHER--

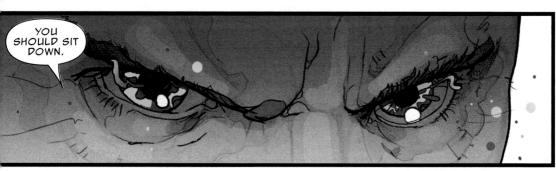

YOU SHOULD SIT DOWN.

...YES.

THAT'S GOOD...SIT DOWN. HAVE A SODA FROM THE EIGHTIES.

JUST TWO GUYS, SITTING DOWN WITH OUR STUFF. IT'S ALL GOOD.

WE SHOULD TALK, YOU AND ME.

WE SHOULD TALK ABOUT ETERNITY.

TREAD CAREFULLY.

HE CAN END YOU WITH A THOUGHT...

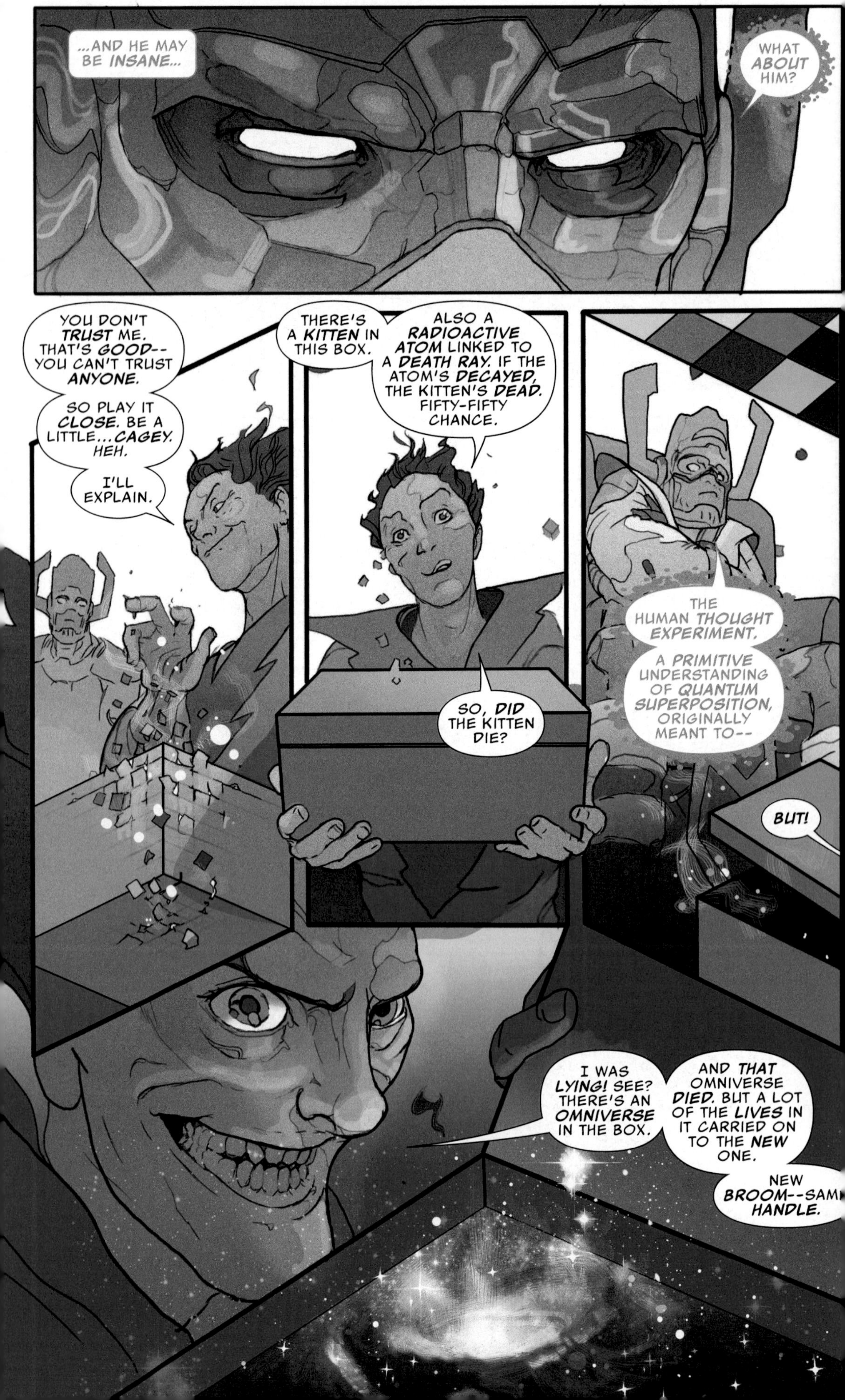

...AND HE MAY BE INSANE...
WHAT ABOUT HIM?
YOU DON'T TRUST ME. THAT'S GOOD-- YOU CAN'T TRUST ANYONE.
SO PLAY IT CLOSE. BE A LITTLE...CAGEY. HEH.
I'LL EXPLAIN.
THERE'S A KITTEN IN THIS BOX.
ALSO A RADIOACTIVE ATOM LINKED TO A DEATH RAY. IF THE ATOM'S DECAYED, THE KITTEN'S DEAD. FIFTY-FIFTY CHANCE.
SO, DID THE KITTEN DIE?
THE HUMAN THOUGHT EXPERIMENT.
A PRIMITIVE UNDERSTANDING OF QUANTUM SUPERPOSITION, ORIGINALLY MEANT TO--
BUT!
I WAS LYING! SEE? THERE'S AN OMNIVERSE IN THE BOX.
AND THAT OMNIVERSE DIED. BUT A LOT OF THE LIVES IN IT CARRIED ON TO THE NEW ONE.
NEW BROOM--SAM HANDLE.

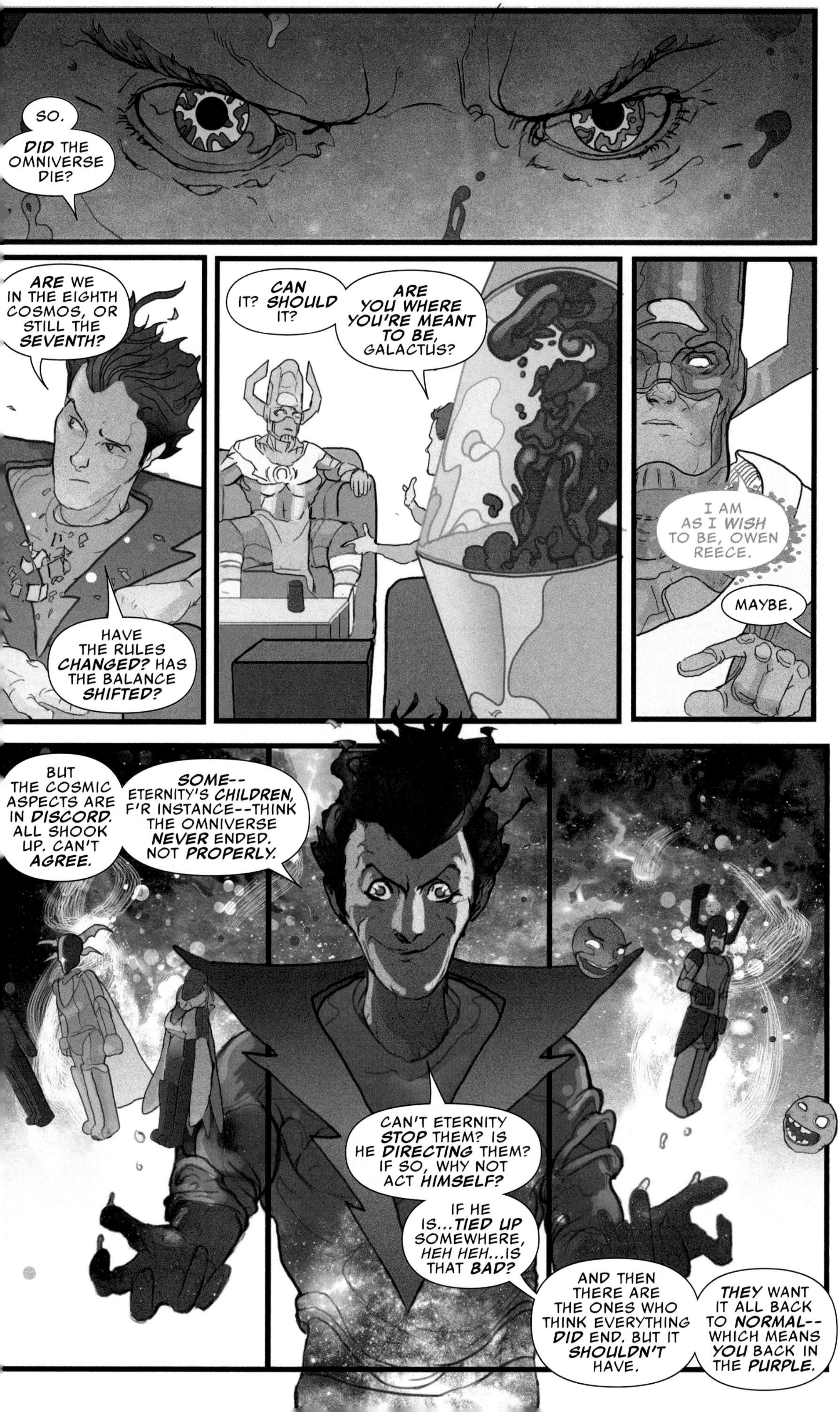
SO.
DID THE OMNIVERSE DIE?
ARE WE IN THE EIGHTH COSMOS, OR STILL THE SEVENTH?
HAVE THE RULES CHANGED? HAS THE BALANCE SHIFTED?
CAN IT? SHOULD IT?
ARE YOU WHERE YOU'RE MEANT TO BE, GALACTUS?
I AM AS I WISH TO BE, OWEN REECE.
MAYBE.
BUT THE COSMIC ASPECTS ARE IN DISCORD. ALL SHOOK UP. CAN'T AGREE.
SOME-- ETERNITY'S CHILDREN, F'R INSTANCE--THINK THE OMNIVERSE NEVER ENDED. NOT PROPERLY.
CAN'T ETERNITY STOP THEM? IS HE DIRECTING THEM? IF SO, WHY NOT ACT HIMSELF?
IF HE IS...TIED UP SOMEWHERE, HEH HEH...IS THAT BAD?
AND THEN THERE ARE THE ONES WHO THINK EVERYTHING DID END. BUT IT SHOULDN'T HAVE.
THEY WANT IT ALL BACK TO NORMAL-- WHICH MEANS YOU BACK IN THE PURPLE.

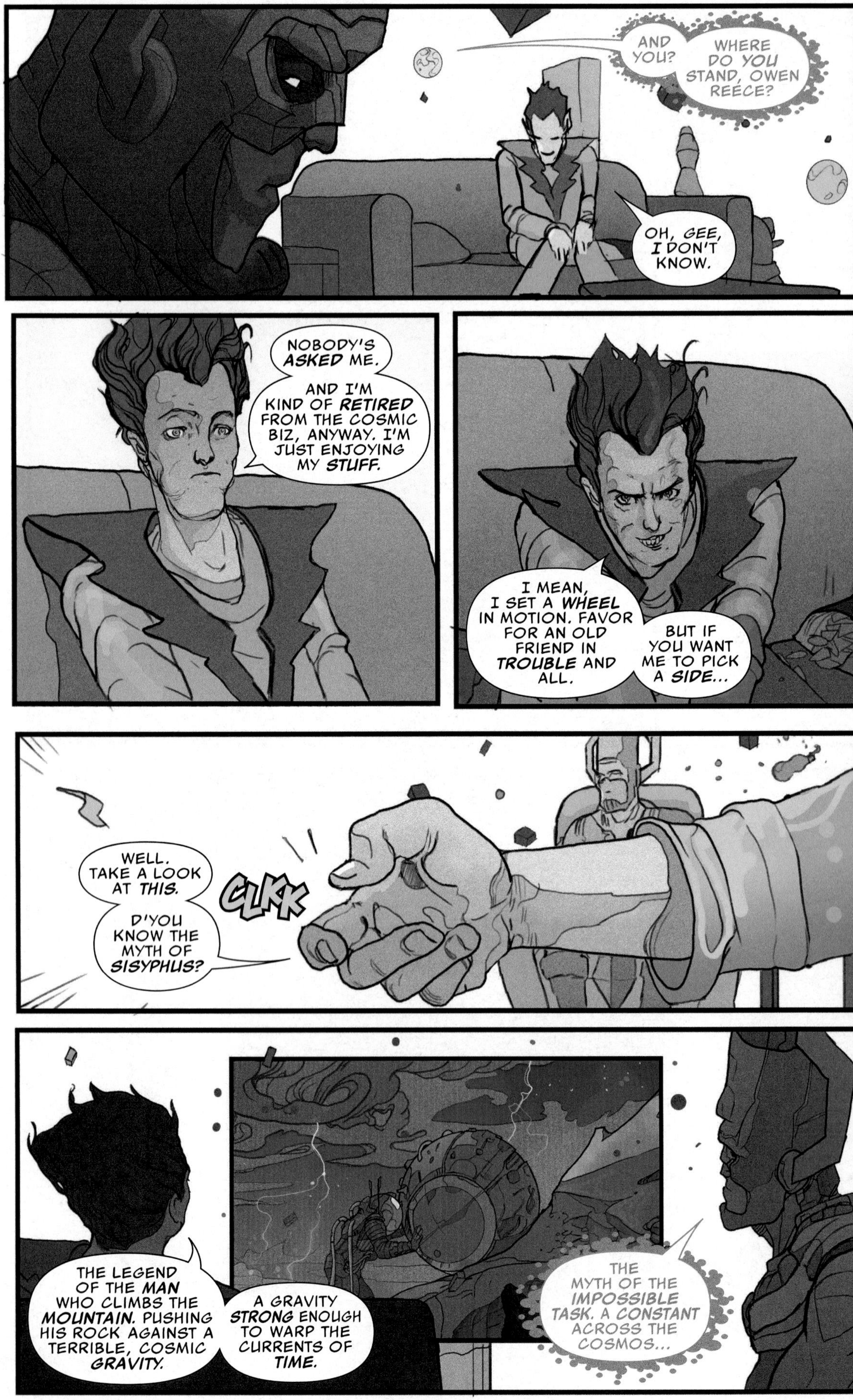
AND YOU?
WHERE DO YOU STAND, OWEN REECE?
OH, GEE, I DON'T KNOW.
NOBODY'S ASKED ME.
AND I'M KIND OF RETIRED FROM THE COSMIC BIZ, ANYWAY. I'M JUST ENJOYING MY STUFF.
I MEAN, I SET A WHEEL IN MOTION. FAVOR FOR AN OLD FRIEND IN TROUBLE AND ALL.
BUT IF YOU WANT ME TO PICK A SIDE...
WELL. TAKE A LOOK AT THIS.
D'YOU KNOW THE MYTH OF SISYPHUS?
CLKK
THE LEGEND OF THE MAN WHO CLIMBS THE MOUNTAIN. PUSHING HIS ROCK AGAINST A TERRIBLE, COSMIC GRAVITY.
A GRAVITY STRONG ENOUGH TO WARP THE CURRENTS OF TIME.
THE MYTH OF THE IMPOSSIBLE TASK. A CONSTANT ACROSS THE COSMOS...

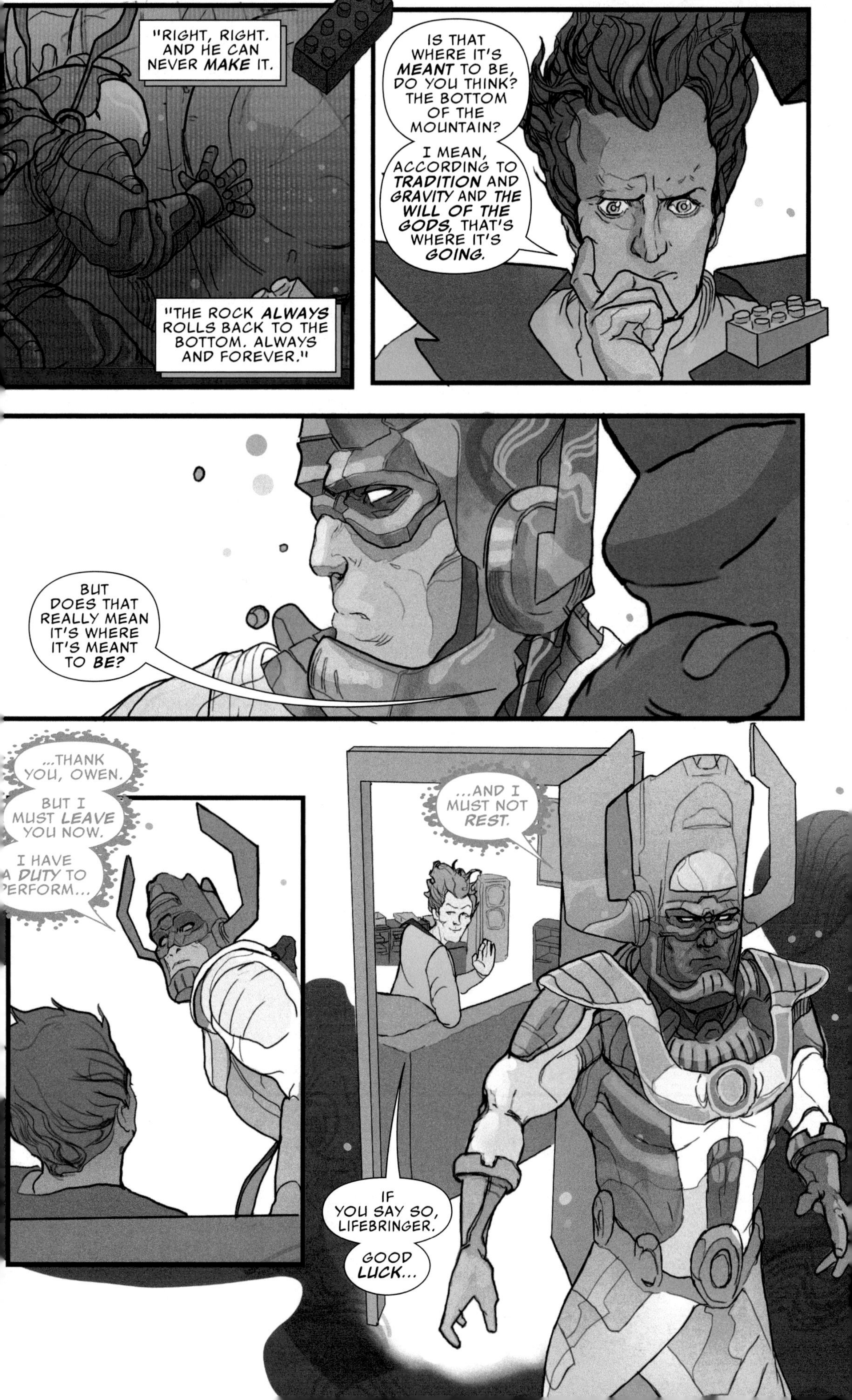
"RIGHT, RIGHT. AND HE CAN NEVER MAKE IT.
"THE ROCK ALWAYS ROLLS BACK TO THE BOTTOM. ALWAYS AND FOREVER."
IS THAT WHERE IT'S MEANT TO BE, DO YOU THINK? THE BOTTOM OF THE MOUNTAIN?
I MEAN, ACCORDING TO TRADITION AND GRAVITY AND THE WILL OF THE GODS, THAT'S WHERE IT'S GOING.
BUT DOES THAT REALLY MEAN IT'S WHERE IT'S MEANT TO BE?
...THANK YOU, OWEN.
BUT I MUST LEAVE YOU NOW.
I HAVE A DUTY TO PERFORM...
...AND I MUST NOT REST.
IF YOU SAY SO, LIFEBRINGER.
GOOD LUCK...

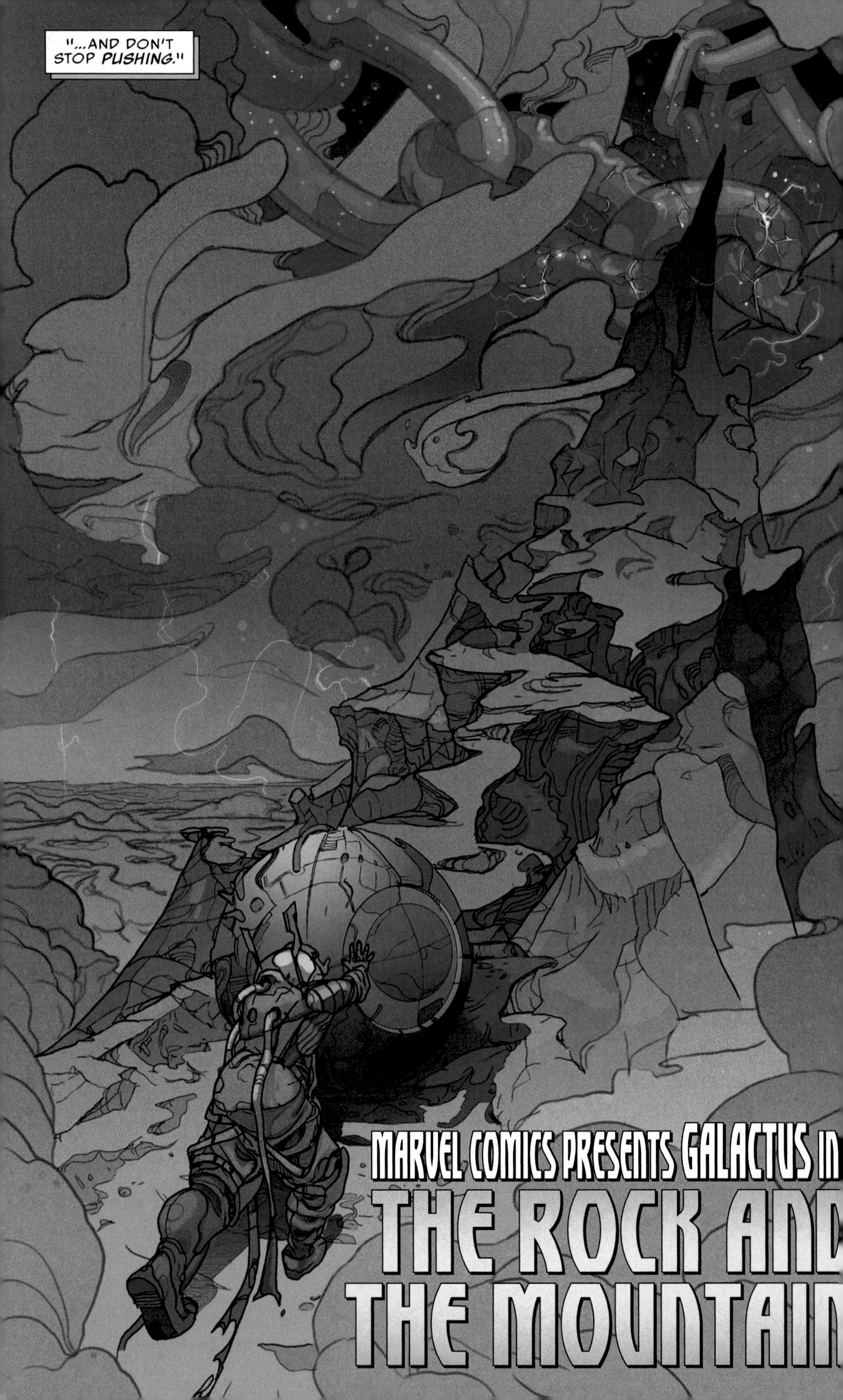
"...AND DON'T STOP PUSHING."
MARVEL COMICS PRESENTS GALACTUS IN
THE ROCK AND THE MOUNTAIN

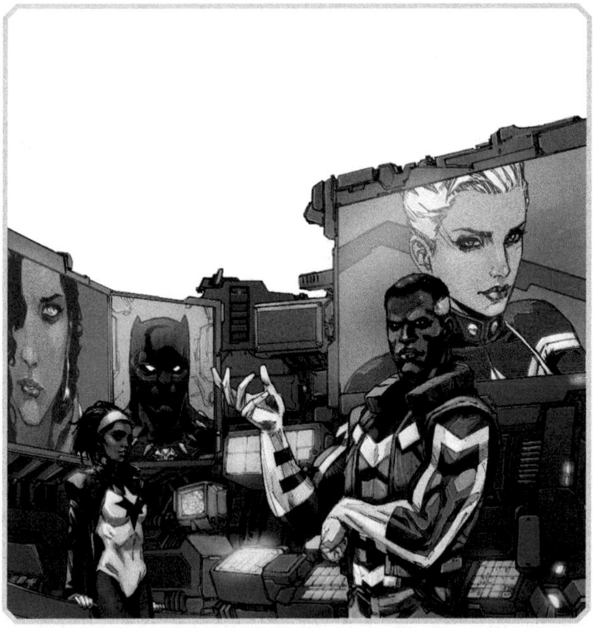

ORIGINAL RECAP ART
BY KENNETH ROCAFORT &
DAN BROWN

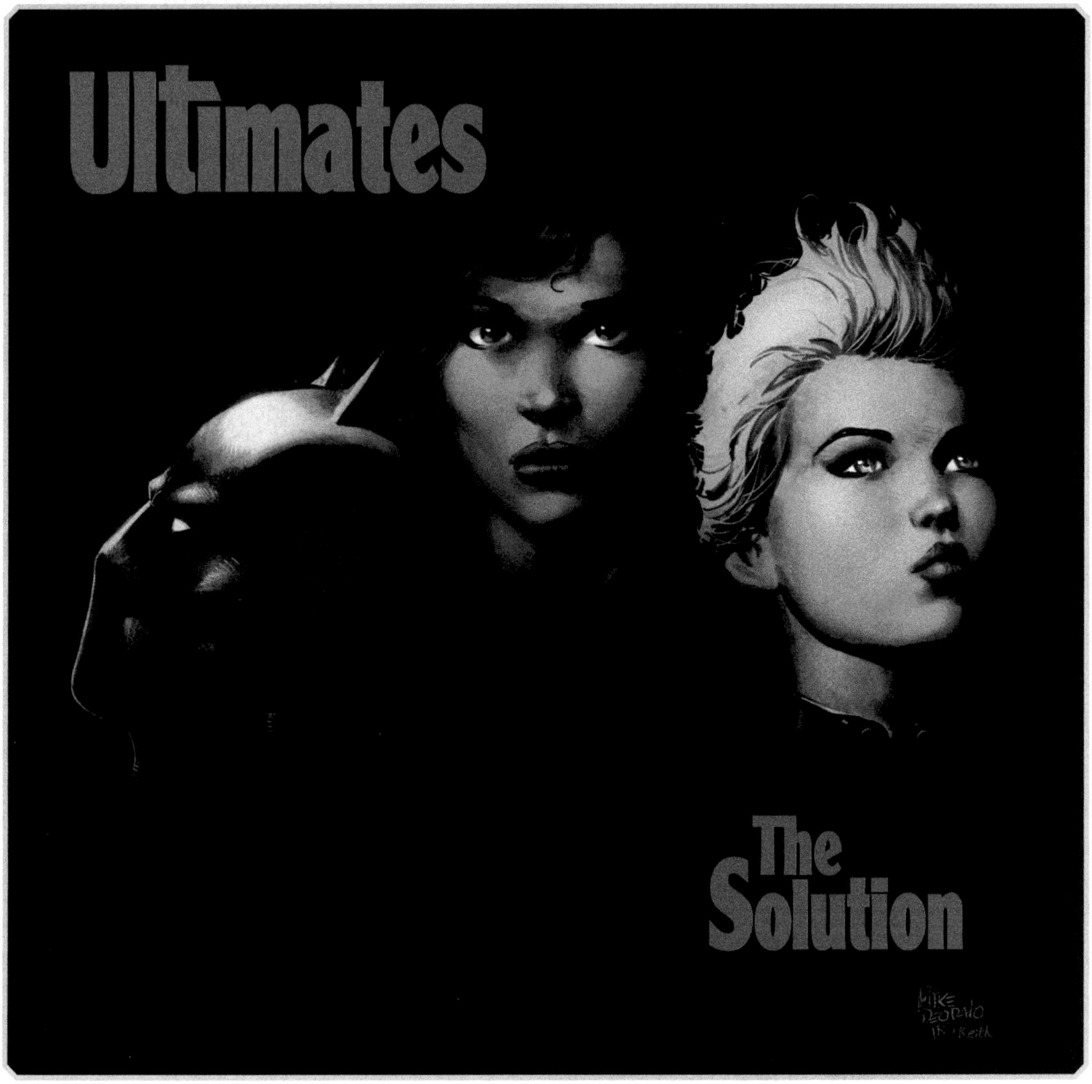
Ultimates
The Solution
MIKE DEODATO

#1 HIP-HOP VARIANT BY
MIKE DEODATO & JASON KEITH

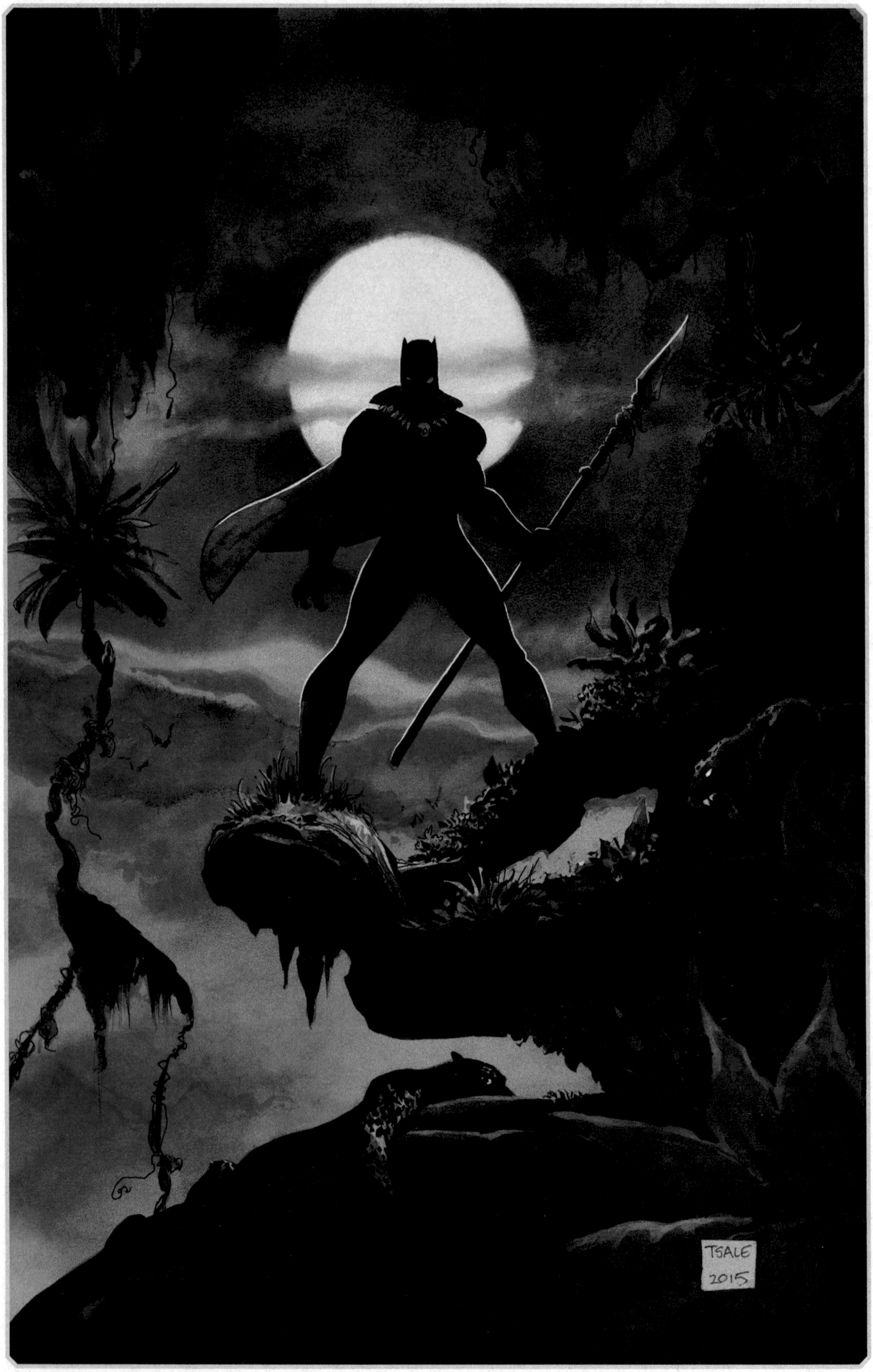
TSALE
2015

#3 BLACK PANTHER 50TH ANNIVERSARY VARIANT BY
TIM SALE & DAVE STEWART